Economics, Bounded Rationality and the Cognitive Revolution

Economics, Bounded Rationality and the Cognitive Revolution

Herbert Simon
Professor of Computer Science and Psychology
Carnegie-Mellon University, Pittsburgh, US
1978 Nobel Laureate, Economic Science

with Massimo Egidi, Robin Marris and Riccardo Viale

Edited by Massimo Egidi and Robin Marris

Edward Elgar

Published by
Edward Elgar Publishing Limited
The Lypiatts
15 Lansdown Road
Cheltenham
Glos GL50 2JA
UK

Edward Elgar Publishing, Inc.
William Pratt House
9 Dewey Court
Northampton
Massachusetts 01060
USA

Paperback edition 2008
Paperback edition reprinted 2016

A catalogue record for this book is available from the British Library

Library of Congress Cataloguing in Publication Data
Economics, bounded rationality and the cognitive revolution/by Herbert
  Simon . . . [et al.]; edited by Massimo Egidi and Robin Marris.
      p. cm.
    1. Decision-making. 2. Economic man. 3. Organizational behaviour.
    4. Neoclassical school of economics. I. Simon, Herbert Alexander,
    1916– . II. Egidi, Massimo. III. Marris, Robin, 1924–.
    HD30.23.E324   1992
    658.4'03–dc20   91–42473
                                                                      CIP

ISBN   978 1 85278 425 6 (cased)
            978 1 84720 896 5 (paperback)

Printed and bound in Great Britain by the CPI Group (UK) Ltd

Contents

v

Figures

Introduction

This book is the indirect result of a discussion organized by Massimo Egidi and Riccardo Viale, held in 1988 at the Rosselli Foundation in Turin, Italy, between Herbert Simon and a distinguished group of Italian economists and social scientists. The whole discussion was recorded, transcribed and made available for others to read. As a result, the present authors became convinced that both the questions raised by the participants and Herbert Simon's rich responses ought to be published. As the transcript itself was not long enough for a book, we approached the present publisher and Herbert Simon with a project for a book which would include not only the discussion but also some past classic papers of Herbert Simon which have appeared in journals not widely read by economists. In addition there would be papers by Raymond Boudon, Massimo Egidi, Riccardo Viale and Robin Marris, these last representing a critique of bounded rationality by an economist who is on the one hand highly sympathetic to Simon critique, but on the other hand not hostile to all maximizing theory.[1] As a result of warm cooperation from Herbert Simon, and strong support from Edward Elgar, the project went ahead and the result follows.

Two points deserve introductory mention. The first is represented in the question, 'What is the book about?' The answer is that the book is about whatever has replaced the unqualified concept of rationality, in response to the assault of Herbert Simon. The concept is generally known as 'bounded' rationality,[2] and is first described, by Herbert Simon, in the opening paragraph of the book: he says the term distinguishes the reality of human behaviour from the 'perfect' rationality implied in classical economic theory.

The second point is represented in the question, 'Where do we go from here?' In other words, what is the new research agenda? It is still generally true that a large part of mainstream economic theory has continued to ignore the cognitive revolution. In consequence, because the economics required in most business schools is largely 'mainstream', there is a considerable number of quite young MBAs, let alone Business-major BAs, who know nothing of satisficing, bounded rationality or any other economic hypotheses beyond simple optimizing. In addition, the cognitive revolution has not up to this point been able to contribute substantially to the field of the theory of conflict. One reason for this state of affairs has been the relative paucity of research lying strictly in the domain of economics that is explicitly based on Simon-like models.[3] What is the best strategy for helping to rectify this situation?

We do not have collective answers to our own questions; mainly we pose them for discussion. With proper modesty, however, the two editors exploit the present opportunity to mention that Egidi in his contribution discusses the implications for organization theory, while Marris, drawing considerably on Boudon and Viale, attempts to respond to the challenge for economics.

Robin Marris
Massimo Egidi

NOTES

1. Marris was not present at the 1988 event.
2. For reasons given in Chapter 10 (p. 199) Marris prefers the term 'intelligent' rationality, but at present he is alone.
3. Of course there are exceptions, such as Cyert and March (1963).

PART ONE
Bounded Rationality: Discussion

1. Introductory Comment

Herbert A. Simon

The term 'bounded rationality' hardly needs definition for the participants in this conference. The term was introduced about thirty years ago to focus attention upon the discrepancy between the perfect human rationality that is assumed in classical and neoclassical economic theory and the reality of human behaviour as it is observed in economic life. The point was not that people are consciously and deliberately *irrational*, although they sometimes are, but that neither their knowledge nor their powers of calculation allow them to achieve the high level of optimal adaptation of means to ends that is posited in economics.

It is not enough, however, to point out that some empirically erroneous assumptions underlie economic theory. In addition (a point for which Milton Friedman has argued), it is necessary to show that it makes a difference – that we would reach different conclusions in our economic analyses if we substituted the concept of bounded rationality for the concept of global optimization. It is also necessary to show how assumptions of bounded rationality could replace assumptions of optimization in actual economic reasoning.

BOUNDED RATIONALITY AND ECONOMIC DYNAMICS

Great progress has been made toward both of these goals. With respect to the former, it has been shown on many occasions that for economics to deal with dynamic phenomena in general, and with the business cycle in particular, it must introduce limits upon the rational calculation of the economic actors. Both the Keynesian and the Lucasian business cycles derive from introducing into the oyster of

3

rationality a small grain of irrational sand that can grow into the pearl of the business cycle. In the case of Keynes, one of these grains of irrationality is the assumption that labour suffers from a money illusion; in the case of Lucas, businessmen suffer from a money illusion.

In general, when economic theory turns from proving theorems about Pareto optimality in competitive equilibrium to dealing with concrete questions in the economic world, the assumptions of optimization have to be supplemented by assumptions about the surrounding conditions of action. These auxiliary assumptions are very frequently assumptions about limits on knowledge or computation-assumptions of bounded rationality. Moreover, they are empirical assumptions whose truth can only be determined by observing the real world outside. They cannot be deduced in an armchair.

THEORY OF DECISION MAKING

What about the second goal: creating a positive theory of bounded rationality that can be used to study economic decision making? Our understanding of how human beings do reason, using limited knowledge and limited computational powers, has been greatly advanced by cognitive psychology during the past generation. Using that knowledge, the discipline of artificial intelligence is now able, in many domains, to build expert systems capable of matching the decision-making performance of human professionals.

We know today that human reasoning, the product of bounded rationality, can be characterized as selective search through large spaces of possibilities. The selectivity of the search, hence its feasibility, is obtained by applying rules of thumb, or heuristics, to determine what paths should be traced and what ones can be ignored. The search halts when a satisfactory solution has been found, almost always long before all alternatives have been examined.

Economic actors are among the experts whose behaviour has been simulated: the choice of stocks and bonds for trust portfolios, determination of the credit-worthiness of borrowers, design of products to customer specifications, policies for determining levels of inventory and factory schedules, and many others. At the micro level, we already have most of the components we need to substitute a realistic theory of the firm for the fictitious theory that now occupies the textbooks. More work will be needed before these results can be aggregated confidently to the macro level. (But aggregations based on empirical observations, even of a sample of one, are surely more dependable than aggregations based on no sample at all.)

Our new understanding of how people solve problems and make decisions is bringing within the scope of economic analysis phenomena of great importance that previously had lain outside it. Neoclassical economic theory assumes that the problem agenda, the way in which problems are represented, the values to be achieved (utility function), and the alternatives available for choice have all been given in advance. It has no systematic way of explaining how problems get on the agenda (e.g. how public attention may be focused on the problem of inflation at one time, on interest rates at another), what it is that people value and how values change, or how action alternatives are created (e.g. new products, new marketing or manufacturing methods, new public policies like the negative income tax). Hence it is incapable of creating a genuine economic dynamics.

Using the approach of bounded rationality and what has been learned about human rational behaviour, all these topics now can be and have been approached. Today, we even have widespread research going forward on the process of scientific discovery. A theory that deals with problem formation and with the design of solution alternatives can provide the basis for a theory of economic change and development.

ORGANIZATIONS IN THE ECONOMY

The concept of bounded rationality also leads us to an understanding of the central role of organizations in economic life. Neoclassical economics focuses almost exclusively on the analysis of markets, with organizations playing a distinctly secondary role. Even the 'new institutional economics' (Williamson, Stiglitz and others) brings in organizations by elaborating 'optimal' contracting schemes to fit private goals to organizational requirements.

But if we look at the actual world around us, we don't find that organizations are simply small lumps in a fabric of markets and contracts. On the contrary, we see that 80 per cent or more of all the people engaged in productive work carry out their work within the boundaries of organizations. Organizations are the prominent features of the landscape, occupying most of the space and connected with a network of market transactions. Economic theory generally presents a caricature of this scene, with the markets much magnified and the firms represented by simplified cost curves and production functions managed by a rudimentary entrepreneur. Nor can the realities of organizational behaviour be explained solely in terms of ordinary motivations of self-interest. Few of the participants in business organizations participate in profits in a significant way; and it was pointed out long ago (by Adolf Berle and Gardner Means) that even the interests of top executives are not wholly consistent with the interests of stockholders. The present era of leveraged buy-out and golden parachutes makes that point even more evident. Hence the appeal of the new institutional economics for using contractual arrangements of various kinds to tie the self-interest of the individual to the profit-maximizing goal of the firm is seriously lacking in credibility.

Empirical research on organizations has shown that self-interest is strongly buttressed by the mechanisms of identification – that is, attachment to the organization and its goals both cognitively and motivationally. Because we human beings cannot see all things at once, we simplify our decision problems by viewing situations within the framework of an organization: the goals of that organization, the factors that are relevant to these goals – a view of the world, so to speak, from the vantage point of the organization. Because of the power of identifications to tie people to organizational goals, organizations are far more coherent and play a far more central role in economic life than classical theory supposes. Within the next few years, we can expect to see economic theories emerging that place markets in the context of organizations, rather than organizations in the context of markets, as current theories do.

PROSPECTS FOR CHANGE

The times have never been more propitious than now for the theory of bounded rationality to have an impact upon mainstream economics. The optimism after World War II, that government policy guided by economic theory could stabilize economies at high levels of employment and a good pace of technological progress, is now muted. The faith in *a priori* theory, uncontaminated by empirical observations, has been weakened – even among 'rational expectationists'. More and more economists are beginning to look for the facts they need in actual observation of business decision making and in laboratory experiments on economic markets and organizations. Translating these changes in attitude into rapid progress in economic science places a special responsibility upon our graduate schools. Today, students of economics are exposed to econometric tools as almost their only technical weapons for attacking empirical questions. They need to be exposed also to the tools of laboratory experimentation and the tools for carrying out field investigations of decision making. With such tools in hand, rapid progress can be sustained in understanding how we human beings use our bounded rationality to make decisions, and in applying that understanding to revising and rebuilding our theories of economics – bringing them into firmer contact with the realities of the world.

2. Colloquium with H. A. Simon

INTRODUCTION by Massimo Egidi

The purpose of this conference is to focus on some of the most important consequences of the bounded rationality approach in economics, methodology and the political sciences.

We will proceed by building a multiple dialogue with Dr Herbert Simon: each participant will discuss a topic and will propose it for a reply to Dr Simon.

Let me propose the first issue: the possible non-equivalence of markets and organizations.

One of the most important achievements entailed by the bounded rationality approach has been to provide a coherent way of interpreting the role of individuals in the market and within organizations. Organizations are viewed as devices, alternative to the market, by which individuals acting with incomplete knowledge and information can satisfactorily reduce their uncertainty and take their decisions.

Traditionally the market is viewed as the institution that coordinates individual decisions. If organizations are also ways by which individuals coordinate their decisions and organize themselves, what differentiates the role of these two forms of human organization?

In the neoclassical view the role of the market is that of synthetizing the relevant information and fully reducing the computing complexity that individuals need to make rational decisions.

Complex strategic behaviours are not needed in this view because perfect markets eliminate the reciprocal interdependence among individuals and reduce behaviours to simple parametric choices.

The problem is that this reduction is widely imperfect; I will try to explore some of the reasons for this and one consequence of it.

The first point to be stressed is that even if we accept the frame of general equilibrium analysis, we cannot conclude that the market fully reduces the computing complexity of human behaviours.

As is well known, in the equilibrium framework not all the information that agents need is provided by the market. It is assumed that there is a sort of 'data base' to which agents should have access (without costs), which contains information about the nature and quality of goods, about technologies and states of nature, and finally about the allocation (both spatial and temporal) of the markets.

This adds up to an unacceptably vast amount of information that individuals should have freely disposable and on which they should compute. What happens if, following the viewpoint of the Austrian school, we assume that agents possess only fragments of information?

Radner has shown that 'if economic decision makers have unlimited computational capacity for choice among strategies, then even if there is uncertainty about the environment, and different agents have different information and different beliefs about environment, then one can apply the standard theorems on the existence and optimality of a competitive equilibrium'.

But the core of the theory lies in the affirmation of the role of markets as mechanisms that decentralize decisions, and obviously this task is necessary only if a bounded human capacity is assumed.

A way to overcome this contradiction is to assume that the basic information needed from individuals is produced and exchanged; it is necessary therefore to show that markets exist in which information on the markets themselves can be acquired, as well as information on technologies, on states of nature, and so on.

Evidence has shown that not all these markets do exist and some of those that exist work mainly in a distorted way (they sell incomplete or unreliable information: take for example advertising).

This is due to the peculiar character of information and knowledge; as Arrow pointed out, information does not respect the characteristics that define the exchange of a 'commodity between private contracting parties: information can only be imperfectly appropriated, is indivisible and imperfectly valuable'.

One consequence of such a situation is that, for lack of some form of legislative guarantee, it may not be worthwhile to produce information. The same goes for invention and innovation.

It follows that generally there is a lack of markets for information (they are drastically fewer than necessary), and consequently the Pareto optimum is not reachable by an economic system.

We can draw one conclusion: even if we accept the frame of

general equilibrium analysis, we cannot attribute to the market the capacity to fully reduce the information and the computing complexity.

The *systematic* failure of markets for information makes it necessary to explain what alternative devices can be employed to reduce complexity.

This is the task that is performed by firms by means of administrative hierarchies. Markets and hierarchies can be viewed as alternative forms by which human activities are performed: I will try to show that they do not perform exactly the same task.

This point can be viewed from two different angles. On the one hand, it is necessary to understand how man's ability to simplify and synthetize information works; this will require a revision of the notion of rationality, and following Professor Simon this notion must be regarded as man's ability to solve problems; on the other hand we have to understand why individuals cooperate and how they do it in order to solve complex problems (this calls for an analysis of the role of human organizations).

Let me start with the first point, recalling the typical example of chess in order to clarify some points about procedural rationality.

There is a winning strategy in chess and we have a method of finding it (the well known von Neumann algorithm); this method entails a complete exploration of all the strategies, and therefore is not *practically* feasible.

We have a typical failure of the classical approach based on the idea of unlimited computational capacity. Curiously real players are able to play and even sometimes to win in spite of the fact that they have not found the best strategy.

A wide literature in the field of artificial intelligence exists on this topic (with important contributions from Professor Simon) and I only will focus on the two following points:

1. Players acting with incomplete information and limited computational capacities need to break the analysis on a given depth of the game (by means of stop rules).
2. They use the so-called static evaluators to simplify the analysis and evaluate the best local strategy.

In such a way they solve the global problem of detecting a winning strategy by means of two different typical steps: one, divide the game tree into sub-trees, and analyse only local strategies in a bounded segment of the tree of the game; two, reduce the choice to a parametric one, by means of appropriate evaluators.

It must be emphasized that in evaluating the strength of their positions, players use subjective criteria which are refined by experience, and generally differ from player to player. Then it is natural that the expectations that each player has about the moves of the other can prove wrong, that is to say, his opponent can make an unexpected move.

Therefore cognitive incompleteness, surprise and expectation inconsistency characterize the behaviour of the players. On the other hand, a great flexibility characterizes their behaviour, because they can revise their strategies and moreover the evaluators on which strategies are selected, by learning from experience.

But the main point in my view is that in any complex game the reduction of complexity that individuals have to cope with is done by dividing the tasks into different functions that, just like the division of labour in an administrative organization, can be performed by different players who cooperate to form a team of experts who represent a single collective player.

Let me synthetize the problem.

In order to formulate and work towards their objectives, individuals who are in situations of computational complexity must reduce them through appropriate procedures.

The typical feature of these procedures is that they reduce strategic behaviours to parametric, by means of state parameters that synthetize the information.

This is exactly what happens with the market, which reduces the strategic nature of individual action to a parametric choice through prices. But this reduction is incomplete, and therefore alternative ways are needed of organizing and coordinating human activity.

This is the task which is performed by organizations: hierarchies can be considered as one of the means by which coordination is achieved in order to solve complex problems.

The nature of the firm, which in the traditional framework was defined by means of the production function, can be redefined on the basis of the bounded rationality approach.

Let me provisionally define the *enterprise* as an organization which performs the task of coordinating the limited capacities of different individuals who cooperate to realize a given goal.

In this definition it seems that the organization plays the same role as the market, since it coordinates individual activities. And yet there is an important difference.

The market in fact coordinates the activities of different individuals and organizations within a given division of labour in the society; but organizations, besides coordinating the activities of different individuals, are able to solve a complex problem by dividing it into different sub-problems, to be solved by different functional sub-systems of the firm.

In this sense the ability to project new forms of division of labour is the characteristic feature of entrepreneurial activity. This difference may be due to the fact that firms, like organizations, exist to pursue given goals, at least partly intentionally, while the market is an unintentional institution. As intentional institutions, firms reflect projecting ability, that is the capacity to plan the forms of cooperation which make it possible to achieve desired goals. We cannot attribute to the market the same functional capacity; therefore we can conclude with a final problem: can the 'transaction cost' approach fully exhaust the problem of explaining the nature of the firm?

Siro Lombardini

Some of the foundations of economics need a profound rethinking. First, economists have focused their attention on the problem of allocation of resources. According to the neoclassical theory, a rational allocation can be attained by individuals having no power of affecting market conditions and behaving independently of one another. Economic development is eventually produced by the same individuals' rational choices assuring optimal allocation of resources. The link with the social system is provided by the assumption that individuals have tastes that economists can assume as given. Thus only a one-way relation between the social and the economic system is considered, as well as between the natural and the economic system. The field of economics is a system of rational choices. How such a system can function has never been properly explained. Various tricks have been devised to solve the problem of how individual decisions are coordinated to produce market results.

Second, rationality is defined in the context of certainty. The choice problem is framed as if the premises can be assumed as certain. Uncertainty has always to be reduced to certainty. Different ways have been suggested from the very simple one proposed by Hicks and Lange to the sophisticated approaches suggested by statistical inference and the theory of games. There may be a variety of possible states of the world. Then probabilistic distributions are assumed that enable us to maintain the models of substantive rationality.

Wiener, Simon and a few others have stressed the need to define proper procedures for rational behaviour. Such procedures cannot be reduced to definition of virtual movements as are those summarized by demand and supply curves: they comprise processes of *learning*, both with regard to the system mechanisms and the data needed to frame and solve the problems. They also comprise definition of goals; choice of strategies that can be either passive or active (usually passive with regard to some stimuli – or information – and active with regard to possible changes that can be produced in the environment); choice of actions conditional not only on exogeneous data but also on the results of individuals' previous actions. All these moments of the procedures are intertwined. Yet rational choice is usually reduced to choice of action conditional only on exogeneous data. Some economists have assumed that it is possible to conceive a world in which all exogeneous data are known with certainty and information is sufficient to frame the choice problem as one of optimization.

To such a concept various kinds of objections can be raised. First, certainty cannot be the context for human rationality. Let us imagine such an experiment: God comes and lets each of us know what will occur to us from now to our death. Should that occur, we would be deprived of all possible context for any rational behaviour. Choice of strategy cannot be reduced to the solution of an optimization problem. It entails, to some extent, some bets, the first being with oneself.

Second, some of the data needed to frame the choice problem are objectively uncertain. The rational-expectations economists have advocated transparency in economic policy. According to them, government can and must make their intentions known and give all required information. But there is no such thing as a conscious and coherent set of intentions that can be referred to that agent evoked by the term 'government'. Other possible events are objectively uncertain. Our expectations about technical innovations have different degrees of uncertainty. Quite a few innovations can be foreseen in some of their essential features and relevant implications; and yet we are not at all sure about when they will occur. The fundamental innovations are mostly unforeseeable. So at least they happened to have been in the past. There is no reason to think that this will no longer occur in the future.

Third, individual goals cannot be defined according to a general and uniform pattern. Suffice it to recall Schumpeter's conception of the entrepreneur distinguished from the rational man of the neoclassical model. Action for its own sake may be the goal of action. To put it in a different way, work does not necessarily entail only pain; it may produce some gratification. Experience may lead to changes in goals. Thus the problem of economic development cannot be reduced either to rational allocation of resources or to some kind of growth that does not change the structure of the economy and can, thereby, be analysed by such models as Leontief's dynamic model and the Harrod–Domar models.

Fourth, neoclassical theoretical models are not only based on the assumption that some mysterious mechanism can ensure simultaneous maximization of individuals' objective functions; they also assume that the model explaining the working of the system is simple enough to enable each of us to foresee the future, provided we know the initial conditions and the values of all exogeneous variables. Any reliable model embodying all relevant knowledge of the working of the economy can only be used to visualize possible scenarios through simulation processes (I am now interested in the kind of research that can be qualified as *computational economics*). Even if all of us agree on the model explaining the working of the economy, different scenarios may be expected. Expectations diverge also because of the different degrees of risk aversion or love of risk. Money makes possible the coexistence of different expectations. At the same time, money may be used to curb expectations in order to avoid unbearable disequilibria.

I can summarize my remarks by saying that it is because uncertainty is an essential feature of the context in which human action can be conceived, that progress (as well as decay) is possible. Speculation and innovation cannot be explained outside such a context. In this new context, some essential peculiar features of production can be analysed, whereas in the neoclassical approach production is assimilated (reduced) to a set of exchanges.

Simon

I agree very much that the troubles of the neoclassical theory begin as soon as we introduce uncertainty, which is a focal concept in the difficulties that arise. Now, uncertainty has a variety of causes. The uncertainty we usually think about is uncertainty about the future, inability to predict because we don't have good models of the future. But we can also classify our computational limits as a form of uncertainty. Even if we had a good model of the future, if our brains wouldn't allow us to run the model as fast as time runs, we would still be uncertain about the future. (The complexity of the models used in meteorology today are limited in precisely this way – by the power of the supercomputers available to run them.) Hence bounded rationality is very closely related to uncertainty.

We also have the peculiar uncertainty of oligopoly, which motivated the work of Chamberlain and Robinson in the 1930s and later inspired game theory. Here we find that the whole definition of rationality is undermined as soon as we have people reacting to other people whose interests conflict with theirs. The big achievement of game theory to date has been to demonstrate how difficult it is to define rationality in the multiperson game of incomplete information. The disagreement about the concept of the solution is precisely a disagreement on what constitutes rationality under the circumstances.

Then we have the other domain of uncertainty emphasized by Professors Egidi and Lombardini: that is, the uncertainty associated with innovation. There's an interesting puzzle or conundrum here: what can you hope for in a science where innovation is very much a part of the system under study? People are fond of pointing out that if you could predict an invention you would already have made it.

That's a very strange situation, but perhaps not without a solution. We can predict that there will be bigger and faster supercomputers five years hence than there are now, and that they'll be cheaper, without being able to design that future supercomputer. You have to separate the ability to predict that things of a certain general kind are going to happen from the ability to predict in detail what they are.

Nevertheless, this puzzle does suggest that if we want to have a theory of technological change, it will have to be a theory of the processes that bring about change rather than a theory of the specific nature of the changes. So again we are forced to move from an economic theory that deals with the result of rational choice to a theory that considers the processes that people use in making their choices. This shift requires a real reconstitution of economic theory.

Luigi Orsenigo

My question concerns the cognitive factors determining firm boundaries.

Conventional explanations emphasize incentive-related and sometimes also cognitive limits as the main factor defining the size and scope of organizations. Yet it still is not clear, both from a theoretical and from an empirical perspective, which is the 'quantitative' limit to the learning capabilities of any one organization.

However, in addition to those considerations, there might also be further limits linked to the nature of learning activities. For instance, many studies in the economics of innovation seem to suggest that such learning processes have strong cumulative features; that they rest on idiosyncratic cognitive frames; and that the knowledge which is thereby created is to a large extent tacit and specific to particular organizations and to particular problems.

Put another way, in the extreme case, the routines developed for the solution of some specific problems cannot be generally applied to other different classes of problems or used by organizations different from those which created them. Or, echoing Williamson, firms face a sort of trade-off between the 'depth and the width' of the problem space that they can explore.

On these grounds, it has been argued (by Nelson, Winter and Teece, for instance) that what defines the boundaries of a firm should be sought precisely in the collection of specific routines, capabilities and cognitive frames embodied in any one organization, rather than in transaction costs. In this approach, the limits to the expansion of firm boundaries would appear to be set essentially by the type of knowledge they are able to understand and use in addition to the quantity of information they are able to process in any given time.

Against this background, what are in your view the limits to firms' size and scope?

Simon

When we begin to raise issues like the question of firm boundaries and firm size, we must be careful not to transform these back into optimization problems. It might be thought, for example, that General Motors, in deciding against vertical integration with its dealerships, was optimizing something; but we must not jump to that conclusion. As we know, firms exist in a great variety of sizes within each industry and with different degrees of integration, and one wonders whether it is easy to explain the enormous variation in the location of firm boundaries simply on the basis of some efficiency criterion.

One's scepticism that these are matters of economic optimization increases on recognizing that there is an alternative explanation of size distributions that puts more stress on history – that says that the world as it exists today can only be explained in terms of historical development. In the work that Yuji Ijiri and I (and quite a few other researchers) have done on this topic, we came to the conclusion that firm size distributions can be explained plausibly on a historical basis by considering the practical limits on rates of growth.

Very rapid growth usually incurs very large costs – almost impossibilities. The amount of money you can borrow today at a reasonable interest rate depends on how much money you have. The position of the decimal point in your statement of wealth is a major determinant of the decimal point in the amount a bank will loan you. Similarly, the absolute rate at which you can increase your sales is somewhat proportional to the size of the marketing organization you already have. A kind of Gibrat's law holds: everything has capacity for growth in proportion to how big it already is. If you build a stochastic model of firm sizes on this principle, with appropriate attention to boundary conditions, the steady-state distribution of the model will be a Pareto distribution, or something very similar. And when we look at firm sizes in the real world they conform to that same Pareto distribution.

My conclusion is that we live in a world where firm boundaries are not determined by considerations of static efficiency, although there are some efficiency constraints on minimum size of firms. (I am talking about firms, not factories. Stronger 'optimal size' arguments can be made for factories, perhaps.) Quality of information, and the cost of transmitting information across organizational boundaries may also sometimes be a consideration. But we must not leave out of account this historical factor: that if you are big you can grow bigger, and if you are little you can grow bigger – but only in proportion to how big or little you already are. A great many empirical facts are explained by that simple Gibrat assumption, and if we ignore the assumption, we are likely to over-explain the phenomenon of firm size on the basis of presumed efficiency considerations that may not be real.

Cristiano Antonelli

The issue of diversity among economic agents is very important in the economics of technological change and in industrial organization. In the market structure you see innovators and non-innovators, early adopters and late adopters, to say nothing of small and large size of firms beyond the levels of efficient size. Now the question, framed in the most simple way, is: does the hypothesis of cognitive heterogeneity fit into the bounded rationality framework, and if so, how?

Simon

One of the virtues of the bounded rationality framework as initially described is that you can fit a lot of things into it by foresight or hindsight. The notion of bounded rationality was developed as a critique of assumptions in classical economics. I think economists have had a valid complaint that a critique isn't enough – you have to say something positive about what should replace the criticized doctrines. In response, over the last decade or two there have been increasing efforts to characterize bounded rationality in a positive way: not simply as the opposite of what neoclassical economists have been thinking, but as a set of principles that explain what goes on in the real world.

For example, I think diversity among economic actors is very important. We take diversity for granted in other domains. There are 'A' students and 'B' students and 'C' students, partly as a matter of endowment and partly as a matter of learning. Diversity is not just a matter of high or low, for people differ in all sorts of qualitative ways, for example, the directions of their interests. Some people become chess masters, others expert chefs, and so on. Since this topic of diversity has been studied a great deal in psychology, both from the motivational and the cognitive sides, economics can get some help from psychology in building models to explain diversity. One product of this psychological research has already crossed the boundaries, if not into economics at least into management science. We are beginning to employ computerized expert systems that are based on what we have learned about human experts over the last 30 years. One of the things we have learned (about individuals, not organizations) is that an expert knows an awful lot and that no one is born an expert in anything, no matter what the initial talent may be. Two 'magic numbers' are now well established on the basis of empirical research.

First, an expert in any domain knows 50 000 things, or as we say in psychology, 50 000 'chunks'. I can illustrate what a chunk is by reference to natural language, for we are all experts in our own language. To estimate your vocabulary, go to the biggest Italian dictionary you can find, count the number of words whose meanings you know on ten pages of the dictionary selected at random, multiply by the number of pages in the dictionary and divide by ten. You will find that your vocabulary – the words whose meanings you will understand if you read them in context – is 50 000 words or more, perhaps even twice that. Chunks are simply familiar units, like the words in your vocabulary.

We find the same thing with chess experts, who can recognize many, many kinds of patterns on a chessboard (again, the number is estimated to be in excess of 50 000), and as a result of those recognitions, can retrieve all sorts of relevant information from memory – information that guides them to a good move. So the expert, in language or chess or any other domain, is among other things a large indexed encyclopedia. The chunks that can be recognized correspond to the index, and the information accessed by the act of recognition constitutes the encyclopedia.

The second magic number for experts is ten years. It has now been validated by careful research in about a dozen fields that no one becomes a world-class expert in less than ten years. But what about child prodigies? For instance, Mozart was writing music at the age of four. But if you've seen or heard that music, you will agree that it is not world-class music: the only reason it is of interest is that it was written by Mozart at the age of four. I think it is generally agreed among musicians that nothing Mozart wrote before age 17 (or, some would say, 21) is world-class. But 4 subtracted from 17 is 13, well over the ten-year limit. We must conclude that Mozart was a slow learner!

We can use facts like these to gain a deeper understanding of organizations. First of all, organization memories must, collectively, contain many more than 50 000 chunks, for organizations have many different kinds of experts in their employ. We can also use our understanding of expertise to find out where the expertness lies in an organization and what it is like: what kinds of knowledge and decision premises people in various parts of the organization can contribute to decision making.

When the expertise is not in one head but in many heads, then we must ask some research questions to which psychology does not yet provide answers. We need to study the flow of information in organizations as part of the decision-making process. I have in mind such work as Philip Bromeley, *Corporate Capital Investment: a Behavioral Approach* (1986). Bromeley, taking the cognitive point of view, tries to discover what executives are involved in the firm's investment decisions and what knowledge and rules of thumb they actually employ.

Now the value of such detailed study within the firm may depend on your goal. If you are trying to understand what firms are and how they operate, you will learn a lot from this kind of very detailed study of the processes of decision. If you are interested in macroeconomics, you may ask: 'How do we aggregate that?' and 'What good is it to study investment decisions in five firms?' Of course, we should not stop with five firms. Biologists have described millions of species of plants and animals in the world, and they think they've hardly started the job. Now, I'm not suggesting that we should go out and describe decision making in a million firms; but we might at least get on with the task and see if we can describe the first thousand. That doesn't immediately solve the aggregation problem, but surely, and in spite of the question of sampling, it is better to form an aggregate from detailed empirical knowledge of a thousand firms, or five, than from direct knowledge of none. But the latter is what we have been doing in economics for too many years.

Fornero

I would like to put to you a problem concerning the way we do research. In the study of human behaviour from an economic point of view, the adoption of a neoclassical model with intertemporal maximization gives us a rich and flexible instrument that can accommodate quite different things.

I think this gives us a useful starting point for clarifying facts, the possibility of walking along many different paths, of organizing our knowledge and our thoughts along different lines.

If I were to leave this model I would feel at a loss; I would be collecting data without a coherent supporting theory.

So, what can be done? If we leave the neoclassical model, where do we start from? Do you think the neoclassical model is flexible enough to accommodate even satisficing or bounded rationality, or would it be better if we left it altogether and started from . . . where?

Simon

I am a great believer in pluralism in science. Any direction you proceed in has a very high *a priori* probability of being wrong; so it is good if other people are exploring in other directions – perhaps one of them will be on the right track. For example, at the moment we are having a controversy in artificial intelligence between researchers who believe in the classical serial architecture for intelligent systems and those who believe in connectionist ('neural network') parallel architectures. I have some firm views (serialist) about which is right, but we took great pains at our university to establish a connectionist group, though we were sceptical that this was the most promising path. Hedging bets is a good rule of science.

So in answer to your question, I am going to take the coward's way out and say that I think both are good things. The first route you proposed – taking neoclassical theory and seeing what happens if you change it a bit by chipping away here and there – is really at the root of the new institutional economics. Even if the steps taken in the new institutional economics are rather conservative moves away from the neoclassical framework, they give you a starting point for thinking about the phenomenon of the firm. You begin to ask: 'Is there a moral hazard in this kind of contractual arrangement? Is there information asymmetry?'

The approach of the new institutional economics provides a checklist of things to look at. That's fine, but I would be sorry if that were all that we did. In terms of our discussion, I believe we are talking about a system that will ultimately look very different from the neoclassical system, and will direct attention to a whole set of phenomena that aren't considered in that system.

How can we search effectively in this open space? As a first point, it isn't completely open, but to see what might fill it, we will need to cross some disciplinary and some methodological boundaries. We must also give our students a chance to cross these boundaries in order to learn methods of research that will be useful when they take new approaches. For example, I don't think economics is going to change rapidly until all graduate students are exposed not only to the best econometric methods but also to field methods that study how decisions are actually made in the firm.

As a second point, we do have a body of knowledge in cognitive science about individual problem solving and decision making. I have tried to suggest through several examples how we can use that knowledge to help frame questions in economics. We also have something called organization theory that is not nearly as highly developed as cognitive science but contains a few homely truths, some of which have even been tested empirically. And so we can look to organization theory, which was the starting point for the behavioural theory of the firm, as a source of ideas to guide our empirical work. We have a good deal to begin with; we are not in a completely hopeless state.

Finally, I think we have been sold a bill of goods with the argument that we must always have a clear-cut theory before we can do empirical work. That belief not only holds sway in economics, but experimental psychology also has a bad case of it. Students are always told that they can't run a successful experiment if they don't have a hypothesis. How could they, without at least a null hypothesis, run a t-test on the data?

I believe that is a very bad criterion for the design of experiments. It is argued that if you don't have a hypothesis you are just counting bricks. But is that a bad thing? If you look down the list of outstanding discoveries in the physical sciences or the biological sciences – look at Nobel awards in those fields – you will note that a considerable number of the prizes are given to people who had the good fortune to experience a surprise.

What are the conditions for surprise? You aren't surprised if you have a well formulated hypothesis, go out and test it, and analyse your data to determine whether the hypothesis is plausible or implausible as measured by tests of statistical significance. I've even seen articles published, more often in psychological than in economics journals, that only reported the results of tests of statistical significance, and not the data at all. None of this provides surprise or anything else of importance in the real world.

What is surprise all about? If you happen to have a key, and you happen to have some photographic paper, you can put the key in a drawer on top of a piece of the photographic paper. Then, a few days later, you can open the drawer and find a picture of the key on the paper, even though they were kept from light. Well, as we all know, that's how X-rays were discovered. The discoverer was surprised.

And what are the conditions for surprise? Pasteur said: 'Accidents only happen to the prepared mind.' You are only surprised if you have 50 000 chunks of relevant knowledge and something happens that doesn't fit those chunks. You have to know a lot to be surprised. You have to have a set of expectations; that's where hypotheses can come in, but not really hypotheses, just knowledge of the world. You are surprised when your expectations about the world are disappointed.

To exploit surprise, you have to know what to do when you experience it. The first thing to do is to find the range of the surprising phenomenon; the second is to search for the mechanism. I have already mentioned the case of Roentgen. The Curies, who found radium, were very much surprised at the level of radiation in some pitchblend they were trying to purify. They continued to purify the ore, and found radium. The discovery of penicillin is a classical case of surprise that began when Fleming found bacteria being dissolved by some mould that had settled on his dirty Petri dish. You can go down the list of important discoveries and find dozens of similar examples among the most highly regarded discoveries in many fields of science.

The only way to experience such a surprise is to go out and look at the world, perhaps with some presumptions about how the world is. It isn't necessary to have a theory, but just to look at the world and say, 'Let's see; there's this coloured stone and that coloured stone . . .'. Of course, you have to be prepared to find something exciting and interesting. How many of you can remember reading an economics paper that was built around a surprise experienced by the investigator? After we've used our theory for all it is worth, after we've borrowed as many theories as we can from cognitive scientists and organization theorists and improved on them, let's also leave a little part of our lives for going out, and with naive childish curiosity, looking at the world. Sometimes it's interesting. Sometimes it will surprise us.

Roberto Tamborini

I would like to ask a question about the distinction between 'environmental uncertainty' and 'strategic uncertainty'. The latter arises because of other people's behaviour and, more deeply, other people's beliefs. As a consequence, when making our decisions, not only do we not know enough about weather forecasts – which seems the most that traditional uncertainty theory can say – but we do not know enough about other people's beliefs and strategies. Of course, this problem is only relevant if we agree that social sciences have to do with relationships among human beings, rather than among mindless 'things'.

The social scientist, the economist in particular, has been given a powerful tool to deal with strategic interaction: game theory. However, it seems that game theory still begs the question that afflicts traditional optimization theory: the extension of cognitive power we are entitled to load on to agents. We are now aware that game theory breaks down as the number of players increases, information is vast and dispersed, and games get more complicated. Playable games indeed include a limited range of ordinary social and economic life. So, my question is simply, how can we assess the contribution of game theory and how can we cope with strategic uncertainty when decision makers are unable, or unwilling, to engage in 'playable games'?

Simon

The principal thing we have learned from game theory, a very important lesson, is that even the very definition of rationality becomes problematic as soon as we have interaction among more than two rational agents with partially or wholly competitive goals. The notion of solution proposed by von Neumann and Morgenstern for n-person games guaranteed neither the existence of a solution nor its uniqueness, and in fact, uniqueness is the rare exception rather than the general case. So what game theory taught us was that there are many patterns of action in most social situations that could claim to be in some sense 'rational'. Strategic uncertainty – uncertainty about what the other players were going to do – proved to be something quite different from uncertainty about the external environment. The latter could be dealt with (conceptually at least, if not in the real world) by probabilities and expected values; the former could not.

Because game theory is intrinsically unable to make specific predictions of behaviour from the postulates of rationality, in order to understand behaviour we must look at the empirical phenomena to see how people actually play games. We must not suppose that there is some way in which we can magically, by pure reason, reduce the number of alternative definitions of rationality that game theory provides us with.

One thing that is obvious (if I may use that dangerous term) is that organizations play a particular role in strategic games, because they provide a mechanism that is not provided by markets for establishing rules of the road. If you have an organization, it can decide that everyone is going to drive on the right side of the street (except the English, but they have their own separate island). Organizations provide a way of dealing with that set of games where there is common interest, but strategic uncertainty – incomplete information – about what the other players are going to do. That is an important fact about organizations.

But when we get into the realm where conflict of interest prevails, we need to observe and to experiment if we are to build a theory of 'rationality'. I am pleased at the rapid expansion now going on in experimental gaming as a research strategy. I don't know if it is currently popular in Italy, but in the United States it is now a vigorous cottage industry. Soon every economics department will feel that it needs at least one faculty member who does experimental gaming or other experimental economics. We will need a lot more empirical investigation to determine what are the empirically interesting definitions of rationality in game situations.

Elisabetta Galeotti

Since I am not an economist, my question is not only slightly outside
the mainstream of the present discussion, but probably rather trivial
to this audience.

I happened to be studying Hayek's methodology and I was struck
by the fact that his notion of imperfect knowledge and human
limitation bears some resemblance to your concept of bounded
rationality. Yet, from similar premises, very different conclusions
seem to follow. What I mean is that, in Hayek, imperfect information and limited rationality bring the rejection of any social
planning and the defence of social spontaneity; in your case, on the
contrary, the concept of bounded rationality is the basis for a theory
of organization. I would like you to expand a little on this point of
departure.

Simon

Until a few months ago, I hadn't thought very much about Austrian
economics, at least since my graduate days. This summer I had
occasion to think about it about in connection with a conference I
attended, and I realized that from one point of view, as you correctly
observed, one could think of the Austrian viewpoint, particularly
von Hayek's version of it, as a form of bounded rationality. Among
other things, the Austrians put a tremendous emphasis on tacit and
personal knowledge, and hence had been very antagonistic to the
development of quantitative and abstract formal economics. But
this very same emphasis ultimately divided them from the notion of
bounded rationality. In particular, it led von Mises to an extreme *a
prioristic* position in which someone – perhaps the good Lord – told
him what the Truth was, and the Truth was neoclassical theory done
non-quantitatively. That led him away from the notion of bounded
rationality and back to utility maximization.

My own beliefs have been that knowledge is something we
produce by processes that can be studied and researched and
explained. If the theory of expert behaviour I proposed earlier is
correct, then the sorts of knowledge that the Austrians would
describe as tacit knowledge are understandable in terms of the
50 000 chunks and the way in which these are accessed through the
recognition process. Recognition is also the process that is often

labelled 'intuition' or 'insight'. So starting, as you shrewdly observed, with what looks like a very similar viewpoint, we rapidly diverge when it comes to attitudes about empiricism. I think that not only are human methods of thought and methods of learning, including tacit knowing, researchable and describable, but also that we have effective methods for accomplishing that research and description, and in fact have already elucidated many of the phenomena. This possibility is denied by the Austrians. And that leads us in quite different directions, for we find, when we do the empirical research, that human beings think in very different ways from those implied by neoclassical theory.

Although von Hayek has this neoclassical side, he has another side as well. The von Hayek I like best is the author of the 1945 paper in the *Proceedings of the American Economic Association* where he argues that the real importance of the market mechanism is not that it produces a Pareto optimum (if it does), but that it conserves information for all of the economic actors, and allows them to behave rationally with relatively simple computations and on the basis of relatively little information. This is an idea that advocates of bounded rationality can accept with enthusiasm, and it is a pity that mainstream economics didn't take this proposal of von Hayek with the seriousness it deserves.

In arguing for markets as mechanisms for simplifying choice, whittling it down to a size where human minds can deal with it, von Hayek undoubtedly exaggerates the role of prices as the only or chief coordinating device in markets. I commented earlier that when we regulate inventories, we do so largely by quantity responses rather than price responses. So perhaps von Hayek was wrong in giving prices the very privileged place they occupy in his article, but he was very right about what markets and economic exchanges are all about – how they make it possible for people of bounded rationality to make reasonable choices. So it is a complex picture. Bounded rationality appears very Austrian in some dimensions and very anti-Austrian in others.

Roberto Cordeschi

I would like to know the reaction of Professor Simon to certain criticisms of the principle of bounded rationality as an explanatory principle of human decision making. These criticisms concern the point that in certain cases it is quite difficult – if not impossible – to define the process of decision making as an heuristic search in the well ordered space of the possible alternative.

This seems to be the case in many real-life problems, for example when the agent does not have sufficient time to make a careful evaluation of these alternatives, and is forced to make a decision quickly. In such a case (this is the core of the criticism) it is the context – or the 'background' – which makes the problem ill structured or even unstructured for the agent; accordingly, his behaviour cannot be adequately described in terms of bounded rationality.

Simon

We are all aware that the decisions we make in our own lives range along a continuum, from very well structured ones to very ill structured ones. At home I eat a standard breakfast: the fruit is melon in summer and grapefruit in winter – that's a trivial decision. The cereal is oatmeal or some kind of wheat cereal. We can decide that by keeping three boxes of cereal on the shelf and taking one down, in order, every morning. That's a very well structured problem.

Then we go to the other extreme: the ill structured decisions. The most horrendous are the life-and-death decisions that national governments make, but there are some pretty difficult ones in everyday life. The theory of heuristic search, and most of the empirical evidence about problem solving gathered during the first fifteen or twenty years of cognitive science was concerned with well structured decisions. We learned a lot about how people solve problems that are well structured. We learned a lot, too, about chess, which in some respects is well structured – its definite rules and goal – and in other respects is ill structured. The number of possibilities is so large that you can't play it by computing the minimax of game theory. So chess represents one step toward understanding ill structured problems, and the progress of AI and cognitive science research has been from the well structured to the ill structured. One of its strategies is to pick some class of ill structured problems that has not been dealt with yet, and to invent a computer program that will solve such problems.

For example, in recent years, researchers in architecture have been trying to write programs that will do architectural design. Already, they are able to lay out floor plans, which is a rather ill structured problem. There are a lot of possibly conflicting criteria that have to be satisfied by a floor plan, and alternative possible arrangements have to be discovered. It isn't just a matter of minimizing or maximizing a well defined criterion over some set of given alternatives.

I can point to a lot of examples of programs that handle ill structured problems. What, for example, can be more ill structured than scientific discovery? But today we have programs that, given sets of data, are capable of finding scientific laws hidden in those data. We have learned a great deal about what is required to solve the kinds of ill structured problem that are connected with scientific discovery. Not all aspects of the scientific endeavour have been examined so far, but a number of them have, and successfully.

You raised the specific problem of making decisions in real time. Here we have some clearcut evidence of what is required, and one part of this evidence led us to the 50 000 chunks. To illustrate, I must go back to the game of chess, which is a serious problem domain, particularly for chess professionals. Chess has become for cognitive science research what the *Drosophila*, fruit fly, is for research in genetics. We need standard organisms so that we can accumulate knowledge. That's my excuse for talking so much about chess.

In a tournament, a chess player has to make twenty moves every hour, an average of three minutes per move. Some moves are obvious, and can be made in a few seconds. On other moves, a player may consider what to do for ten or fifteen minutes: you often see grand masters doing that in tournament games. Now put that same grand master in a room with 50 lesser players whom he must play simultaneously. He'll move from board to board, averaging perhaps twenty seconds for a move at each, and he will win all or almost all of the 50 games.

You can show that the grand master in the simultaneous demonstration is not playing at grand master level, for if you put another grand master at one of the 50 boards, the latter will almost certainly win. But experts, the next grade below masters, will almost always lose. This means that most, though not all, of the grand master's skill is still there, even without the three minutes. How does he do it? He uses precisely those recognition processes we describe earlier; there is lots of empirical evidence for that. As the grand master moves to a board, if he doesn't notice anything unusual or interesting on it, he makes a standard developing move (there are certain sensible things to do when you can't think of anything better – move your pieces to positions of greater mobility, for example). Every grand master has lots of heuristics that suggest standard moves when there is nothing better.

Sooner or later, the other player, since he is not a grand master, will create a feature on the board that the grand master, but not the weaker player, will recognize as a weakness – there is a doubled pawn, or the King's position is loose, for example. The moment the grand master sees one of these familiar friends, one of the 50 000 chunks, it reminds him of all sorts of things to do about it, to exploit it. In five more moves the game is lost for his opponent.

So the answer to the question of real-time responses, and the answer to the question of how experts behave intuitively, is that they have the 50 000 chunks. When they don't have time to solve problems by careful analysis, they solve them by recognition. Sometimes they make mistakes, but less often than you and I, who have fewer recognition cues to draw upon.

Giovanni Dosi

The issue of equivalence or non-equivalence of market and organizational structure is crucial, both in terms of general theoretical modelling and in terms of explaining such phenomena as the one that you mentioned before, namely firm distributions by size.

I think Professor Egidi has already mentioned the possible non-equivalence between the two counts especially under conditions that are not stationary.

In a stationary world, however complex, both market and organization essentially perform the role of coordination and the problem of non-equivalence may arise in relation to issues quite familiar in standard literature, such as imperfect information, incentives, etc.

The non-equivalence of organization and market under non-stationarity is amplified by the fact that organizations embody a permanent tension between coordination and innovative learning.

You might have, for example, a loosely coordinated organization composed of crazy scientists, that learns a lot but coordinates very badly. Or, the other way around, you might have organizations that are very efficient in coordinating on given tasks but totally incapable of learning.

Conversely, it might be, under certain circumstances, that markets perform satisfactorily in allowing decentralized innovative 'explorations' or 'trials', irrespective of how efficient they are in allocating given resources.

In general, what I am hinting at here is that, in non-stationary environments as far as our experience of contemporary capitalism is concerned, one is likely to find different modes, and relative importance, or organizational learning versus decentralized trials and errors.

An implication that I suggest is that the set of neutral equilibria between markets and organizations is only a sub-set of the possible combinations of market/organization that are logically conceivable.

In between you have path-dependent processes and you don't know where you are going to end up, unless you have a detailed knowledge of initial conditions and history. Then if this is so, I always wonder whether purely stochastic interpretations of observed regularities as Gibrat's law on the size distribution of firms are enough.

Certainly they can give a good representation of what happens in large aggregates. Moreover, one may invoke Occam, on the parsimoniousness of explanations, and you might not want anything more.

Still, I would like to know what kind of evolutionary process is leading there. We share the view that learning is one of the crucial phenomena to be investigated theoretically. But, then what about the learning process, what about cognitive structures and their changes? Suppose you want to represent cognition processes leading from playing chess to playing poker: what kind of generalizations can one make on that, both in terms of individual cognitive structures and, even more linked with economics, the forms of learning inside the organization?

Simon

Learning is a very active area for research today. A few years ago, I tried to persuade a student to write a thesis about how one would transfer to a game like poker what he already knew about the game of chess. After further discussion, it became clear that that wasn't a feasible research problem at that time – a decade ago. Today it might well be.

At present, however, the area of learning is very active, including the problem of how we learn new structures, or representations, for problems. Let me cite examples of what we now know about this task. There are computer programs which, if given the description in natural language of a well structured, puzzle-like problem, one that the system has never seen before, will be able to construct in memory a representation of the problem: a description of the objects it involves, the relations between the objects, what constitutes a move, what constitutes a goal. The problem representation is sufficiently complete that a problem-solving program can go to work on it. For simple situations, then, we know how to build a system that can extract that kind of information from language and use it to construct a representation.

We also know how to make use of knowledge about things in the world to construct repesentations of particular situations that involve those kinds of things. For example, a program called Isaac can be given a natural language statement of problems in physics, statics problems, and on the basis of the knowledge Isaac already has about levers and masses, and the like, it will construct in its memory a representation of this particular physics problem. It will then go to work to solve it by setting up the appropriate equations. We know much less about how a really major change in representation occurs. At the time of Faraday, scientists interested in electricity and magnetism thought about it in Newtonian terms, in analogy to gravitation with central forces and action at a distance. Faraday thought instead in terms of continuous fields of force. His metaphor was taken over by Maxwell and the other Cambridge mathematicians and became field theory, which is our modern preferred way of representing physical situations. Why did Faraday make the change? Ideas of field were around since Greek times, as were ideas of atomicity. How did Faraday decide that his problem should be treated in terms of fields? These questions have hardly been touched yet. You will have to give the cognitive psychologists a few more years to answer them. Or you may want to try yourself.

Bruno Contini

First of all, I would like to make sure that I understand one basic message that comes from Dr Simon's lecture. I think that he has unveiled for us a strategy that will enhance our own chances of becoming Nobel prize candidates. The strategy is 'look for surprises in your research programs'. It's a very simple heuristic indeed.

I would like to make a comment on my own research that relates to Professor Simon's observation about surprises earlier. If one observes what's going on all over the industrial world, there seems to be a strong trend towards the vertical disintegration of production (at the plant level) and an increased division of labour. This implies higher recourse to the market and less reliance on the organizational hierarchy. I was surprised to find out how little attention is being paid to this phenomenon in the United States. Nor is there (here and there) much analytical insight on how such a process comes about.

One direction of research which I think might be of use is the analysis of panel data of business firms, in the search for adequate indicators of the organizational structure.

Panel data are available, but most economists seem to be thinking of other uses for these data. May I mention one little surprise that I had when looking at panel data of Italian firms?

If one sorts out groups of profitable firms and groups of unprofitable firms, what does one find? One finds that the profitable firms have all decided to go out and 'buy'. The unprofitable ones instead are those that 'make'. Now, this correlation is obviously not sufficient to clarify what the process at work is, but it is an important hint and may develop into satisfactory explanations in future research.

Simon

The problem of degree of integration of business firms might be an attractive one for computer modelling, and I gather that you and possibly others are doing some of that. I am not going to try to second guess what will come out of such empirical studies. Dozens of hypotheses have been put forth about the optimal degree of integration or separation. In the United States it appears that many of the firms that are being dismembered are precisely the ones that were put together a few years ago as conglomerates, and never had any reasons except financial ones for being integrated. But I don't know empirically whether that is actually the case.

The correlation you have discovered between profitability and the decision to buy rather than make requires some interpretation. What the processes and drives are that would lead unprofitable firms to keep things in house and profitable firms to contract outside (if that's the way the causation goes) are not immediately evident. Particularly, we would need to know how integrated the firms were initially.

But I don't see any difficulty in principle in getting empirical evidence about what people are thinking when they make these decisions. Newspaper reporters frequently get such information. Sometimes they are misled, but reporters are pretty shrewd and usually fairly knowledgeable. With the guarantees of anonymity that we can give in our research, I think we can successfully inquire into the processes that went on, and which led to the decisions. You see, having preached empiricism in all my remarks today, I don't want to offer guesses as to what you will see when you go into the firms. I hope you will be surprised – as you suggest you already have been.

Miriam Campanella

I would like to comment on a very interesting statement on the subject of political rationality that I found in the 1985 Lecture at APSA. Let me quote the passage. In politics – you say – 'the key premises are the empirical assumptions about goals and, even more important, about the ways in which people characterize the choice situations that face them. These goals and characterizations do not rest on immutable first principles, but are functions of time and place that can only be ascertained by empirical inquiry. In this sense, political science is necessarily a historical science – in the same way and for the same reason as astronomy.' Could I have your views on the following?

First, I find that the way in which analysts collect data about choice situations has something in common with the self-referential notion of cognition analysed by Maturana, Foerster, Glazarsfeld and Varela.

Second, if this is so, I would like to know how it is possible in this case to avoid the tautological, or self-justificatory representation implied by this methodology.

Third, while I share your thesis on the major reality of the procedural or segmented rationalities, at the same time I am afraid (I am thinking of these Italian politicians who behave in a Machiavellian way) that the heuristic fruitfulness of that realistic self-oriented representation is not sufficient to cover the need for normative account.

I mean that the next stop could be, almost theoretically, to network (map) the actions of one actor or more actors in order to realize a deeper learning about actors and decision making and the actual consequences arising in related time–space parameters. But this kind of learning is quite different from the knowledge considered in the Olympic rationality. Perhaps it is properly learning, while the outcome of that learning is not optimal choice, but something near to 'responsibility' of choices.

If you have done some thinking about the differences between knowledge and learning, can you let me know what your understanding of this is?

Simon

I will comment briefly on each of the three questions.

First, any information we gather about the world, whether through a telescope or a microscope or by interviewing or observing business executives, is filtered through our eyes and ears, hence influenced by our representations of reality. A major task of all the sciences, physical, biological, or social, is to make the filter relatively innocuous, so that scientific knowledge can be public and objective. We can accomplish this only as a matter of degree, and hence our descriptions of our observations will always be subject to modification.

But many of us are persuaded that the process is a convergent one, that we can incrementally approach objectivity in observing – long before we have anything approaching a correct scientific picture of the phenomena we are observing. Thus anthropologists are trained to describe the values and behaviours of the societies they are studying even if these are quite different from the values and behaviours of their own society, and quite independently of a theory of what determines such values and behaviours. Political scientists are trained to predict elections accurately even when the predictions are contrary to their own political preferences, and even though they may have no good theory to explain the electorate's preferences. While the elimination of bias is never quite complete, reducing it to a minimal level is a major objective of scientific training, and objectivity a mark of the professional.

In particular, achieving a relatively high level of objectivity in observing does not have to wait until we have a correct theory of the phenomena we are observing. We can have good telescopes long before we have a veridical theory of astrophysics, or even of optics. Similarly, we can observe businessmen's decision-making behaviour objectively without having a complete theory of either their decisions or ours.

I do not mean to argue that bias in observation is not a problem, but simply that we have learned a great deal about how to reduce the problem to manageable proportions – to a level where it does not prevent us from gathering relatively objective data about our world, physical and social.

Second, since my previous answer expresses scepticism about the premise of this question, I have little to add. I do not think that the information we gain by observing the world need be (or, if we are well trained scientists, is likely to be) either tautological or self-justificatory.

Third, since representations do change, it is useful to think in terms of learning as well as knowledge. Let me take as a concrete example the methodology of taking thinking-aloud protocols as a source of data in problem-solving or decision-making research. The interpretation of thinking-aloud data is certainly not wholly independent of our theory of human cognition. Rejected at one time as 'introspective', hence subjective and unreliable, thinking-aloud protocols are now used widely in cognitive research. They are usually interpreted as reports of the contents of short-term memory, itself a construct of cognitive theory. Hence we have learned to interpret thinking-aloud protocols in the course of improving our theory of cognition, specifically our theory of how short-term memory works.

But notice that it is the *interpretation* of the thinking-aloud data, and not the data themselves, that is the subject of the learning. The data themselves (up to the limits of noisy tapes or transcription errors) are nearly perfectly objective (although filtered through our eyes and ears). They will be the same data a generation from now even if we reinterpret their significance in terms of improved cognitive theories.

I don't believe that the viewpoint I am taking here implies any kind of Olympian rationality. It simply implies that we can observe with reasonable objectivity even phenomena that we do not fully understand, or may understand differently tomorrow than today. The learning has to do with the significance of the phenomena, not with whether they have been observed.

PART TWO

Herbert Simon Reprints

3. Rational Choice and the Structure of the Environment* (1956)[1]

A growing interest in decision making in psychology is evidenced by the recent publication of Edwards's review article in the *Psychological Bulletin* (Edwards 1954) and the Santa Monica Conference volume, *Decision Processes* (Thrall et al. 1954). In this work, much attention has been focused on the characterization of *rational* choice, and because the latter topic has been a central concern in economics, the theory of decision making has become a natural meeting ground for psychological and economic theory.

A comparative examination of the models of adaptive behaviour employed in psychology (e.g. learning theories), and of the models of rational behaviour employed in economics, shows that in almost all respects the latter postulate a much greater complexity in the choice mechanisms, and a much larger capacity in the organism for obtaining information and performing computations, than do the former. Moreover, in the limited range of situations where the predictions of the two theories have been compared (See Thrall et al. 1954, Chapters 9, 10, 18), the learning theories appear to account for the observed behaviour rather better than do the theories of rational behaviour.

Both from these scanty data and from an examination of the postulates of the economic models it appears probable that, however adaptive the behaviour of organisms in learning and choice situations, this adaptiveness falls far short of the ideal of 'maximizing' postulated in economic theory. Evidently, organisms adapt well enough to 'satisfice'; they do not, in general, 'optimize'.

*Reprinted with the permission of the copyright holder from *The Psychological Review*, No. 63, 1956.

If this is the case, a great deal can be learned about rational decision making by taking into account, at the outset, the limitations upon the capacities and complexity of the organism, and by taking account of the fact that the environments to which it must adapt possess properties that permit further simplification of its choice mechanisms. It may be useful, therefore, to ask: how simple a set of choice mechanisms can we postulate and still obtain the gross features of observed adaptive choice behaviour?

In a previous paper (Simon 1955) I have put forth some suggestions as to the kinds of 'approximate' rationality that might be employed by an organism possessing limited information and limited computational facilities. The suggestions were 'hypothetical' in that, lacking definitive knowledge of the human decisional processes, we can only conjecture on the basis of our everyday experiences, our introspection, and a very limited body of psychological literature what these processes are. The suggestions were intended, however, as empirical statements, however tentative, about some of the actual mechanisms involved in human and other organismic choice.[2]

Now if an organism is confronted with the problem of behaving approximately rationally, or adaptively, in a particular environment, the kinds of simplifications that are suitable may depend not only on the characteristics – sensory, neural and other – of the organism, but equally upon the structure of the environment. Hence we might hope to discover, by a careful examination of some of the fundamental structural characteristics of the environment, some further clues as to the nature of the approximating mechanisms used in decision making. This is the line of attack that will be adopted in the present paper.

The environment we shall discuss initially is perhaps a more appropriate one for a rat than for a human. For the term *environment* is ambiguous. We are not interested in describing some physically objective world in its totality, but only those aspects of the totality that have relevance as the 'life space' of the organism considered. Hence what we call the 'environment' will depend upon the 'needs', 'drives', or 'goals' of the organism, and upon its perceptual apparatus.

THE ENVIRONMENT OF THE ORGANISM

We consider first a simplified (perhaps 'simple-minded') organism that has a single need – food – and is capable of three kinds of activity: resting, exploration and food getting. The precise nature of these activities will be explained later. The organism's life space may be described as a surface over which it can locomote. Most of the surface is perfectly bare, but at isolated, widely scattered points there are little heaps of food, each adequate for a meal.

The organism's vision permits it to see, at any moment, a circular portion of the surface about the point in which it is standing. It is able to move at some fixed maximum rate over the surface. It metabolizes at a given average rate and is able to store a certain amount of food energy, so that it needs to eat a meal at certain average intervals. It has the capacity, once it sees a food heap, to proceed toward it at the maximum rate of locomotion. The problem of rational choice is to choose its path in such a way that it will not starve.

Now I submit that a rational way for the organism to behave is the following: (a) it explores the surface at random, watching for a food heap; (b) when it sees one, it proceeds to it and eats (food getting); (c) if the total consumption of energy during the average time required, per meal, for exploration and food getting is less than the energy of the food consumed in the meal, it can spend the remainder of its time in resting.[3]

There is nothing particularly remarkable about this description of rational choice, except that it differs so sharply from the more sophisticated models of human rationality that have been proposed by economists and others. Let us see what it is about the organism and its environment that makes its choice so simple.

1. It has only a single goal: food. It does not need to weigh the respective advantages of different goals. It requires no 'utility function' or set of 'indifference curves' to permit it to choose between alternatives.
2. It has no problem of maximization. It needs only to maintain a certain average rate of food intake, and additional food is of no use to it. In the psychologist's language, it has a definite, fixed aspiration level, and its successes or failures do not change its aspirations.

3. The nature of its perceptions and its environment limit sharply its planning horizon. Since the food heaps are distributed randomly, there is no need for pattern in its searching activities. Once it sees a food heap, it can follow a definite 'best' path until it reaches it.

4. The nature of its needs and environment create a very natural separation between 'means' and 'end'. Except for the food heaps, one point on the surface is as agreeable to it as another. Locomotion has significance only as it is a means to reaching food.[4]

We shall see that the first point is not essential. As long as aspirations are fixed, the planning horizon is limited, and there is a sharp distinction between means and ends; the existence of multiple goals does not create any real difficulties in choice. The real complications ensue only when we relax the last three conditions; but to see clearly what is involved, we must formulate the model a little more precisely.

PERCEPTUAL POWERS, STORAGE CAPACITY AND SURVIVAL

It is convenient to describe the organism's life space not as a continuous surface, but as a branching system of paths, like a maze, each branch point representing a choice point. We call the selection of a branch and locomotion to the next branch point a 'move'. At a small fraction of the branch points are heaps of food.

Let p, $0 < p < 1$ be the percentage of branch points, randomly distributed, at which food is found. Let d be the average number of paths diverging from each branch point. Let v be the number of moves ahead the organism can see. That is, if there is food at any of the branch points within v moves of the organism's present position, it can select the proper paths and reach it. Finally let H be the maximum number of moves the organism can make between meals without starving.

At any given moment, the organism can see d branch points at a distance of one move from his present position, d^2 points two moves away, and in general, d^k points k moves away. In all, it can see $d + d^2 + \ldots + d^v = d(d^v - 1)/(d - 1)$ points. When it chooses a branch and makes a move, d^v new points become visible on its horizon. Hence, in the course of m moves, md^v new points appear. Since it can make a maximum of H moves, and since v of these will be required to reach food that it has discovered on its horizon, the probability, $Q = 1 - P$, that it will *not* survive will be equal to the probability that no food points will be visible in $(H - v)$ moves. (If p is small, we can disregard the possibility that food will be visible inside its planning horizon on the first move.) Let ρ be the probability that none of the d^v new points visible at the end of a particular move is a food point.

$$\rho = (1 - p)d^v \qquad (3.1)$$

Then:

$$1 - P = Q = \rho(H - v) = (1 - \rho)^{(H - v)d^v} \qquad (3.2)$$

We see that the survival chances from meal to meal, of this simple organism depend on four parameters, two that describe the organism and two the environment: p, the richness of the environment in food; d, the richness of the environment in paths; H, the storage capacity of the organism; and v, the range of vision of the organism.

To give some impression of the magnitudes involved, let us assume that p is $1/10\,000$, $(H - v)$ is 100, d is 10 and v is 3. Then the probability of seeing a new food point after a move is $1 - p = 1 - (1 - p)^{1000} \sim 880/10\,000$, and the probability of survival is $P = 1 - \rho^{100} \sim 9999/10\,000$. Hence there is in this case only one chance in 10 000 that the organism will fail to reach a food point before the end of the survival interval. Suppose now that the survival time $(H - v)$ is increased one-third, that is, from 100 to 133. Then a similar computation shows that the chance of starvation is reduced to less than one chance in 100 000. A one-third increase in v will, of course, have an even greater effect, reducing the chance of starvation from one in 10^{-4} to one in 10^{-40}.

Using the same values, $p = .0001$, and $(H - v) = 100$, we can compute the probability of survival if the organism behaves completely randomly. In this case $P' = [1 - (1 - p)^{100}] = .009$. From these computations, we see that the organism's modest capacity to perform purposive acts over a short planning horizon permits it to survive easily in an environment where random behaviour would lead to rapid extinction. A simple computation shows that its perceptual powers multiply by a factor of 880 the average speed with which it discovers food.

If p, d and v are given, and in addition we specify that the survival probability must be greater than some numbers close to unity $(P \geq 1 - \varepsilon)$, we can compute from (3.2) the corresponding minimum value of H:

$$\log (1 - P) = (H - v) \log \rho \tag{3.3}$$
$$H \geq v + \log \varepsilon / \log \rho \tag{3.4}$$

For example, if $\rho = .95$ and $\varepsilon = 10^{-10}$, then $\log \rho = -.022$, $\log \varepsilon = -10$ and $(H - v) \geq 455$. The parameter, H, can be interpreted as the 'storage capacity' of the organism. That is, if the organism metabolizes at the rate of α units per move, then a storage of αH food units, where H is given by Equation (3.4), would be required to provide survival at the specified risk level ε.

Further insight into the meaning of H can be gained by considering the average number of moves, M, required to discover food. From Equation (3.1), the probability of making $(k - 1)$ moves without discovering food, and then discovering it on the kth is:

$$P_k = (1 - \rho)\rho^{(k-1)} \tag{3.5}$$

Hence the average number of moves, M, required to discover food is:

$$M = \sum_{k=1}^{\infty} k(1 - \rho)\rho^{(k-1)} = (1 - \rho)/(1 - \rho)^2 = 1/(1 - \rho) \tag{3.6}$$

Since $(1 - \rho)$ is the probability of discovering food in any one move, M is the reciprocal of this probability. Combining (3.3) and (3.6) we obtain:

$$M/(H - v) = (\log\rho)/((1 - \rho)\log(1 - P)) \tag{3.7}$$

Since ρ is close to one, $\log \hat{e} \ p \simeq (1 - \rho)$, and (3.7) reduces approximately to:

$$M/(H - v) \simeq 1/\log_e(1 - P) \tag{3.8}$$

For example, if we require $(1 - P) = \varepsilon \leq 10^{-4}$ (one chance in 10 000 of starvation), then $M/(H - v) \leq .11$. For this survival level we required food storage approximately equal to $\alpha(v + 9M)$ – food enough to sustain the organism for nine times the period required, on the average, to discover food, plus the period required to reach the food.[5]

CHOICE MECHANISM FOR MULTIPLE GOALS

We consider now a more complex organism capable of searching for and responding to one or more kinds of goal objects. In doing this we could introduce any desired degree of complexity into the choice process; but the interesting problem is how to introduce multiple goals with a minimum complication of the process – that is, to construct an organism capable of handling its decision problems with relatively primitive choice mechanisms.

At the very least, the presence of two goals will introduce a consistency requirement – the time consumed in attaining one goal will limit the time available for pursuit of the other. But in an environment like the one we have been considering, there need be no further relationship between the two goals. In our original formulation, the only essential stipulation was that H, the storage capacity, be adequate to maintain the risk of starvation below a stipulated level $(1 - P)$. Now we introduce the additional stipulation that the organism should only devote a fraction, λ, of its time to food-seeking activities, leaving the remaining fraction, $1 - \lambda$, to other activities. This new stipulation leads to a requirement of additional storage capacity.

In order to control the risk of starving, the organism must begin its exploration for food whenever it has reached a level of H periods of food storage. If it has a total storage of $(\mu + H)$ periods of food, and if the food heaps are at least $\alpha(\mu + H)$ in size, then it need begin the search for food only μ periods after its last feeding. But the food search will require, on the average, M periods. Hence, if a hunger threshold is established that leads the organism to begin to explore μ periods after feeding, we will have:

$$\lambda = M/M + \mu \tag{3.9}$$

Hence, by making μ sufficiently large, we can make λ as small as we please. Parenthetically, it may be noted that we have here a close analogue to the very common two-bin system of controlling industrial inventories. The primary storage, H, is a buffer stock to meet demands pending the receipt of new orders (with risk, $1 - P$, of running out); the secondary storage, μ, defines the 'order point'; and $\mu + M$ is the average order quantity. The storage μ is fixed to balance storage 'costs' against the cost (in this case, time pressure) of too frequent reordering.

If food and the second goal object (water, let us say) are randomly and independently distributed, then there are no important complications resulting from interference between the two activities. Designate by the subscript 1 the variables and parameters referring to food getting (e.g. μ_1 is the food threshold in periods), and by the subscript 2 the quantities referring to water seeking. The organism will have adequate time for both activities if $\lambda_1 + \lambda_2 < 1$.

Now when the organism reaches either its hunger or thirst threshold, it will begin exploration. We assume that if *either* of the goal objects becomes visible, it will proceed to that object and satisfy its hunger or thirst (this will not increase the number of moves required, on the average, to reach the other object); but if *both* objects become visible at the same time, and if S_1 and S_2 are the respective quantities remaining in storage at this time, then it will proceed to food or water as M_1/S_1 is greater or less than M_2/S_2. This choice will maximize its survival probability. What is required, then, is a mechanism that produces a drive proportional to M_i/S_i.

A priority mechanism of the kind just described is by no means the only or simplest one that can be postulated. An even simpler rule is for the organism to persist in searching for points that will satisfy the particular need that first reached its threshold and initiated exploratory behaviour. This is not usually an efficient procedure, from the standpoint of conserving goal-reaching time, but it may be entirely adequate for an organism generously endowed with storage capacity.

We see that an organism can satisfy a number of distinct needs without requiring a very elaborate mechanism for choosing among them. In particular we do not have to postulate a utility function or a 'marginal rate of substitution'.

We can go even further, and assert that a primitive choice mechanism is adequate to take advantage of important economies, if they exist, which are derivable from the interdependence of the activities involved in satisfying the different needs. For suppose the organism has n needs, and that points at which he can satisfy each are distributed randomly and independently through the environment, each with the same probability, p. Then the probability that no points satisfying *any* of the needs will be visible on a particular move is p^n, and the mean number of moves for discovery of the *first* need-satisfying point is:

$$m_n = 1/(1 - p^n) \tag{3.10}$$

Suppose that the organism begins to explore, moves to the first need-satisfying point it discovers, resumes its exploration, moves to the next point it discovers that satisfies a need other than the one already satisfied, and so on. Then the mean time required to search for all n goals will be:

$$M_n = m_n + m_{n-1} + \ldots = \sum_{i=1}^{\infty} 1/(1 - p^i) << n/(1 - p) \tag{3.11}$$

In particular, if p is close to one, that is, if need-satisfying points are rare, we will have:

$$M_n - M_{n-1} = 1/(1 - p^n) = 1/[(1 - p) \sum_{i=0}^{n} p^i] \simeq M_1/n \tag{3.12}$$

and

$$M \simeq M_1 \sum_{i=1}^{n} (1/i) \tag{3.13}$$

Now substituting particular values for n in (3.13) we get: $M_2 = 3/2\ M_1$; $M_3 = 11/6\ M_1$; $M_4 = 25/12\ M_1$, etc. We see that if the organism has two separate needs, its exploration time will be only 50 per cent greater than – and not twice as great as – if it has only one need; for four needs the exploration time will be only slightly more than twice as great as for a single need, and so on. A little consideration of the program just described will show that the joint exploratory process does not reduce the primary storage capacity required by the organism but does reduce the secondary storage capacity required. Indeed, there would be no necessity at all for secondary storage.

This conclusion holds only if the need-satisfying points are *independently* distributed. If there is a negative correlation in the joint distribution of points satisfying different needs, then it may be economical for the organism to pursue its needs separately, and hence to have a simple signalling mechanism, involving secondary storage, to trigger its several exploration drives. This point will be developed further in the next section.

A word may be said here about 'avoidance needs'. Suppose that certain points in the organism's behaviour space are designated as 'dangerous'. Then it will need to avoid those paths that lead to these particular points. If r per cent of all points, randomly distributed, are dangerous, then the number of available paths, among those visible at a given move, will be reduced to $(1 - r)d^v$. Hence, $\rho' = (1 - \rho)^{(1-r)d^v}$ will be smaller than ρ (Equation 3.1), and M (Equation 3.6) will be correspondingly larger. Hence, the presence of danger points simply increases the average exploration time and, consequently, the required storage capacity of the organism.

FURTHER SPECIFICATION OF THE ENVIRONMENT: CLUES

In our discussion up to the present point, the range of the organism's anticipations of the future has been limited by the number of behaviour alternatives available to it at each move (d) and the length of the 'vision' (v). It is a simple matter to introduce into the model the consequences of several types of learning. An increase in the repertoire of behaviour alternatives or in the length of vision can simply be represented by changes in d and v, respectively.

A more interesting possibility arises if the food points are not distributed completely at random, and if there are clues that indicate whether a particular intermediate point is rich or poor in paths leading to food points. First, let us suppose that on the path leading up to each food point the k preceding choice points are marked with a food clue. Once the association between the clue and the subsequent appearance of the food point is learned by the organism, its exploration can terminate with the discovery of the clue, and it can follow a determinate path from that point on. This amounts to substituting $v' = (v + k)$ for v.

A different kind of clue might operate in the following fashion. Each choice point has a distinguishable characteristic that is associated with the probability of encountering a food point if a path is selected at random leading out of this choice point. The organism can then select at each move the choice point with the highest probability. If only certain choice points are provided with such clues, then a combination of random and systematic exploration can be employed. Thus the organism may be led into 'regions' where the probability of goal attainment is high relative to other regions, but it may have to explore randomly for food within a given region.

A concrete example of such behaviour in humans is the 'position play' characteristic of the first phase of a chess game. The player chooses moves on the basis of certain characteristics of resulting positions (e.g. the extent to which his pieces are developed). Certain positions are adjudged richer in attacking and defensive possibilities than others, but the original choice may involve no definite plan for the subsequent action after the 'good' position has been reached.

Next, we turn to the problem of choice that arises when those regions of the behaviour space that are rich in points satisfying one need (p_1 is high in these regions) are poor in points satisfying another need (p_2 is low in these same regions). In the earlier case of goal conflict (two or more points simultaneously visible mediating different needs), we postulated a priority mechanism that amounted to a mechanism for computing relative need intensity and for responding to the more intense need. In the environment with clues, the learning process would need to include a conditioning mechanism that would attach the priority mechanism to the response to competing clues, as well as to the response to competing visible needs.

Finally, we have thus far specified the environment in such a way that there is only one path leading to each point. Formally, this condition can always be satisfied by representing as two or more points any point that can be reached by multiple paths. For some purposes, it might be preferable to specify an environment in which paths converge as well as diverge. This can be done without disturbing the really essential conditions of the foregoing analysis. For behaviour of the sort we have been describing, we require of the environment only:

1. that if a path is selected *completely* at random the probability of survival is negligible;
2. that there exist clues in the environment (either the actual visibility of need-satisfying points or anticipatory clues) which permit the organism, sufficiently frequently for survival, to select specific paths that lead with certainty, or with very high probability, to a need-satisfying point.

CONCLUDING COMMENTS ON MULTIPLE GOALS

The central problem of this paper has been to construct a simple mechanism of choice that would suffice for the behaviour of an organism confronted with multiple goals. Since the organism, like those of the real world, has neither the senses nor the wits to discover an 'optimal' path – even assuming the concept of optimal to be clearly defined – we are concerned only with finding a choice mechanism that will lead it to pursue a 'satisficing' path, a path that will permit satisfaction at some specified level of all its needs.

Certain of the assumptions we have introduced to make this possible represent characteristics of the organism. First, it is able to plan short purposive behaviour sequences (of length not exceeding v), but not long sequences. Second, its needs are not insatiable, and hence it does not need to balance marginal increments of satisfaction. If all its needs are satisfied, it simply becomes inactive. Third, it possesses sufficient storage capacity so that the exact moment of satisfaction of any particular need is not critical.

We have introduced other assumptions that represent characteristics of the environment, the most important being that need satisfaction can take place only at 'rare' points which (with some qualifications we have indicated) are distributed randomly.

The most important conclusion we have reached is that blocks of the organism's time can be allocated to activities related to individual needs (separate means–end chains) without creating any problem of overall allocation or coordination or the need for any general 'utility function'. The only scarce resource in the situation is time, and its scarcity, measured by the proportion of the total time that the organism will need to be engaged in *some* activity, can be reduced by the provision of generous storage capacity.

This does not mean that a more efficient procedure cannot be constructed, from the standpoint of the total time required to meet the organism's needs. We have already explored some simple possibilities for increasing efficiency by recognizing complementarities among activities (particularly the exploration activity). But the point is that these complications are not essential to the survival of an organism. Moreover, if the environment is so constructed (as it often is in fact) that regions rich in possibilities for one kind of need satisfaction are poor in possibilities for other satisfactions, such efficiencies may not be available.

It may be objected that even relatively simple organisms appear to conform to efficiency criteria in their behaviour, and hence that their choice mechanisms are much more elaborate than those we have described. A rat, for example, learns to take shorter rather than longer paths to food. But this observation does not affect the central argument. We can introduce a mechanism that leads the organism to choose time-conserving paths, where multiple paths are available for satisfying a given need, without any assumption of a mechanism that allocates time among *different* needs. The former mechanism simply increases the 'slack' in the whole system, and makes it even more feasible to ignore the complementarities among activities in programming the overall behaviour of the organism.

This is not the place to discuss at length the application of the model to human behaviour, but a few general statements may be in order. First, the analysis has been a static one, in the sense that we have taken the organism's needs and its sensing and planning capacities as given. Except for a few comments, we have not considered how the organism develops needs or learns to meet them. One would conjecture, from general observation and from experimentation with aspiration levels, that in humans the balance between the time required to meet needs and the total time available is maintained by the raising and lowering of aspiration levels. I have commented on this point at greater length in my previous paper.[6]

Second, there is nothing about the model that implies that the needs are physiological and innate rather than sociological and acquired. Provided that the needs of the organism can be specified at any given time in terms of the aspiration levels for the various kinds of consumer behaviour, the model can be applied.

The principal positive implication of the model is that we should be sceptical in postulating for humans, or other organisms, elabor-

ate mechanisms for choosing among diverse needs. Common deno-
minators among needs may simply not exist, or may exist only in
very rudimentary form; and the nature of the organism's needs in
relation to the environment may make their non-existence entirely
tolerable.

There is some positive evidence bearing on this point in the work
that has been done on conflict and frustration. A common method
of producing conflict in the laboratory is to place the organism in a
situation where: (a) it is stimulated to address itself simultaneously
to alternative goal-oriented behaviours, or (b) it is stimulated to
goal-oriented behaviour, but restricted from carrying out the behaviours it usually evinces in similar natural situations. This suggests
that conflict may arise (at least in a large class of situations) from
presenting the animal with situations with which it is not 'programmed' to deal. Conflict of choice may often be equivalent to an
absence of a choice mechanism in the given situation. And while it
may be easy to create such situations in the laboratory, the absence
of a mechanism to deal with them may simply reflect the fact that the
organism seldom encounters equivalent situations in its natural
environment.[7]

CONCLUSION

In this paper I have attempted to identify some of the structural
characteristics that are typical of the 'psychological' environments
of organisms. We have seen that an organism in an environment
with these characteristics requires only very simple perceptual and
choice mechanisms to satisfy its several needs and to assure a high
probability of its survival over extended periods of time. In particular, no 'utility function' needs to be postulated for the organism; nor
does it require any elaborate procedure for calculating marginal
rates of substitution among different wants.

The analysis set forth here casts serious doubt on the usefulness of
current economic and statistical theories of rational behaviour as
bases for explaining the characteristics of human and other organismic rationality. It suggests an alternative approach to the description of rational behaviour that is more closely related to psychological theories of perception and cognition, and that is in closer

agreement with the facts of behaviour as observed in laboratory and field.

NOTES

1. I am indebted to Allen Newell for numerous enlightening conversations on the subject of this paper, and to the Ford Foundation for a grant that permitted me leisure to complete it.
2. Since writing the paper referred to I have found confirmation for a number of its hypotheses in the interesting and significant study, by A. de Groot (1946), of the thought processes of chess players. I intend to discuss the implications of these empirical findings for my model in another place.
3. A reader who is familiar with W. Grey Walter's mechanical turtle, *Machina speculatrix* (Walter 1953), will see as we proceed that the description of our organism could well be used as a set of design specifications to assure the survival of his turtle in an environment sparsely provided with battery chargers. Since I was not familiar with the structure of the turtle when I developed this model, there are some differences in their behaviour – but the resemblance is striking.
4. It is characteristic of economic models of rationality that the distinction between 'means' and 'ends' plays no essential role in them. This distinction cannot be identified with the distinction between behaviour alternatives and utilities, for reasons that are set forth at some length in the author's *Administrative Behaviour*, Chaps 4 and 5 (Simon 1947).
5. I have not discovered any very satisfactory data on the food storage capacities of animals, but the order of magnitude suggested above for the ratio of average search time to storage capacity is certainly correct. It may be noted that, in some cases at least, where the 'food' substance is ubiquitous, and hence the search time negligible, the storage capacity is also small. Thus in terrestrial animals there is little oxygen storage and life can be maintained in the absence of air for only a few minutes. I am not arguing as to which way the causal arrow runs, but only that the organisms, in this respect, are adapted to their environments and do not provide storage that is superfluous.
6. See Simon (1955, pp. 111, 117–18). For an experiment demonstrating the adjustment of the rat's aspiration levels to considerations of realizability, see Festinger (1953).
7. See, for example, Neal E. Miller, 'Experimental Studies of Conflict' in Hunt 1944, Chapter 14.

REFERENCES

Edwards, W. (1954) 'The theory of decision making', *Psychological Bulletin*, 51, pp. 380–417.

Festinger, L. (1953) 'Development of differential appetite in the rat.' *J. Exp. Psychol.*, 32, pp. 226–34.

De Groot, A. (1946) *Het Denken van den Schaker*. Amsterdam: North-Holland.

Hunt, J. McV. (1944) *Personality and the behavior disorders*. New York: Ronald.

Simon, H. A. (1947) *Administrative behavior.* New York: Macmillan.
Simon, H. A. (1955) 'A behavioral model of rational choice.' *Quart. J. Econ.,* 59, pp. 99–118.
Thrall, R. M., Coombs, C. H. and Davis, R. L. (eds) (1954) *Decision processes.* New York: Wiley.
Walter, W. G. (1953) *The living brain.* New York: Norton.

4. Thinking by Computers (1966)*

> That is the aim of that great science which I am used to calling Charac-
> teristic, of which what we call Algebra, or Analysis, is only a very small
> branch, since it is this Characteristic which gives words to languages,
> letters to words, numbers to Arithmetic, notes to Music. It teaches us
> how to fix our reasoning, and to require it to leave, as it were, visible
> traces on the paper of a notebook for inspection at leisure. Finally, it
> enables us to reason with economy, by substituting characters in the
> place of things in order to relieve the imagination . . .
>
> Leibniz, *On the Method of Universality* (1674)

It is hardly possible to talk about thinking by computers without
saying something first about thinking by people. There are two
reasons why this is so. First, the only definitions of thinking that are
of any use at all are ostensive ones. We can point to a person in a
certain state of activity and say, 'Thinking is a set of processes like
those now taking place in the central nervous system of that person.'
Alternatively, we can point to the statement of a problem and to its
solution and say, 'Thinking is a set of processes like those which
enabled a person to produce this problem solution from this
problem statement.' I do not mean that these two definitions are
necessarily equivalent, but they might serve equally well as a basis
for delimiting the set of phenomena we wish to understand when we
investigate thinking.

The second reason why we must talk about thinking by people in

*This chapter is reprinted with the permission of the copyright holder from *Mind and
Cosmos: Essays in Contemporary Science and Philosophy*, Vol. III in the University
of Pittsburgh Series in the Philosophy of Science. Copyright C, 1966, University of
Pittsburgh Press.

The work on this chapter is based was supported in part by a grant from the
Carnegie Corporation and in part by Research Grant MH-07722-01 from the
National Institutes of Health. Several of my examples are drawn from joint work
with K. Kotovsky, P. A. Simon and L. W. Gregg. My debts to Allen Newell are too
numerous to acknowledge in detail. To all of these, I give thanks and offer absol-
ution for the particular conclusions reached here, which are my own.

order to talk about thinking by computers is that the history of the latter phenomenon is inextricably interwoven with research efforts to understand the former. In most cases where a computer has done something that might reasonably be called 'thinking', the occasion for this activity was an investigation aimed at explaining human thinking.

HUMAN THINKING

I have defined human thinking as a set of processes occurring in the central nervous system, and *par excellence* in the human central nervous system. What do we know about these processes? It is conventional to refer to our abysmal ignorance of them. It would not surprise me if a word count revealed that the adjective most commonly associated with the phrase 'thought processes' is 'mysterious'.[1]

That adjective is no longer appropriate. Today we have a substantial and rapidly growing body of knowledge about thinking processes, both at the neurological level and at the level of what I shall call elementary information processes. There are still very large gaps in this knowledge – and particularly gaps between the two levels, as I shall point out. But I think it more useful to follow the example of the physical sciences – to describe what we already know before moving on to the frontier of knowledge – than to observe the vow of ignorance that has been traditional in the social sciences.

NEUROLOGICAL AND INFORMATION PROCESSING EXPLANATIONS

The notion of levels of explanation is familiar from physics, chemistry and biology. From classical Greek times, if not before, unobservable atomic particles have been hypothesized to explain the observable processes going on in chemical reactions. The atomic hypothesis, quantified by Dalton and his contemporaries at the beginning of the nineteenth century, led to one triumph after another in the regularization, systemization, and explanation of chemical phenomena during the course of that century. Only in our own century did atoms acquire an existence partially independent of their hypothesized participation in chemical reactions. Thus, we had a highly developed explanation of chemical reactions at the level of atomic processes long before the latter processes received explanation and confirmation, in turn, at the level of nuclear physics.[2] Genetics provides an example of levels of explanation that is even more instructive than atomic theory for our purposes. In its initial introduction as the unit of inheritance, the gene had exactly the same hypothetical status as did the atom in Dalton's theory.[3] If one assumed there were genes with certain properties, one could explain some of the gross macroscopic phenomena of inheritance. The gene hypothesis, in its initial form, did not require the genes to be localized in space or to have any specific existence as chemical or protoplasmic entities. The gene hypothesis was compelling because it regularized, systemized and explained those macroscopic phenomena.

The gene, like the atom, turned out to be 'realer' than any of those who proposed it had defensible reasons for predicting. Some of the most beautiful achievements of biology in our generation have been the advances toward the explanation of genes in terms of more microscopic and fundamental levels of biochemical process. The great strides toward deciphering the so-called genetic code within the past few years are only the most recent of these achievements.

Two lessons can be drawn from these examples. First, explanation in science is frequently achieved in successive levels. We explain reactions in terms of atoms and molecules, atoms and molecules in terms of the so-called 'elementary' particles. We explain inherited characteristics in terms of genes, genes in terms of organic molecules and their reactions.

Second, the fact that we have succeeded in 'reducing' a first-level explanation by means of a more fundamental explanation of its entities and laws does not make the original explanation otiose or dispensable. It is important and gratifying to know that complex chemical reactions can *in principle* be explained by the laws of quantum mechanics. In practice, of course, the chemist could not get along without an intermediate level of chemical theory, for the in-principle reduction has been carried out *in practice* only in the very simplest cases.[4] Similarly, there is no reason to suppose that direct explanation of inheritance in terms of cellular biochemical processes will ever in practice replace explanations in terms of genes. Hierarchy is as essential to the organization and application of knowledge as to its original discovery.

These two examples provide encouraging historical precedents for what is now going on in psychology. Today, the explanation of thinking is progressing at two levels. We are succeeding in explaining ever-widening spheres of human mental activity in terms of hypothesized 'atoms' called *elementary processes*. At the same time, we are making substantial progress toward explaining the fundamental electrochemical processes of synaptic action and nerve signal transmission, and the organization of these processes in various parts of the peripheral and central nervous system.[5] If there is a significant difference between these developments in psychology and the corresponding developments that I have described in genetics and chemistry, it is that the work of constructing explanations at the two levels is going on more nearly simultaneously in psychology than it did in the two other instances cited.

Perhaps the greatest gulf of ignorance today is not *within* neurophysiology or *within* information-processing psychology – although there is no lack of work to be done in each of these areas – but *precisely between them*. Although we can give a considerable account of thinking in terms of elementary information processes, we know almost nothing about the specific physiological basis for these information processes. We do not know what the engram is – how and where symbolized information is stored in the brain. We do not know how symbols are compared, copied, or associated. Neurophysiologists boring from one side of the mountain have not yet made contact with information-processing psychologists boring from the other side.

Yet this state of affairs should be no cause for discouragement, especially for the psychologist who is interested in using psychological theory to understand and work with human higher mental processes. He is no worse off, in his theoretical foundations, than chemists were during the period of most vigorous development of their science. He is no worse off than geneticists were during the 1920s. And basing his prognostications on those sciences, he can look forward to a future in which the symbols and symbolic processes hypothesized by information-processing theory will be encased in such hard 'reality' as chemistry can provide to entities.

There is one respect in which the information-processing psychologist today is distinctly better off than the geneticist was a generation ago. Belief in the possibility of a mechanistic explanation for the gene hypothesis was then largely an act of faith.[6] Today, although we do not know what protoplasmic processes correspond to the elementary information processes, or how these processes fit into the architecture of the brain, we do have a proof that such processes *can* be provided with mechanistic explanations. For although we do not know how the elementary symbolic processes that are capable of explaining thinking are accomplished in the brain, we do know how they are accomplished electronically in a digital computer. The possibility of providing a mechanistic explanation for thinking has been demonstrated by programming computers to think.

AN INFORMATION-PROCESSING EXPLANATION OF THINKING

Thinking is a dynamic process – using that term in its technical sense. Classical dynamical theories, of which Newtonian mechanics is the standard example, have generally taken the form of differential equations. The *state* of the system at any given moment of time is specified by the values of a set of variables, the state variables, at that moment. Then the differential equations determine how the state variables will change; they predict the state of the system at the 'next' moment as a function of the present state.[7]

Before a system can be described in differential equations of the classical sort, a set of state variables must be discovered. One of the difficulties that has plagued psychology is that no satisfactory way has been found for characterizing thought processes in terms of the kinds of state variables that are suitable for classical differential equations. That difficulty has now been bypassed with the invention of information-processing languages, a special class of computer programming languages, whose variables are not numbers but symbolic structures.[8]

A computer program is quite analogous, at an abstract level, to a system of differential equations (more precisely, of difference equations). Given the memory contents of the computer at any given moment of time (these characterizing its state at that moment), the program determines how the memory contents will change during the next computing cycle and what the contents will be at the end of the cycle. Thus a computer program can be used as a theory of a dynamic system in exactly the same way as can a set of differential equations. The basic methodological problems of theory construc-

Figure 4.1 Some simple symbol structures

$$A \longrightarrow B \longrightarrow M \longrightarrow C \longrightarrow D \longrightarrow M$$

A *list*. Each item is associated with the previous one by the relation of next (→).

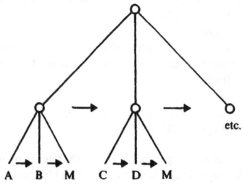

A *tree*, or list of lists. Each item on the main list is itself a list (in this case, a list of three items).

tion and theory testing are identical in the two cases. The theory is tested by providing a specific set of initial and boundary conditions for the system, using the equations to predict the resulting time path, and comparing this predicted path with the actual path of the system.

The advantage of an information-processing language over classical mathematical languages for formulating a theory of thinking is that an information-processing language takes symbolic structures rather than numbers as its variables. Since thinking processes are processes for manipulating symbols and structures of symbols (Figure 4.1), these processes can be represented directly, without requiring elaborate translations or scaling techniques, in an information-processing language.

Let us make this point more specific by considering a particular thinking task.[9] Suppose that a human subject in the psychological laboratory is confronted with a sequence of symbols – ABMCD-MEFM, say – and asked to continue it. After a few moments, he will very likely give the continuation GHMIJM, and so on. Now one way in which he might accomplish this – and, from the available evidence, the way in which most subjects do accomplish it – is the following:

Figure 4.2   A pattern. Each triad (list) can be generated from the previous one by using the relations of next (--) and same (= = =) on the English alphabet

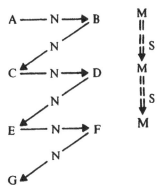

1. He scans the original list looking for repetitions of identical symbols, discovering that each third symbol is M.
2. He constructs a symbolic structure in memory that represents the periodicity and the recurrence of the M. In order to talk about this structure, let us represent it as (**M), where the asterisks stand for unspecified symbols. Of course, we should not suppose that the symbolic structure in memory 'looks' like this sequence in any literal sense, but we can use the sequence in our theory as a fairly straightforward representation of the structure in memory.
3. Now the subject again scans the original list to see whether there are consistent relations between pairs of symbols that occupy corresponding positions in different periods of the sequence. We may think of him as now representing the given sequence thus: ABM CDM EFM, so that A, C and E are in the first positions in their respective periods, and B, D and F in the second positions. The relations he searches for are relations of *identity* and of *next on a familiar alphabet* (Figure 4.2). In the example

before us, he will discover that the second symbol in each period is next to the first symbol, in the English alphabet, and that the first symbol in each period is next to the second symbol in the preceding period. These relations, then, provide a general description of the sequence, as well as a means for extrapolating it. Leaving out details, we might describe the sequence symbolically as (nnM), where 'n' stands for 'next on the English alphabet.' Given one period of the sequence, the subject can now construct an indefinite number of the following periods.

It is easy to write a program in an information-processing language that explains this dynamic process in terms of elementary information processes. We need processes for copying symbols, for constructing compound symbols (lists and 'trees') from simple symbols, for comparing symbols for identity, for finding the next symbol on a list, and a few others.

A review of the steps that the subjects were described as taking in the example shows that these processes are essentially the ones mentioned. In step 1, the original list of symbols could be scanned by a process for finding the *next* symbol on a list. The repetitions of the letter M could be detected by a process for comparing symbols for identity. Step 2 could be carried out by a process for constructing compound symbols – in this case, the list **M. Step 3 again calls for processes that compare symbols for identity and find the next symbol on a list and processes that construct the final pattern nnM from the incomplete pattern **M. The extrapolation of the sequence, finally, calls for applications of the same kinds of processes, under the control of the pattern.

Thus, the program constructed from these processes, and organized to carry out the steps 1 through 3, provides an explanation of how humans detect the patterns in sequences like the one illustrated, how they represent such patterns in memory, and how they use the pattern representations to extrapolate the sequences. It is a theory of human information processing in the series generation task.

This theory has been tested by programming a computer to behave in the manner described and examining the behaviour of the computer when it is given the same series completion tasks that were given to the human subjects. The predictions of the theory – that is, the output of the computer under these conditions – can be compared directly with the human behaviour. No mathematization of the human behaviour is required. One gross test is to check whether the problems the program solves are the same ones that were solved by the largest number of human subjects. Much more specific tests – comparison, for example, of the specific errors made by program and subjects – are possible. With the evidence available to date, the theory has given a fairly good account of itself.

The information-processing explanation of series completion would have only rather narrow interest if it were not for the fact that the same small set of processes that represents the core of this explanation also turns up in a central role in the information-processing theories that have been devised to explain human thinking in quite different contexts. In the first place, the program for the series completion task can be generalized without too much difficulty to apply to a much wider range of pattern recognizing tasks:

1. With a few additions (primarily of the numerical operations of addition, subtraction, multiplication and division), it will handle number series – e.g. 1 4 9 16 25 . . .
2. It can be extended to various kinds of analogy tasks – e.g. '*a* is to *c* as *r* is to _____?' or '*a* rectangle is to a square as a parallelogram is to a _____?'

Similar programs, employing the same elementary information processes, have had considerable success in explaining subjects' behaviour in partial reinforcement experiments.[10]

Finally, quite distinct information-processing programs which, however, employ essentially the same elementary processes, explain a considerable number of other kinds of human thinking: among them, discovering proofs for theorems in logic, geometry and trigonometry, playing chess and bridge, harmonizing a musical theme, making investment decisions, memorizing nonsense syllables, or learning foreign language vocabulary.[11]

On the basis of experience with these theories, it now appears highly probable that elementary processes like the ones described, operating on symbols and structures of symbols (that is, lists and trees of symbols), are the fundamental means by which human thinking is accomplished. Because the theories take the form of programs in information-processing languages, and because we can program digital computers to execute such programs, we have incontrovertible evidence that these processes are *sufficient* to account for performance of the kinds of tasks that have been mentioned. And because the computers so programmed do prove theorems, play games, compose music, make investment decisions, and memorize, the theories provide examples of thinking by computers that, from the evidence at hand, closely parallel some kinds of thinking by human beings.[12]

SOME CHARACTERISTICS OF THINKING PROCESSES

What are some of the generalizations about thinking that have emerged from the information-processing theories? It will not be necessary, in stating these generalizations, to distinguish particularly between human thinking and computer thinking, because the computer thinking referred to occurs in the context of programs designed to simulate human thinking as closely as possible. The generalizations apply to both.

One qualification should be made, however. Existing information-processing theories of thinking undoubtedly fall far short of covering the whole range of thinking activities in man. It is not just that the present theories are only approximately correct. Apart from limits on their correctness in explaining the ranges of behaviour to which they apply, much cognitive behaviour still lies beyond their scope.

The first generalization – that all thinking processes are constructed out of a small set of elementary information processes – has already been sufficiently stressed. Nothing has been said about the organization of these processes, the way in which they are put together in programs. Two additional generalizations apply here:

First, the processes are organized hierarchically.[13] A sequence of elementary processes can be combined into a compound process. Sequences of compound and elementary processes can be combined again into still more elaborate and complex processes, and so on. If there is a limit on the number of levels in such a hierarchy, experimentation thus far has not revealed that limit – or even indicated that it exists.

In the example of the sequence completion program, the three main program steps represent compound processes organized from elementary ones. The first step determines the periodicity of the sequence; the second step constructs an incomplete representation of the pattern; the third step completes the representation. These three 'sub-routines', to use computer terminology, are combined into the complete pattern-detection process. The pattern-detection process, in turn, is combined with the extrapolation process in order to carry out the experimental task – continuing the series.

Second, the processes are executed *serially*. Implicit in the principal information-processing theories that have been constructed is the hypothesis that the central nervous system can only do one or a few things at a time. 'At a time' means in an interval of a few milliseconds.

Because existing digital computers are serially organized devices, it is simplest to construct information-processing theories that operate serially.[14] However, there is considerable evidence that the human system is organized in the same way – or at least that large parts of it are. The observably narrow limits on span of human attention are one symptom of the serial organization of thinking. There exists also some contrary evidence – for example, the ability of a person to hear his own name softly spoken even when he is attending to something else. On balance, however, it does not appear inaccurate to describe thinking as essentially a serial process.

The generalizations stated thus far – that thinking is a hierarchically organized, serially executed symbol-manipulating process – apply to virtually all the information-processing theories that have been constructed to date. There are several additional important generalizations that refer more specifically to the kinds of thinking activities called 'problem solving'.

Problem solving involves a highly selective trial-and-error search for solution possibilities. The terms 'highly selective' and 'trial and error' may seem contradictory. They are not. Problem-solving searches require trial and error in that they generally do not go directly to the solution without traversing and retracing some blind alleys – sometimes many, sometimes few. When a person solves a problem without any backtracking whatsoever, we are apt to deny that he needed to think at all. We say, 'He knew the answer', or 'he didn't have to think; he did it by rote'.

Problem-solving searches are selective in that they generally explore only a miniscule fraction of the total (and usually immense) number of possibilities. In most cases of interest, the selection of the paths to be searched is not governed by foolproof, systematic procedures, but by rules of thumb we call *heuristics*.

In a few cases a good deal is known about the size of the problem space, about the heuristics that are used to explore it selectively, and about the quantitative reduction in search that these heuristics achieve.[15] The game of chess is one such case. It is known that a player typically has freedom to choose among about twenty or thirty legal moves. To each of these, the opponent may have a similar number of replies. Thus the tree of possible game continuations branches geometrically nearly a thousand-fold for a single set of move possibilities and their replies. A complete analysis of continuations two moves deep would typically require the exploration of nearly one million branches; three moves deep, one billion, and so on.

It is now pretty well established that experienced chess players, even in difficult middle-game positions or in exploring deep combinations, seldom examine as many as 100 continuations. The number examined appears to be almost independent of the player's skill. What distinguishes very good players from less good players is not the amount of exploration they do, but their relative success in identifying the significant continuations to be explored – the selective power of their heuristics.

A detailed investigation of this question has been made for mating combinations – sequences of moves that force a checkmate.[16] An information-processing program has been written that examines continuations in potential mating positions very selectively, using heuristics gleaned from the chess literature and chess experience. This program is able to find combinations as many as eight or more moves deep by examining far fewer than 100 branches of the game tree. The program, examined in comparison with records of historical chess games, appears to capture successfully some of the main heuristics that are actually used by strong players in complex mating positions.

The positions to which the mating combinations program is relevant allow the players less freedom than many other chess positions, and our previous estimate of the branching rate of the game tree – a thousand-fold per move – is probably too high when applied to them. Let us take 100 as a more conservative estimate. With this branching rate, *exhaustive* exploration of an eight-move combination would mean examining 10^{16} positions! A program that examines only 100 is therefore more efficient by a factor of 10^{14} – one hundred thousand billion – than a random search program that tries all possibilities.

Similar calculations have been made for the power of the heuristics in some of the theorem-proving programs, with the finding, again, of gain factors of orders of magnitude similar to those in chess.

Means–end analysis is one of the basic heuristics in human problem solving.[17] Means–end analysis, as it appears in human behaviour, and as it is formalized in information-processing theories of problem solving, is organized somewhat as follows:

1. The present situation is compared with the desired situation (problem goal), and one or more *differences* between them noticed. (E.g. 'I have a board five feet long; I want a two-foot length; there is a difference in length.')
2. Memory is searched for an *operator* or operators associated with one of the differences that has been detected. By 'operator' is meant some process that will change the present situation. (E.g. 'sawing', 'planing', 'drilling'.) Operators become associated with particular differences as a result of experiences that show that these operators are capable of reducing or eliminating the differences in question. (E.g. 'Sawing changes lengths.')
3. An attempt is made to apply the operator to change the present situation. Sometimes, in the course of making the attempt, it is discovered that the operator cannot be applied until some other aspect of the situation has been altered. (E.g. 'A board must be held fast in order to saw it.') In these cases a new goal of type (1) may be set up, with satisfaction of the conditions for applying the operator as the 'desired situation'. (E.g. 'Hold the board fast.')

Examination of a large number of human protocols in problem-solving situations reveals that the largest part of the activity is means–end analysis. Considerable success in simulating such problem-solving behaviour has been achieved in an information-processing program called the General Problem Solver.

Means–end analysis is a special case of a selective heuristic. By identifying the specific differences between the present and desired situation, it becomes unnecessary to consider all possible ways in which the situation might be changed. Only those operations need be examined that are relevant (at least potentially, on the basis of past experience) to the actual differences that exist. When a tailor alters a suit, he obtains, at the fitting, not only the qualitative nature of the difference – whether the sleeves are too short or long – but the precise amount of the alteration that is needed. He thereby achieves a laudable reduction in the amount of trial and error that is required to make the suit fit.

Intermingled with means–end analysis in problem solving are heuristics that may be called *planning*.[18] Planning consists in omitting some of the detail of the actual problem by abstracting its essential features, solving the simplified problem, then using the solution of the simplified problem as a guide, or plan, for the solution of the full problem. Again, it can be shown quantitatively that planning can increase speed of solution in favourable circumstances by many orders of magnitude. Speaking generally, the larger the number of steps in the complete problem solution, the greater the increase in efficiency achievable through planning.

Another heuristic of wide applicability is the procedure of factoring a problem into sub-problems, and tackling first the sub-problems containing the smallest number of 'unknowns'. In this way the number of combinations of possible solutions that have to be examined is greatly reduced. Consider, for example, puzzles of the following kind:

$$
\begin{array}{r}
\text{DONALD} \\
+ \ \underline{\text{GERALD}} \\
\text{ROBERT}
\end{array}
$$

The problem task is to substitute distinct digits – from 0 to 9 – for distinct letters in such a way that the resulting expression will be a correct example of addition. The hint is given that $D = 5$.[19]

Only one unknown now remains in the last column, and this is immediately solved to give $T = 0$, with a carry to the fifth column. Also, the value 5 for D can be substituted in the first column. Now, subjects generally turn their attentions to columns two, four or five, since each of these has a duplication of letters, hence, only two unknowns each. They soon discover that $E = 9$, and that R must be an odd number greater than 5, hence $R = 7$. The process is continued until the answer is obtained:

$$
\begin{array}{r}
526485 \\
+\ \ 197485 \\
\hline
723970
\end{array}
$$

The significant point about the example is that successful subjects almost never explore at random or consider possible combinations of digits that might 'work'. They carry through the solution with a minimum of combinations by always working at points where there are only a few unknowns to be determined.

In some very well structured problem domains, formal procedures, usually called algorithms, are available for finding systematically the solution that is best or maximal by some criterion. Elementary calculus provides an example of a simple algorithm of this kind: to find the maximum of a function, take the first derivative, set it equal to zero, and solve the resulting equation.

In most problem-solving domains of everyday life, however, and even in many formal ones, like chess, no such algorithm has been discovered. A modest number of possible solutions can be considered, and there is no way of telling whether a given solution is the best, since many other possibilities must, perforce, go unexamined. In these domains, human problem solvers and the computer programs that simulate them do not search for the 'best' solution, but for a solution that is 'good enough' by some criterion. Heuristics that proceed on this basis are sometimes called 'satisficing' heuristics.[20]

Suppose, for example, that someone wishes to sell a house. He does not know exactly how much he can get for it, but he can make an estimate. If bids come in close to this figure, he holds to it; if they do not, he gradually reduces it. When a bid comes in that meets the revised figure, he accepts it.

The criterion of 'good enough' that adjusts in this way is called an *aspiration level*. Satisficing behaviour that makes use of aspiration levels is prominent in the selection of chess moves. We have already seen that there is no practical possibility of evaluating all possible moves. Instead, the player can form a preliminary estimate of the value of his position and look for a move that meets this estimate. As his search continues, if he does not find such a move, he revises the estimate downward. Satisficing heuristics are widely applicable and widely applied in problem domains where the number of possible solutions is far too great to permit exhaustive search and where an efficient maximizing algorithm is not available.

MOTIVATION AND EMOTION IN THINKING

Satisficing heuristics bring us to a consideration of the relation between thinking processes and those aspects of human behaviour that we call motivation and emotion. Thinking is activity directed toward goals, and as we have just seen, involves considerations of whether a proposed solution is the best, or is good enough, in terms of a criterion. If the level of aspiration is very high, search for a satisfactory solution will be more prolonged than if it is low. The thinking program will also contain parameters, or constants, that determine how long exploration will continue in a particular direction and when it will turn to a new direction. (E.g. 'If not successful in five minutes, try something else'.) It may contain procedures to determine which of several alternative sub-problems will be explored next (the 'minimize-unknowns' heuristic is an example of this).

Thus, thinking programs, whether for human or computer, contain motivational components.[21] This is not to say that the aspects of motivation that have been represented in information-processing theories to date come anywhere near to representing the totality of motivational factors in human behaviour. Ulric Neisser has pointed out that, as compared with human behaviour in the large, the behaviour predicted by existing information-processing theories is exceedingly single-minded, stubborn, but otherwise unemotional.[22] He observes that human beings are capable of turning from one activity to another and of being interrupted in an activity.

Can information-processing theories be broadened to encompass the motivational and emotional mechanisms we observe in human behaviour? Although there has been little concrete progress in this direction, there have been some speculations suggesting the directions that progress might take.

Imagine a computer with a rather large memory – a combination of magnetic core and tape, say – that contains, among others, the general problem-solving program augmented by programs for specific tasks like playing chess, detecting serial patterns, solving differential equations, inverting matrices, calculating correlation coefficients, and so on. Each job that is input to the computer is examined and assigned a priority (on some basis that need not concern us) that gradually changes with the length of time the job has been waiting to be processed. When the priority of a job reaches a sufficiently high level, the job that is currently being processed is interrupted and replaced by the high priority job.

Such a computer (and, of course, systems organized in this general way are already in existence) would exhibit, in its behaviour, motivation and a set of values. If we noticed that it gave high priorities to matrix inversions, we would say that this was an activity it preferred. Suppose we also noticed that when certain brief new jobs were input, it immediately interrupted what it was doing to undertake one of the new tasks before returning to the original one. We might say that it was easily distracted, or even that it was exhibiting emotion.

I do not propose here to develop in detail the idea that the core of the behaviour we call emotional derives from a mechanism for interrupting the ongoing stream of activity. However, this notion is consistent with a good deal of empirical evidence about the nature of emotion and provides an interesting avenue of exploration into the relation of emotion to cognitive activity. It suggests that we shall not be able to write programs for computers that allow them to respond flexibly to a variety of demands, some with real-time priorities, without thereby creating a system that, in a human, we would say exhibited emotion.

CONCLUSION

In the foregoing I have tried to describe some of the general characteristics of human thinking, as we know them from constructing and testing information-processing theories. These are also, of course, the characteristics of computer thinking, since most computers that think, think in simulation of man.

I have not tried to answer the standard objections that 'of course' computers do not think at all. To most of these objections, very satisfactory answers have been given by others – the delightful article by Alan Turing, for example, and the paper by Professor J. J. C. Smart.[23] The best answers probably, are given by the structure of the programs themselves that embody our information-processing theories of human thinking.

I cannot forbear, however, a brief comment on one of the commonest objections: that computers do only what they are programmed to do. The assertion is undoubtedly true, but it does not imply that computers cannot think. That conclusion would only follow if it were true that human beings, when they are thinking, do *not* do what they are programmed to do. The progress of information-processing theories of human thinking requires a denial of this latter premise. The processes of human thinking, in fact, can be very effectively stated in the form of programs. We do not know what physiological mechanisms store these programs in the brain and execute them; but we have as much reason to believe there are such mechanisms as earlier generations had to believe that there are mechanisms underlying the valences of atoms and the control of heredity by genes.

A human being is able to think because, by biological inheritance and exposure to a stream of experience in the external world, he has acquired a program that is effective for guiding thought processes. If we wish to seek an efficient cause for his behaviour, it lies in that program in its interaction with ongoing stimuli.

We know a great deal today about the structure and content of human thinking programs. We know very little about which parts of these programs are inherited and which parts are acquired. We know little about the biological substrate for the programs. We know far less than we need to know about how thinking programs can be modified and improved through education and training. Computers, programmed to stimulate human thinking, continue to offer a powerful research tool in investigating these unanswered questions. And programs in information-processing languages offer powerful means for expressing our theories of human thought processes.

NOTES

1. A typical example is Edna Heidbreder's concluding comment in her article on 'Thinking' in the 1960 *Encyclopedia Britannica*: 'Thinking remains one of the unsolved problems of psychology.'
2. It might be mentioned that although there was much resistance to the atomic hypothesis through the first two-thirds of the nineteenth century, the grounds for this resistance were not what a radical operationalist might suppose. There were few objections to atoms because of their hypothetical character – only a few philosophers of science, like Mach, Poincaré and Russell, anachronistically stressed this toward the end of the century. The main objection was to the neglect of the 'qualities', like colour, in a theory that took mass as the significant atomic property. The sceptics were humanists, not operationalists. See Toulmin

and Goodfield (1962), pp. 234–7, 263–8; or Conant and Nash (1950), pp. 215–321.

3. Toulmin and Goodfield (1962), pp. 365–8.

4. Compare Kekulé's prescient observation, 'Should the progress of science lead to a theory of the constitution of chemical atoms, it would make but little alteration in chemistry itself. The chemical atoms will always remain the chemical unit . . .' (quoted by Toulmin and Goodfield (1962), p. 265). 'Little alteration' sounds too strong in the light of modern physical chemistry, but the import of the statement, that there is a distinct 'chemical' level, is still substantially correct.

5. Symbolic of this progress was the award of the 1963 Nobel Prize in Physiology and Medicine to Eccles, to Hodgkin, and to Huxley for their work on transmission of neural signals. See the brief appreciation of this work in Fuortes (1963), pp. 468–70.

6. Toulmin and Goodfield (1962), pp. 365–8.

7. Of course 'next' must be put in quotation marks since the differential equations describe the changes in the limit as the time interval is taken shorter and shorter.

8. See Newell et al. (1964).

9. The analysis here is based on Simon and Kotovsky (1963), pp. 534–46. For similar theories applied to closely related tasks, see Feldman, Tonge and Kanter (1963), pp. 55–100; and Laughery and Gregg (1962), pp. 265–82.

10. In the partial reinforcement experiment, the subject is asked to predict whether the next stimulus in a series will be a 'plus' or 'minus'. The sequence is in fact random, each symbol having a certain probability of occurring. Subjects, however, typically search for patterns: 'a run of pluses', 'an alteration of plus and minus', or the like. See the chapter by Feldman in Feigenbaum and Feldman (1964).

11. For a survey of these theories see Newell and Simon (1963) and the references therein.

12. See references in 'Computers in Psychology', note 11, to the work of Hiller and Isaacson on musical composition, Clarkson on investment decisions, and Feigenbaum and Simon on memorizing.

13. See Simon (1962), pp. 467–82; and Toulmin and Goodfield (1962), pp. 301–2.

14. For reasons both of economics and organizational simplicity, a typical computer has only a few 'active' memory locations (sometimes called accumulators) where processing can be carried out. Information is brought in from 'passive' storage locations, processed, then returned to storage. Thus, the steps involved in adding the number in storage location A to the number in storage location B and storing the sum in C might be the following: (1) copy contents of A into accumulator, (2) add contents of B to contents of accumulator, (3) store contents of accumulator in C. With only one or a few active accumulators, the action of such a system is necessarily serial rather than parallel. Increasing the number of accumulators is expensive; it also creates an extremely difficult problem of coordinating their activity.

15. For some quantitative analysis, see Newell, Shaw and Simon (1962), Chap. 3; and Simon and Simon (1962), pp. 425–9.

16. Simon and Simon (1962).

17. The organization of thinking around means–end analysis has been extensively explored with a program called the General Problem Solver (GPS). Descriptions of GPS have been published in several places, including 'Computers in Psychology', note 11 and 'The Processes of Creative Thinking', note 15.

18. The planning heuristic is described briefly in 'The Processes of Creative Thinking', note 15, pp. 91–6.

19. Data on the behaviour of subjects performing the Donald–Gerald task will be found in Bartlett (1958), Chap. 4.
20. A discussion of satisficing heuristics and aspiration levels will be found in Simon 1957, Introduction to Pt IV and Chaps 14 and 15.
21. Taylor (1960); Reitman (1963) and Tomkins (1963).
22. Neisser (1963), pp. 193–7.
23. Turing (1950), pp. 433–60, reprinted in Newmann 1956, IV, and in Feigenbaum and Feldman (1964); Smart (1961), pp. 105–10.

REFERENCES

Bartlett, Sir Frederic (1958) *Thinking*. New York: Basic Books.

Chomsky, Noam (1957) *Syntactic Structures*. The Hague: Mouton.

Conant, James B. and Nash, Leonard K. (eds) (1950) *Harvard Case Histories in Experimental Science*.

Feigenbaum, E. A. and Feldman, J. (eds) (1964) *Computers and Thought*. New York: McGraw-Hill.

Feldman, J., Tonge, F. and Kanter, H. (1963) 'Empirical Explorations of a Hypothesis-Testing Model of Binary Choice Behavior' in Hoggatt, A. C. and Balderston, F. E. *Symposium on Simulation Models*. Cincinnati: South-Western Publishing.

Fuortes, M. G. F. (1963) 'Neural Signals: The Work of Hodgkin and Huxley', *Science*, 142, pp. 468–70.

Laughery, K. R. and Gregg, L. W. (1962) 'Simulation of Human Problem-Solving Behavior', *Psychometrika*, 27.

Neisser, Ulric (1963) 'The Imitation of Man by Machine', *Science*, 139.

Newell, A., Shaw, J. C. and Simon, H. A. (1962) 'The Processes of Creative Thinking' in Gruber, Terrell and Wertheimer (eds) *Contemporary Approaches to Creative Thinking*. New York: Atherton Press.

Newell, A. and Simon, H. A. (1963) 'Computers in Psychology' in Luce, Bush and Galanter (eds) *Handbook of Mathematical Psychology*, New York: Wiley.

Newell, A. et al. (1964) *IPL-V Programmers' Reference Manual*. New York: Prentice-Hall, 2nd ed.

Newmann, James R. (ed.) (1956) *The World of Mathematics*. New York: Simon & Schuster.

Reitman, Walter R. (1963) 'Personality as a Problem-Solving Coalition' in Tomkins, S. S. and Messick (eds) *Computer Simulation of Personality*. New York: Wiley.

Simon, H. A. (1957) *Models of Man*. New York: Wiley.

Simon, H. A. (1962) 'The Architecture of Complexity', *Proceedings of the American Philosophical Society*, 106.

Simon, H. A. and Kotovsky, K. (1963) 'Human Acquisition of Concepts for Sequential Patterns', *Psychological Review*, 70.

Simon, H. A. and Simon, P. A. (1962) 'Trial and Error Search in Solving Difficult Problems: Evidence from the Game of Chess', *Behavioral Science*, 7.

Smart, J. J. C. (1961) 'Gödel's Theorem, Church's Theorem, and Mechanism', *Synthèse*, 13, June.

Taylor, D. W. (1960) 'Toward an Information Processing Theory of Motivation', in Jones (ed.) *Nebraska Symposium on Motivation*. Lincoln: University of Nebraska Press.

Tomkins, Silvan S. (1963) 'Simulation of Personality' in Tomkins, S. S. and Messick *Computer Simulation of Personality*. New York: Wiley.

Toulmin, Stephen and Goodfield, June (1962) *The Architecture of Matter*. New York: Harper & Row.

Turing, A. M. (1950) 'Computing Machinery and Intelligence', *Mind*, 59.

5. Information Processing in Computer and Man (1964)*

Organizing a computer to perform complex tasks depends very much more upon the characteristics of the task environment than upon the 'hardware' – the specific physical means for realizing the processing in the computer. Thus, all past and present digital computers perform basically the same kinds of symbol manipulations.

In programming a computer it is substantially irrelevant what physical processes and devices – electromagnetic, electronic, or what not – accomplish the manipulations. A program written in one of the symbolic programming languages, like ALGOL or FORTRAN, will produce the same symbolic output on a machine that uses electron tubes for processing and storing symbols, one that incorporates magnetic drums, one with a magnetic core memory, or one with completely transistorized circuitry. The program, the organization of symbol-manipulating processes, is what determines the transformation of input into output. In fact, provided with only the program output, and without information about the processing speed, one cannot determine what kinds of physical devices accomplished the transformations: whether the program was executed by a solid-state computer, an electron-tube device, an electrical relay machine, or a room full of statistical clerks! Only the organization of the processes is determinate. Out of this observation arises the possibility of an independent science of information processing.

By the same token, since the thinking human being is also an information processor, it should be possible to study his processes

*Reprinted with the permission of the copyright holder from *American Scientist*, vol. 52, no. 3, September 1964. Copyrighted 1964, by The Society of the Sigma Xi and reprinted by permission of the copyright owner.

and their organization independently of the details of the biological mechanisms – the 'hardware' – that implement them. The output of the processes, the behaviour of *Homo cogitans*, should reveal how the information processing is organized, without necessarily providing much information about the protoplasmic structures or biochemical processes that implement it. From this observation follows the possibility of constructing and testing psychological theories to explain human thinking in terms of the organization of information processes; and of accomplishing this without waiting until the neurophysiological foundations at the next lower level of explanation have been constructed.

Finally, there is a growing body of evidence that the elementary information processes used by the human brain in thinking are highly similar to a sub-set of the elementary information processes that are incorporated in the instruction codes of present-day computers. As a consequence it has been found possible to test information-processing theories of human thinking by formulating these theories as computer programs – organizations of the elementary information processes – and examining the outputs of computers so programmed. The procedure assumes no similarity between computer and brain at the 'hardware' level, only similarity in their capacities for executing and organizing elementary information processes. From this hypothesis has grown up a fruitful collaboration between research in 'artificial intelligence', aimed at enlarging the capabilities of computers, and research in human cognitive psychology.

These, then, are the three propositions on which this discussion rests:

1. A science of information processing can be constructed that is substantially independent of the specific properties of particular information-processing mechanisms.
2. Human thinking can be explained in information-processing terms without waiting for a theory of the underlying neurological mechanisms.
3. Information-processing theories of human thinking can be formulated in computer programming languages, and can be tested by simulating the predicted behaviour with computers.

LEVELS OF EXPLANATION

No apology is needed for carrying explanation only to an intermediate level, leaving further reduction to the future progress of
science. The other sciences provide numerous precedents, perhaps
the most relevant being nineteenth-century chemistry. The atomic
theory and the theory of chemical combination were invented and
developed rapidly and fruitfully during the first three-quarters of the
nineteenth century – from Dalton, through Kekulé, to Mendeleev –
without any direct physical evidence for or description of atoms,
molecules, or valances. To quote Pauling (1960):

> Most of the general principles of molecular structure and the nature of
> the chemical bond were formulated long ago by chemists by induction
> from the great body of chemical facts ... The study of the structure of
> molecules was originally carried on by chemists using methods of investi-
> gation that were essentially chemical in nature, relating to the chemical
> composition of substances, the existence of isomers, the nature of the
> chemical reactions in which a substance takes part, and so on. From the
> consideration of facts of this kind Frankland, Kekulé, Couper, and
> Butlerov were led a century ago to formulate the theory of valence and to
> write the first structural formulas for molecules, van't Hoff and le Bel
> were led to bring classical organic stereochemistry into its final form by
> their brilliant postulate of the tetrahedral orientation of the four valence
> bonds of the carbon atom, and Werner was led to his development of the
> theory of the stereochemistry of complex inorganic substances. (pp. 3–4)

The history this passage outlines is worth pondering, because the
last generation of psychologists has engaged in so much methodological dispute about the nature, utility, and even propriety, of theory.
The vocal methodologically self-conscious, behaviourist wing of
experimental psychology has expressed its scepticism of 'unobserved
entities' and 'intermediate constructs'.[1] Sometimes it has seemed to
object to filling the thinking head with anything whatsoever. Psychologists who rejected the empty-head viewpoint, but who were
sensitive to the demand for operational constructs, tended to
counter the behaviourist objections by couching their theories in
physiological language.[2]

The example of atomic theory in chemistry shows that neither
horn of this dilemma need be seized. On the one hand, hypothetical
entities, postulated because they were powerful and fruitful for
organizing experimental evidence, proved exceedingly valuable in
that science, and did not produce objectionable metaphysics.

Indeed, they were ultimately legitimized in the present century by 'direct' physical evidence.

On the other hand, the hypothetical entities of atomic theory initially had no *physical* properties (other than weight) that could explain why they behaved as they did. While an electrical theory of atomic attraction predated valence theory, the former hypothesis actually impeded the development of the latter and had to be discredited before the experimental facts could fall into place. The valence of the mid-century chemist was a 'chemical affinity' without any underlying physical mechanism. So it remained for more than half a century until the electron-shell theory was developed by Lewis and others to explain it.

Paralleling this example from chemistry, information-processing theories of human thinking employ unobserved entities – symbols – and unobserved processes – elementary information processes. The theories provide explanations of behaviour that are mechanistic without being physiological. That they are mechanistic – that they postulate only processes capable of being effected by mechanism – is guaranteed by simulating the behaviour predicted on ordinary digital computers. (See the Appendix, 'Computer Programs as Theories.') Simulation provides a basis for testing the predictions of the theories, but does not imply that the protoplasm in the brain resembles the electronic components of the computer.

A SPECIFIC INFORMATION-PROCESSING THEORY: PROBLEM SOLVING IN CHESS

Information-processing theories have been constructed for several kinds of behaviour, and undertake to explain behaviour in varying degrees of detail. As a first example, we consider a theory that deals with a rather narrow and special range of human problem-solving skill, attempting to explain the macroscopic organization of thought in a particular task environment.

Good chess players often detect strategies – called in chess 'combinations' – that impose a loss of a piece or a checkmate on the opponent over a series of moves, no matter what the latter does in reply. In actual game positions where a checkmating possibility exists, a strong player may spend a quarter of an hour or more discovering it, and verifying the correctness of his strategy. In doing so, he may have to look ahead four or five moves, or even more.[3] If the combination is deep, weaker players may not be able to discover it at all, even after protracted search. How do good players solve such problems? How do they find combinations?

A theory now exists that answers these questions in some detail. First, I shall describe what it asserts about the processes going on in the mind of the chess player as he studies the position before him, and what it predicts about his progress in discovering an effective strategy. Then we can see to what extent it accounts for the observed facts. The actual theory is a computer program couched in a list-processing language, called Information Processing Language V (IPL-V). Our account of the theory will be an English-language translation of the main features of the program.[4]

The statement of the theory has five main parts. The first two of these specify the way in which the chess player stores in memory his representation of the chess position, and his representation of the moves he is considering, respectively. The remaining parts of the theory specify the processes he has available for extracting information from these representations and using that information: processes for discovering relations among the pieces and squares of the chess position, for synthesizing chess moves for consideration, and for organizing his search among alternative move sequences. We shall describe briefly each of these five parts of the theory.

The theory asserts, first of all, that *the human chess player has means for storing internally, in his brain, encoded representations of the stimuli presented to him*. In the case of a highly schematized stimulus like a chess position, the internal symbolic structure representing it can be visualized as similar to the printed diagram used to represent it in a chess book. The internal representation employs symbols that name the squares and the pieces, and symbolizes the relations among squares, among pieces, and between squares and pieces.

For example, the internal representation symbolizes rather explicitly that a piece on the King's square is a Knight's-move away, in a SSW direction, from a piece on the third rank of the Queen's file. Similarly, if the King's Knight is on the King's Bishop's Third square (KB3), the representation associates the symbol designating the Knight with the symbol designating the KB3 square, and the symbol designating the square with that designating the Knight. On the other hand, the representation does not symbolize directly that two pieces stand on the same diagonal. Relations like this must be discovered or inferred from the representation by the processes to be discussed below.

Asserting that a position is symbolized internally in this way does not mean that the internal representations are verbal (any more than the diagrams in a chess book are verbal). It would be more appropriate, in fact, to describe the representations as a 'visual image', provided that this phrase is not taken to imply that the chess player has any conscious explicit image of the entire board in his 'mind's eye'.

The chess player also has means for representing in memory the moves he is considering. He has symbol-manipulating processes that enable him, from his representations of a position and of a move, to use the latter to modify the former – the symbolic structure that describes the position – into a new structure that represents what the position would be *after* the move. The same processes enable him to 'unmake' a move – to symbolize the position as it was before the move was considered. Thus, if the move that transfers the King's Knight from his original square (KN1) to the King's Bishop's Third square (KB3) is stored in memory, the processes in question can alter the representation of the board by changing the name of the square associated with the Knight from KN1 to KB3, and conversely for unmaking the move.

The chess player has processes that enable him to discover new relations in a position, to symbolize these, and to store the information in memory. For example, in a position he is studying (whether the actual one on the board, or one he has produced by considering moves), he can discover whether his King is in check – attacked by an enemy man; or whether a specified piece can move to a specified square; or whether a specified man is defended. The processes for detecting such relations are usually called perceptual processes. They are characterized by the fact that they are relatively direct: they obtain the desired information from the representation with a relatively small amount of manipulation.

The chess player has processes, making use of the perceptual processes, that permit him to generate or synthesize for his consideration moves with specified properties – for example, to generate all moves that will check the enemy King. To generate moves having desired characteristics may require a considerable amount of processing. If this were not so, if any kind of move could be discovered effortlessly, the entire checkmating program would consist of the single elementary process: DISCOVER CHECKMATING MOVES.

An example of these more complex, indirect processes is a procedure that would discover certain forking moves (moves that attack two pieces simultaneously) somewhat as follows.

Find the square of the opposing Queen. Find all squares that lie a Knight's-move from this square. Determine for each of these squares whether it is defended (whether an opposing piece can move to it). If not, test all squares a Knight's-move away from it to see if any of them has a piece that is undefended or that is more valuable than a Knight.

Finally, the chess player has processes for organizing a search for mating combinations through the 'tree' of possible move sequences. This search makes use of the processes already enumerated, and proceeds as follows.

The player generates all the checking moves available to him in the given position, and for each checking move, generates the legal replies open to his opponent. If there are no checking moves, he concludes that no checkmating combination can be discovered in the position, and stops his search. If, for one of the checking moves, he discovers there are no legal replies, he concludes that the checking move in question is a checkmate. If, for one of the checking moves, he discovers that the opponent has more than four replies, he concludes that this checking move is unpromising, and does not explore it further.

Next, the player considers all the checking moves (a) that he has not yet explored and (b) that he has not yet evaluated as 'CHECK-MATE', or 'NO MATE'. He selects the move that is most promising – by criteria to be mentioned presently – and pushes his analysis of that move one move deeper. That is, he considers each of its replies in turn, generates the checking moves available after those replies, and the replies to those checking moves. He applies the criteria of the previous paragraph to attach 'CHECKMATE' or 'NO MATE' labels to the moves where he can. He also 'propagates' these labels to antecedent moves. For example, a reply is labelled CHECKMATE if at least one of its derivative checking moves is CHECKMATE; it is labelled NO MATE if all the consequent checking moves are so labelled. A checking move is labelled CHECKMATE if all of the replies are so labelled; it is labelled NO MATE if at least one reply is so labelled.

The most promising checking move for further exploration is selected by these criteria: that checking move to which there are the fewest replies receives first priority.[5] If two or more checking moves are tied on this criterion, a double check (check with two pieces) is given priority over a single check. If there is still a tie, a check that does not permit a recapture by the opponent is given priority over one that does. Any remaining ties are resolved by selecting the check generated most recently.

A number of details have been omitted from this description, but it indicates the theory's general structure and the kinds of processes incorporated. The theory predicts, for any chess position that is presented to it, whether a chess player will discover a mating combination in that position, what moves he will consider and explore in his search for the combination, and which combination (if there are several alternatives, as there often are) he will discover. These predictions can be compared directly with published analyses of historical chess positions or tape recordings of the thinking-aloud behaviour of human chess players to whom the same position is presented.

Now it is unlikely that, if a chess position were presented to a large number of players, all of them would explore it in exactly the same way. Certainly strong players would behave differently from weak players. Hence, the information-processing theory, if it is a correct theory at all, must be a theory only for players of a certain strength. On the other hand, we would not regard its explanation of chess playing as very satisfactory if we had to construct an entirely new theory for each player we studied.

Matters are not so bad, however. First, the interpersonal variations in search for chess moves in middle-game positions appear to be quite small for players at a common level of strength as we shall see in a moment. Second, some of the differences that are unrelated to playing strength appear to correspond to quite simple variants of the program – altering, for example, the criteria that are used to select the most promising checking move for exploration. Other differences, on the other hand, have major effects on the efficacy of the search, and some of these, also, can be represented quite simply by variants of the program organization. Thus, the basic structure of the program, and the assumptions it incorporates about human information-processing capacities, provide a general explanation for the behaviour, while particular variants of this basic program allow specific predictions to be made of the behavioural consequences of individual differences in program organization and content.

The kinds of information the theory provides, and the ways in which it has been tested, can be illustrated by a pair of examples. Adrian de Groot (1964) has gathered and analysed a substantial number of thinking-aloud protocols, some of them from grand masters. He uniformly finds that, even in complicated positions, a player seldom generates a 'tree' of more than 50 or 75 positions before he chooses his move. Moreover, the size of the tree does not depend on the player's strength. The thinking-aloud technique probably underestimates the size of the search tree somewhat, for a player may fail to mention some variations he has seen, but the whole tree is probably not an order of magnitude greater than that reported.

In 40 positions from a standard published work on mating combinations where the information-processing theory predicted that a player would find mating strategies, the median size of its search tree ranged from 13 positions for two-move mates, to 53 for five-move mates. A six-move mate was found with a tree of 95 positions; and an eight-move mate with a tree of 108. (The last two mates, as well as a number of the others, were from historically celebrated games between grand masters, and are among the most 'brilliant' on record.) Hence, we can conclude that the predictions of the theory on amount of search are quite consistent with de Groot's empirical findings on the behaviour of highly skilled human chess players.

The second example tests a much more detailed feature of the theory. In the eight-move mate mentioned above, it had been known that by following a different strategy the mate could have been achieved in seven moves. Both the human grand master (Edward Lasker in the game of Lasker-Thomas, 1912) and the program found the eight-move mate. Examination of the exploration shows that the shorter sequence could only have been discovered by exploring a branch of the tree that permitted the defender two replies before exploring a branch that permitted a single reply. The historical evidence here confirms the postulate of the theory that players use the 'fewest replies' heuristic to guide their search. (The evidence was discovered after the theory was constructed.) A second piece of evidence of the same sort has been found in a game between experts reported in *Chess Life* (December 1963). The winner discovered a seven-move mate, but overlooked the fact that he could have mated in three moves. The annotator of the game, a master, also over-looked the shorter sequence. Again, it could only have been found by exploring a check with two replies before exploring one with a single reply.

The 'fewest replies' heuristic is not a superficial aspect of the players' search, nor is its relevance limited to the game of chess. Most problem-solving tasks – for example, discovering proofs of mathematical theorems – require a search through a branching 'tree' of possibilities. Since the tree branches geometrically, solving a problem of any difficulty would call for a search of completely unmanageable scope (numbers like 10^{120} arise frequently in esti-mating the magnitude of such searches), if there were not at hand powerful heuristics, or rules of thumb, for selecting the promising branches for exploration. Such heuristics permit the discovery of proofs for theorems (and mating combinations) with the limited explorations reported here.

The 'fewest replies' heuristic is powerful because it combines two functions: it points search in those directions that are most restric-tive for the opponent, giving him the least opportunity to solve his problems; at the same time, it limits the growth of the search tree, by keeping its rate of branching as low as possible. The 'fewest replies' heuristic is the basis for the idea of retaining the initiative in military strategy, and in competitive activities generally, and is also a central heuristic in decision making in the face of uncertainty. Hence its appearance in the chess-playing theory, and in the behaviour of the human players, is not fortuitous.

PARSIMONIOUS AND GARRULOUS THEORIES

Granting its success in predicting both some general and some very specific aspects of human behaviour in chess playing, like the exam-ples just described, the theory might be confronted with several kinds of questions and objections, It somehow fails to conform to our usual notions of generality and parsimony in theory. First, it is highly specific – the checkmating theory purports to provide an explanation only of how good chess players behave when they are confronted with a position on the board that calls for a vigorous mating attack. If we were to try to explain the whole range of human behaviour, over all the enormous variety of tasks that particular human beings perform, we should have to compound the explanations from thousands of specific theories like the checkmate program. The final product would be an enormous compendium of 'recipes' for human behaviour at specific levels of skill in specific task environments.[6]

Second, the individual theories comprising this compendium would hardly be parsimonious, judged by ordinary standards. We used about a thousand words above to provide an approximate description of the checkmate program. The actual program – the formal theory – consists of about three thousand computer instructions in a list-processing language, equivalent in information content to about the same number of English words. (It should be mentioned that the program includes a complete statement of the rules of chess, so that only a small part of the total is given over to the description of the player's selection rules and their organization.)

Before we recoil from this unwieldy compendium as too unpleasant and unaesthetic to contemplate, let us see how it compares in bulk with theories in the other sciences. With the simplicity of Newtonian mechanics (why is this always the first example to which we turn?), there is, of course, no comparison. If classical mechanics is the model, then a theory should consist of three sentences, or a couple of differential equations.[7]

But chemistry, and particularly organic chemistry, presents a different picture. It is perhaps not completely misleading to compare the question 'How does a chess player find a checkmating combination?' with a question like 'How do photoreceptors in the human eye operate?' or 'How is the carbohydrate and oxygen intake of a rabbit transformed into energy usable in muscular contraction?'

The theory of plant metabolism provides a striking example of an explanation of phenomena in terms of a substantial number of complex mechanisms. Calvin and Bassham (1962), in their book on *The Photosynthesis of Carbon Compounds*, introduce a figure entitled 'carbon reduction pathways in photosynthesis' with the statement: 'We believe the *principal* pathways for photosynthesis of simple organic compounds from CO_2 to be those shown in Figure 2.' (pp 8–11, italics ours.) The figure referred to represents more than 40 distinct chemical reactions and a corresponding number of compounds. This diagram, of course, is far from representing the whole theory. Not only does it omit much of the detail, but it contains none of the quantitative considerations for predicting reaction rates, energy balances, and so on. The verbal description accompanying the figure, which also has little to say about the quantitative aspects, or the energetics, is over two pages in length – almost as long as our description of the chess-playing program. Here we have a clearcut example of a theory of fundamental importance that has none of the parsimony we commonly associate with scientific theorizing.

The answer to the question of how photosynthesis proceeds is decidedly long-winded – as is the answer to the question of how chess players find mating combinations. We are often satisfied with such long-winded answers because we believe that the phenomena are intrinsically complex, and that no brief theory will explain them in detail. We must adjust our expectations about the character of information-processing theories of human thinking to a similar level. Such theories, to the extent that they account for the details of the phenomena, will be highly specific and highly complex. We might call them 'garrulous theories' in contrast with our more common models of parsimonious theories.

ELEMENTARY INFORMATION PROCESSES

We should like to carry the analogy with chemistry a step further. Part of our knowledge in chemistry – and a very important part of the experimental chemist – consists of vast catalogues of substances and reactions, not dissimilar in bulk to the compendium of information processes we are proposing. But, as we come to understand these substances and their reactions more fully, a second level of theory emerges that explains them (at least their general features) in a more parsimonious way. The substances, at this more basic level, become geometrical arrangements of particles from a small set of more fundamental substances – atoms and sub-molecules – held together by a variety of known forces whose effects can be estimated qualitatively and, in simple cases, quantitatively.

If we examine an information-processing theory like the check-mating program more closely, we find that it, too, is organized from a limited number of building blocks – a set of elementary information processes – and some composite processes that are compounded from the more elementary ones in a few characteristic ways. Let us try to describe these building blocks in general terms. First, we shall characterize the way in which symbols and structures of symbols are represented internally and held in memory. Then, we shall mention some of the principal elementary processes that alter these symbol structures.[8]

Symbols, Lists and Descriptions

The smallest units of manipulable information in memory are *symbol tokens*[9] or symbol occurrences. It is postulated that tokens can be compared, and that comparison determines that the tokens are occurrences of the same symbol (*symbol type*), or that they are different.

Symbol tokens are arranged in larger structures, called *lists*. A list is an ordered set, a sequence, of tokens. Hence, with every token on a list, except the last, there is associated a unique *next* token. Associated with the list as a whole is a symbol, its *name*. Thus, a list may be a sequence of symbols that are themselves names of lists – a list of lists. A familiar example of a list of symbols that all of us carry in memory is the alphabet. (Its name is 'alphabet'.) Another is the list of days of the week, in order – Monday is next to Sunday, and so on.

Associations also exist between symbol types. An association is a two-termed relation, involving three symbols, one of which names the relation, the other two its arguments. 'The colour of the apple is red' specifies an association between 'apple' and 'red' with the relation 'colour'. A symbol's associations *describe* that symbol.

Some Elementary Processes

A symbol, a list and an association are abstract objects. Their properties are defined by the elementary information processes that operate on them. One important class of such processes are the *discrimination* processes. The basic discrimination process, which compares symbols to determine whether or not they are identical, has already been mentioned. Pairs of compound structures – lists and sets of associations – are discriminated from each other by matching processes that apply the basic tests for symbol identity to symbols in corresponding positions in the two structures. For example, two chess positions can be discriminated by a matching process that compares the pieces standing on corresponding squares in the two positions. The outcome of the match might be a statement that 'the two positions are identical except that the White King is on his Knight's square in the first but on his Rook's square in the second.'

Other classes of elementary information processes are those capable of *creating* or *copying* symbols, lists and associations. These processes are involved, for example, in fixating or memorizing symbolic materials presented to the sense organs – learning a tune. Somewhat similar information processes are capable of modifying existing symbolic structures by *inserting a symbol* into a list, by *changing a term of an association* (from 'its colour is red' to 'its colour is green'), or by *deleting a symbol* from a list.

Still another class of elementary information processes *finds* information that is in structures stored in memory. We can think of such a process, schematically, as follows: to answer the question, 'What letter follows "g" in the alphabet?', a process must find the list in memory named 'alphabet'. Then, another process must search down that list until (using the match for identity of symbols) it finds a 'g'. Finally, a third process must find the symbol *next* to 'g' in the list. Similarly, to answer the question, 'what colour is the apple?' there must be a process capable of finding the second term of an association, given the first term and the name of the relation. Thus, there must be processes for finding named objects, for finding symbols on a list, for finding the next symbol on a list, and for finding the value of an attribute of an object.

This list of elementary information processes is modest, yet provides an adequate collection of building blocks to implement the chess-playing theory as well as the other information-processing theories of thinking that have been constructed to date: including a general problem-solving theory, a theory of rote verbal learning, and several theories of concept formation and pattern recognition, among others.[10]

Elementary Processes in the Chess Theory

A few examples will show how the mechanisms employed in the chess-playing theory can be realized by symbols, lists, associations and elementary information processes. The player's representation of the chess board is assumed to be a collection of associations: with each square is associated the symbol representing the man on that square, and symbols representing the adjoining squares in the several directions. Moves are similarly represented as symbols with which are associated the names of the squares from which and to which the move was made, the name of the piece moved, the name of the piece captured, if any, and so on.

Similarly, the processes for manipulating these representations are compounded from the elementary processes already described. To make a move, for example, is to modify the internal representation of the board by deleting the association of the man to be moved with the square on which he previously stood, and creating the new association of that man with the square to which he moved; and, in case of a capture, by deleting also the association of the captured man with the square on which he stood. Another example: testing whether the King is in check involves finding the square associated with the King, finding adjoining squares along ranks, files and diagonals, and testing these squares for the presence of enemy men who are able to attack in the appropriate direction. (The latter is determined by associating with each man his *type*, and associating with each type of man the directions in which such men can legally be moved.)

We see that, although the chess-playing theory contains several thousand program instructions, these are comprised of only a small number of elementary processes (far fewer than the number of elements in the periodic table). The elementary processes combine in a few simple ways into compound processes and operate on structures (lists and descriptions) that are constructed, combinatorially, from a single kind of building block – the symbol. There are two levels of theory: an 'atomic' level, common to all the information-processing theories, of symbols, lists, associations and elementary processes, and a 'macro-molecular' level, peculiar to each type of specialized human performance, of representations in the form of list structures and webs of associations, and of compound processes for manipulating these representations.

Processes in Serial Pattern Recognition

A second example of how programs compounded from the elementary processes explain behaviour is provided by an information-processing theory of serial pattern recognition.

Consider a sequence like:

ABMCDMEFM –.

An experimental subject in the laboratory, asked to extrapolate the series, will, after a little thought, continue:

GHM, etc.

To see how he achieves this result, we examine the original sequence. First, it makes use of letters of the Roman alphabet. We can assume that the subject holds this alphabet in memory stored as a list, so that the elementary list process for finding the NEXT item on a list can find B, given A, or find S, given R, and so on. Now we note that any letter in the sequence, after the first three, is related to previous letters by relations NEXT and SAME. Specifically, if we organize the series into periods of three letters each:

ABM   CDM   EFM

we see that:

1. The first letter in each period is NEXT in the alphabet to the second letter in the previous period.
2. The second letter in each period is NEXT in the alphabet to the first letter in that period.
3. The third letter in each period is the SAME as the corresponding letter in the previous period.

The relations of SAME and NEXT also suffice for a series like:

AAA   CCC   EEE

or for a number series like:

1 7 2 8 3 9 4 0

In the last case, the 'alphabet' to which the relation of NEXT is applied is the list of digits, 0 to 9, and NEXT is applied circularly, i.e. after 9 comes 0 and then 1 again.

Several closely related information-processing theories of human pattern recognition have been constructed using elementary processes for finding and generating the NEXT item in a list (see Feldman, Tonge and Kanter 1964; Laughery and Gregg 1962, and

Simon and Kotovsky 1963). These theories have succeeded in explaining some of the main features of human behaviour in a number of standard laboratory tasks, including so-called binary choice tasks, and series-completion and symbol-analogy tasks from intelligence tests.

The nature of the series-completion task has already been illustrated. In the binary choice experiment, the subject is confronted, one by one, with a sequence of tokens – each a ' + ' or 'V', say. As each one is presented to him, he is asked what the next one will be. The actual sequence is, by construction, random. The evidence shows that, even when the subjects are told this, they rarely treat it as random. Instead, they behave as though they were trying to detect a serial pattern in the sequence and extrapolate it. They behave essentially like subjects faced by the series-completion task, and basically similar information-processing theories using the same elementary processes can explain both behaviours.

A BROADER VIEW OF THINKING PROCESSES

A closer look at the principal examples now extant of information-processing theories suggests that another level of theory is rapidly emerging, intermediate between the 'atomic' level common to all the theories and the 'macro-molecular' level idiosyncratic to each. It is clear that there is no prospect of eliminating all idiosyncratic elements from the individual theories. A theory to explain chess-playing performances must postulate memory structures and processes that are completely irrelevant to proving theorems in geometry, and vice versa.

On the other hand, it is entirely possible that human performances in different task environments may call on common components at more aggregative levels than the elementary processes. This, in fact, appears to be the case. The first information-processing theory that isolated some of these common components was called the General Problem Solver (Newell and Simon 1964).

Means–End Analysis

The General Problem Solver is a program organized to keep separate (1) problem-solving processes that, according to the theory, are possessed and used by most human beings of average intelligence when they are confronted with any relatively unfamiliar task environment, from (2) specific information about each particular task environment.

The core of the General Problem Solver is an organization of processes for *means–end analysis*. The problem is defined by *specifying a given situation (A)*, and a *desired situation (B)*. A discrimination process incorporated in the system of means–end analysis compares A with B, and detects one or more *differences (D)* between them, if there are any. With each difference, there is associated in memory a set of *operators*, (O_D) or processes, that are possibly relevant to removing differences of that kind. The means–end analysis program proceeds to try to remove the difference by applying, in turn, the relevant operators.

Using a scheme of means–end analysis, a proof of a trigonometric identity like $\cos \Theta \tan \Theta = \sin \Theta$ might proceed like this: The right-hand side contains only the sine function; the left-hand side other trigonometric functions as well. The operator that replaces tan by sin/cos will eliminate one of these. Applying it we get $\cos \Theta (\sin \Theta/\cos \Theta) = \sin \Theta$. The left-hand side still contains an extraneous function, cosine. The algebraic cancellation operator, applied in the two cosines, might remove this difference. We apply the operator, obtaining the identity $\sin \Theta = \sin \Theta$.

Planning Process

Another class of general processes discovered in human problem-solving performances and incorporated in the General Problem Solver are *planning* processes. The essential idea in planning is that the representation of the problem situation is simplified by deleting some of the detail. A solution is now sought for the new, simplified, problem, and if one is found, it is used as a plan to guide the solution of the original problem, with the detail reinserted.

Consider a simple problem in logic. Given: (1) '*A*', (2) '*not A or B*', (3) '*if not C then not B*'; to prove '*C*'. To plan the proof, note that the first premise contains *A*, the second *A* and *B*, the third, *B* and *C*, and the conclusion, *C*. The plan might be to obtain *B* by combining *A* with (*AB*), then to obtain *C* by combining *B* with (*BC*). The plan will in fact work, but requires (2) to be transformed into

'*A* implies *B*' and (3) into '*B* implies *C*', which transformations follow from the definitions of 'or' and 'if . . . then'.

Problem-Solving Organization

The processes for attempting sub-goals in the problem-solving theories and the exploration processes in the chess-playing theory must be guided and controlled by executive processes that determine what goal will be attempted next. Common principles for the organization of the executive processes have begun to appear in several of the theories. The general idea has already been outlined above for the chess-playing program. In this program the executive routine cycles between an exploration (*search*) phase and an evaluation (*scan*) phase. During the exploration phase, the available problem-solving processes are used to investigate sub-goals. The information obtained through this investigation is stored in such a way as to be accessible to the executive. During the evaluation phase, the executive uses this information to determine which of the existing sub-goals is the most promising and should be explored next. An executive program organized in this way may be called a search–scan scheme, for it searches an expanding tree of possibilities, which provides a common pool of information for scanning by its evaluative processes.[11]

The effectiveness of a problem-solving program appears to depend rather sensitively on the alternation of the search and scan phases. If search takes place in long sequences, interrupted only infrequently to scan for possible alternative directions of exploration, the problem solver suffers from stereotypy. Having initiated search in one direction, it tends to persist in that direction as long as the sub-routines conducting the search determine, locally, that the possibilities for exploration have not been exhausted. These determinations are made in a very decentralized way, and without benefit of the more global information that has been generated.

On the other hand, if search is too frequently interrupted to consider alternative goals to the one being pursued currently, the exploration takes on an uncoordinated appearance, wandering indecisively among a wide range of possibilities. In both theorem-proving and chess-playing programs, extremes of decentralized and centralized control of search have shown themselves ineffective in comparison with a balanced search–scan organization.

Discrimination Trees

Common organizational principles are also emerging for the rote memory processes involved in almost all human performance. As a person tries to prove a theorem, say, certain expressions that he encounters along the way gradually become familiar to him and his ability to discriminate among them gradually improves. An information-processing theory (EPAM) was constructed several years ago to account for this and similar human behaviour in verbal learning experiments (e.g. learning nonsense syllables by the serial anticipation or paired associate methods) (see Feigenbaum 1964). This theory is able to explain, for instance, how familiarity and similarity of materials affect rates of learning. The essential processes in EPAM include processes for discriminating among compound objects by sorting them in a 'discrimination tree'; and familiarization processes for associating pairs or short sequences of objects.

Discrimination processes operate by applying sequences of tests to the stimulus objects, and sorting them on the basis of the test results – a sort of 'twenty questions' procedure. The result of discrimination is to find a memory location where information is stored about objects that are similar to the one sorted. *Familiarization processes* create new compound objects out of previously familiar elements. Thus, during the last decade, the letter sequence 'IPL' has become a familiar word (to computer programmers!) meaning 'information processing language'. The individual letters have been *associated* in this word. Similarly, the English alphabet, used by the serial pattern-recognizing processes, is a familiar object compounded from the letters arranged in a particular sequence. All sorts of additional information can be associated with an object, once familiarized (for example, the fact that IPLs organize symbols in lists can be associated with 'IPL').

Because discrimination trees play a central role in EPAM, the program may also be viewed as a theory of pattern detection, and EPAM-like trees have been incorporated in certain information-processing theories of concept formation. It also now seems likely that the discrimination tree is an essential element in problem-solving theories like GPS, playing an important role in the gradual modification of the subject's behaviour as he familiarizes himself with the problem material.

CONCLUSION

Our survey shows that within the past decade a considerable range of human behaviours has been explained successfully by information-processing theories. We now know, for example, some of the central processes that are employed in solving problems, in detecting and extrapolating patterns, and in memorizing verbal materials.

Information-processing theories explain behaviour at various levels of detail. In the theories now extant, at least three levels can be distinguished. At the most aggregative level are theories of complex behaviour in specific problem domains: proving theorems in logic or geometry, discovering checkmating combinations in chess. These theories tend to contain very extensive assumptions about the knowledge and skills possessed by the human beings who perform these activities, and about the way in which this knowledge and these skills are organized and represented internally. Hence each of these theories incorporates a rather extensive set of assumptions, and predicts behaviour only in a narrow domain.

At a second level, similar or identical information-processing mechanisms are common to many of the aggregative theories. Means–end analysis, planning, the search–scan scheme, and discrimination trees are general-purpose organizations for processing that are usable over a wide range of tasks. As the nature of these mechanisms becomes better understood, they, in turn, begin to serve as basic building blocks for the aggregative theories, allowing the latter to be stated in more parsimonious form, and exhibiting the large fraction of machinery that is common to all, rather than idiosyncratic to individual tasks.

At the lowest, 'atomic', level, all the information-processing theories postulate only a small set of basic forms of symbolic representation and a small number of elementary information processes. The construction and successful testing of large-scale programs that simulate complex human behaviours provide evidence that a small set of elements, similar to those now postulated in information-processing languages, is sufficient for the construction of a theory of human thinking.

Although none of the advances that have been described constitute explanations of human thought at the still more microscopic, physiological level, they open opportunities for new research strategies in physiological psychology. As the information-processing theories become more powerful and better validated, they disclose to the physiological psychologist the fundamental mechanisms and processes that he needs to explain. He need no longer face the task of building the whole long bridge from microscopic neurological and molecular structures to gross human behaviour, but can instead concentrate on bridging the much shorter gap from physiology to elementary information processes.

The work of Lettvin, Maturana, McCulloch and Pitts on information processing in the frog's eye (1959), and the work of Hubel and Wiesel on processing of visual information by the cat (1962) already provide some hints of the form this bridging operation may take.

NOTES

1. The best-known exponent of this radical behaviourist position is Professor B.F. Skinner. He has argued, for example, that 'an explanation is the demonstration of a functional relationship between behavior and manipulable or controllable variables,' in Wann (1964), p. 102.
2. A distinguished example of such a theory is Hebb's (1949) formulation in terms of 'cell assemblies'. Hebb does not, however, insist on an exclusively physiological base for psychological theory, and his general methodological position is not inconsistent with that taken here. See also Hebb (1958), Chap. 13.
3. A 'move' means here a move by one player followed by a reply by his opponent. Hence to look ahead four of five moves is to consider sequences of eight or ten successive positions.
4. A general account of this program, with the results of some hand simulations, can be found in Simon and Simon (1962), pp. 425–9. The theory described there has subsequently been programmed and the hand-simulated findings confirmed on a computer.
5. This is perhaps the most important element in the strategy. It will be discussed further later.
6. The beginnings of such a compendium have already appeared. A convenient source for descriptions of a number of the information-processing theories is the collection by Feigenbaum and Feldman (1964).
7. Of course, even Newtonian mechanics is not at all this simple in structure. See Simon (1947), pp. 888–905.
8. Only a few of the characteristics of list-processing systems can be mentioned here. For a fuller account, see Newell and Simon (1963), especially pp. 273–376, 380–84, 419–24.
9. Evidence as to how information is symbolized in the brain is almost non-existent. If the reader is assisted by thinking of different symbols as different macromolecules, this metaphor is as good as any. A few physiologists think it may even be the correct explanation. See Hyden (1961), pp. 18–39. Differing patterns of neural activity will do as well. See Adey, Kador, Didio and Schindler (1963), pp. 259–81.

10. For examples, see Feigenbaum and Feldman (1964), Part 2.
11. Perhaps the earliest use of the search–scan scheme appeared in the Logic Theorist, the first heuristic theorem-proving program. See Newell and Simon (1964).

REFERENCES

Adey, W. R., Kador, R. T., Didio, J. and Schindler, W. J. (1963) 'Impedance Changes in Cerebral Tissue Accompanying a Learned Discriminative Performance in the Cat', *Experimental Physiology*, 7.

Calvin, M. and Bassham, J. A. (1962) *The Photosynthesis of Carbon Compounds*. New York: W. A. Benjamin.

De Groot, A. (1964) *Thought and Choice in Chess*. The Hague: Mouton.

Feigenbaum, E. A. (1964) 'The Simulation of Verbal Learning Behavior' in Feigenbaum and Feldman (1964).

Feigenbaum, E. A. and Feldman, J. (eds) (1964) *Computers and Thought*. New York: McGraw-Hill.

Feldman, J., Tonge, F. and Kanter, H. (1963) 'Empirical Explorations of Hypothesis-Testing Model of Binary Choice Behavior' in Hoggatt, A. C. and Balderston, F. E. (eds) *Symposium on Simulation Models*. Cincinnati: South-Western Publishing.

Hebb, D. O. (1949) *The Organization of Behavior*. New York: Wiley.

Hebb, D. O. (1958) *Textbook of Psychology*. Philadelphia: Saunders.

Hubel, D. H. and Wiesel, T. N. (1962) 'Receptive Fields, Binocular Interaction and Functional Architecture in the Cat's Visual Cortex', *Journal of Physiology*, 160, pp. 106–54.

Hyden, Holger (1961) 'Biochemical Aspects of Brain Activity' in Farber, S.M. and Wilson, R. H. L. (eds) *Control of the Mind*. New York: McGraw-Hill.

Laughery, K. R. and Gregg, L. W. (1962) 'Simulation of Human Problem-Solving Behaviour', *Psychometrika*, 27.

Lettvin, J. Y., Maturana, H. R., McCulloch, W. S. and Pitts, W. H. (1959) 'What the Frog's Eye Tells the Frog's Brain', *Proceedings of the Institute of Radio Engineers*, 47, pp. 1940–51.

Newell, A. and Simon, H. A. (1963) 'Computers in Psychology' in Luce, Bush and Galanter (eds) *Handbook of Mathematical Psychology*, vol. 1. New York: Wiley.

Newell, A. and Simon, H. A. (1964) 'Empirical Explorations with the Logic Theory Machine: A Case Study in Heuristics' in Feigenbaum and Feldman (1964).

Newell, A. and Simon, H. A. (1964) 'GPS, A Program that Simulates Human Thought' in Feigenbaum and Feldman (1964).

Pauling (1960) *The Nature of the Chemical Bond*. Ithaca: Cornell University Press, 3rd ed.

Simon, H. A. (1947) 'The Axioms of Newtonian Mechanics', *Phil. Mag.*, Ser. 7, 38 (December).

Simon, H. A. and Kotovsky, K. (1963) 'Human Acquisition of Concepts for

Sequential Patterns', *Psychological Review*, 70 (November), pp. 534–46.

Simon, H. A. and Simon, P. A. (1962) 'Trial and Error Search in Solving Difficult Problems: Evidence from the Game of Chess', *Behavioral Science*, 7 (October).

Wann, T. W. (ed.) (1964) *Behaviorism and Phenomenology*. Chicago: University of Chicago Press.

APPENDIX: COMPUTER PROGRAMS AS THEORIES

Since the use of computer programs as formal theories, in the manner described in this chapter, is still somewhat novel, this appendix sketches briefly the relation between this formalism and the formalisms that have been used more commonly in the physical sciences.

In the physical sciences, theories about dynamical systems usually take the form of systems of differential equations. This is the form of classical Newtonian mechanics, of Maxwell's electromagnetic theory, and of many other theories of central importance. In the classical dynamics of mass points, for example, it is assumed that the initial positions and velocities of a set of bodies (mass points) are given, and that the forces acting on the bodies are known, instantaneous functions of the positions, say, of the bodies. Then, by Newton's Second Law, the acceleration (second derivative of position) of each body is proportional to the resultant force acting on it. The paths of the bodies over time are calculated by integrating twice the differential equations that express the Second Law.

More generally, a system of differential or difference equations is a set of conditional laws that determine the state of the system 'a moment later' as a function of its state at a given time. Repeated application of the laws, equivalent to integrating the equations, then determines the path of the system over time.

A computer program is also literally a system of difference equations – albeit of a rather unorthodox kind. For it determines the behaviour of the computer in the next instruction cycle as a function of the current contents of its memory. Executing the program is formally equivalent to integrating (numerically) the difference equations for a specified initial state of the computer. Thus, information-processing theories, expressed as programs in computer languages, are not merely analogous to more familiar kinds of dynamical theories; formally, they are of an equivalent type.

Very simple systems of differential and integral equations can sometimes be integrated formally, so that general properties can be inferred about the paths of the systems they describe, independent of particular initial and boundary conditions. There are no known methods for integrating formally systems of difference equations like those discussed in this chapter. Hence, the principal means for making predictions about such systems is to simulate their behaviour for particular initial and boundary conditions. This is the method of investigation that we have relied on here.

6.   Scientific Discovery as Problem Solving (1988)*

Scientific discovery is a central topic both for the philosophy of science and for the history of science, but it has been treated in very different ways by the two disciplines. Philosphers of science have been concerned mainly with the verification (or falsification) of scientific theories rather than with the origins of the theories or the processes by means of which they were derived. In fact, until very recently, most philosophers of science denied that a theory of discovery processes was possible, and that is probably still the majority view in the discipline (Popper 1961). Within the past decade or so, however, a weak trickle of interest in discovery has grown into a sizeable stream (Nickles 1978).

Historians of science, on the other hand, have long been interested in the discovery process, and have experienced no special difficulty in studying it. I do not mean by this that it is easy to study. Since data are mostly lacking at the more microscopic level – the hour-by-hour progress of an investigation – they have viewed it on a more global scale, usually relying on publications as a principal source of data. Sometimes, however, and especially in recent years, they have gained access to more detailed accounts of scientific work: for example the

*Peano Lecture, Rosselli Foundation, Turin, 1988, reprinted with the permission of the copyright holder.

This research was supported by the Personnel and Training Programs, Psychological Sciences Division, Office of Naval Research, under Contract no. N00014-86-K-0768; and by the Defense Advanced Research Projects Agency, Department of Defense, ARPA Order 3597, monitored by the Air Force Avionics Laboratory under contract F33615-81-k-1539.

In this chapter I have drawn extensively upon *Scientific Discovery: Computational Explorations of the Creative Process*, Cambridge, Mass.: MIT Press, 1987, an account of research carried out over a decade with my co-authors Pat Langley, Gary L. Bradshaw and Jan M. Zytkow. Of course, I alone am responsible for this particular expression of our views, but the ideas are a wholly joint product.

diaries and correspondence of Darwin (Gruber 1974), and the laboratory notebooks of Faraday (1932–36) and Hans Krebs (Holmes 1980). These sources allow a discovery to be traced, if not minute by minute, at least experiment by experiment.

Cognitive psychology is a third discipline that has long had an interest in scientific discovery. Since psychology is especially concerned with thinking at the micro level, progress toward understanding the discovery process has been impeded by the absence of appropriate data. To make up for this lack, psychologists have sometimes had to rely upon anecdotal accounts of discovery, never wholly reliable, or upon experiments which elicited behaviours that might or might not be correctly regarded as creative (Glass, Holyoak and Santa 1979, pp. 432–40).

The development of modern cognitive science, combining research methods drawn from psychology and artificial intelligence, has produced a new burst of activity in the study of scientific discovery (Giere 1988). The substantive innovation sparking this activity is a theory of human problem solving that has been constructed over the past 30 years which might be capable of accounting for scientific discovery as well as for more mundane kinds of human mental activity. The methodological innovation sparking the new research has been the use of electronic computers to simulate human thinking, and accordingly, the use of computer programs as theories (systems of difference equations) of thinking (Newell and Simon 1972).

I will begin my account of these developments by trying to define what we would mean by a 'theory of scientific discovery', what the shape or form of such a theory, descriptive or normative, might be. Next, I will describe the theory of human problem solving that has emerged from the research in modern cognitive psychology (or, to include the simulation aspects, cognitive science). With these preliminaries out of the way, I will say something about the theory of discovery that has emerged, its relation to the theory of problem solving and the evidence that supports it.

SHAPE OF A THEORY OF DISCOVERY

Arguments against the possibility of constructing a theory of scientific discovery fall into two main categories. Stated simply, the first argument is that a successful theory of discovery processes would predict discoveries, hence make them – an obvious impossibility. The second argument is that discovering a theory requires a 'creative' step, and that creativity is inherently unexplainable in terms of natural processes.

I will not spend much time in debating these points, for they can be refuted by a constructive proof. After one has described a giraffe to a sceptical listener and been assured that 'there ain't no such animal' the best reply is to exhibit a living and breathing example. Computer programs exist today that, given the same initial conditions that confronted certain human scientists, remake the discoveries the scientists made. Bacon, described at length in Langley et al. (1987), is one such program; Kekada (Kulkarni and Simon 1988) is another. Neither Bacon nor Kekada has made (predicted?) a wholly new discovery, but there is no reason in principle why they should not. Other computer programs, e.g. Dendral, in fact have done so (Feigenbaum et al. 1971).

What do we mean by claiming that these programs are theories of scientific discovery? We mean, first, that a computer program is formally describable as a system of difference equations; hence it has essentially the same logical structure as those theories in the physical and biological sciences that take the form of systems of differential or difference equations. For any given state of the system under study, such a theory predicts the subsequent state. We mean, second, that the symbolic processes that enable the programs to make discoveries, or to reproduce historical ones, can be shown empirically to resemble the processes used by human scientists. I will have more to say about this evidence presently.

Exhibiting 'living and breathing' computer programs that actually make discoveries also refutes the argument that creativity cannot be explained or simulated. To maintain this claim in the face of the programs' accomplishments would imply that Kepler, and Joseph Black, and Snell, and Dalton, and Avogadro, and Faraday, and Hans Krebs, and many others whose discovery processes have been simulated, were not creative. If they were not, then creativity is obviously not required for making scientific discoveries of first magnitude. If they were, then the creative processes have been simulated. Preferring the latter alternative, I will have more to say presently about the nature of creativity.

What kind of evidence would allow us to conclude that the processes in a computer program were basically the same as the processes used by a human being in the course of thinking? We have every reason to believe that while some thought processes are conscious, so that their inputs and outputs can be reliably reported by the thinker (Ericsson and Simon 1984), other essential processes are subconscious and not open to direct observation or even self-observation. Since the unobservable processes will be as essential to the theory as the observable ones, we are faced with the necessity of inferring their presence by indirect means.

This difficulty is no different from those faced continually in all the sciences. If, for example, the information processes that allow a person to recognize a familiar object are inaccessible to direct observation, as they are, it is equally true that electrons, atoms, and certainly quarks, are inaccessible to direct observation. The task of inducing theories from data and the task of persuading ourselves of the validity of these theories, is no different in the case before us than in any other domain of science.

The task of a theory of discovery is to postulate an organization of processes sufficient to account for the discoveries and for the observable behavioural phenomena that accompany them. The task of a theory of verification (I will take a Popperian position here, but a Bayesian one would do as well) is to test that the theory is not falsified by any of the observations of the relevant phenomena. In this formulation, a theory of scientific discovery, like any other theory, is falsifiable but not irrevocably verifiable. The theory I shall propose here is a theory of both conscious and unconscious thought processes described at the level of information processes or symbolic processes. If it is false, that can be shown by demonstrating serious mismatches of the behaviour of the program that embodies it with the behaviour of human beings engaged in creative activity.

THE THEORY OF HUMAN THINKING

One claim implicit in Bacon, Kekada, and similar models of the discovery process is that the thought processes of scientists are basically the same as the human thought processes that have been modelled and simulated in more 'mundane' task environments. The scientist does not think in ways that are qualitatively different from the ways in which other professionals think, or the ways in which college students think when confronted with puzzles to solve in the psychological laboratory, or the ways in which T. C. Mits (The Common Man in The Street) thinks.

Today we have empirically validated theories of the thought processes of chess players, of medical diagnosticians, of subjects solving the Tower of Hanoi and Missionaries and Cannibals puzzles, of students solving algebra and physics problems, and of thinkers and problem solvers in many other domains. For reviews of some of the evidence, see Newell and Simon (1972), or Simon (1979, 1989). These theories, like the theories of scientific discovery that are under discussion here, take the form of computer programs that actually perform the tasks in question. Hence in each case they postulate a set of processes that is at least *sufficient* to perform the task. In addition, a large body of evidence, including evidence from thinking-aloud protocols and eye-movement records, shows that the processes are closely similar to those used by human subjects.

A reassuring feature of these models is that they are closely similar in structure from task to task. What distinguishes thinking in one task domain from that in another is specific substantive knowledge of the domain, and not the processes used to apply this knowledge to the task. This commonality of process throughout the range of tasks that has been studied gives us initial confidence – a high Bayesian prior – that the same processes will also show up in the study of scientific discovery. What are the underlying common features of this theory of thinking?

Physical Symbol Systems

The foundation for all of the models is the Physical Symbol System Hypothesis. The hypothesis states that physical symbol systems, and only such systems, are capable of thinking. A *physical symbol* is a pattern (of chalk, ink, neuronal connections, electromagnetic fields, or what not) that refers to or designates another pattern or a detectable external stimulus. Printed words on a page are symbols, so are pictures or diagrams, so are numbers. A *physical symbol system* is a system that is capable of *inputting* symbols, *outputting* them, *storing* them in memory, *forming* and *modifying structures* of symbols in memory, *comparing* pairs of symbols for identity or difference, and *branching* in its subsequent behaviour on the basis of the outcomes of such tests.

A computer is obviously a physical symbol system. Its ability to perform these processes (and only these processes) can be verified easily from its physical properties and operation. A human brain is (less obviously) a physical symbol system. It can certainly carry out the processes specified in the definition of such a system, but perhaps other processes as well.

How Do Computers Think?

That human beings can think is regarded as well established. If we wish to test this capability in any instance, we give the person a task of the kind that is regarded as requiring thought and observe his or her performance. That computers can think is sometimes regarded as debatable. If we wish to test this hypothesis, we give the computer a task of the kind used to test whether people think and observe its performance. The empirical evidence is by now overwhelming that computers can perform successfully in many task environments that call for thinking in humans. Hence we must conclude that appropriately programmed computers think.

The more interesting and difficult question is whether a thinking computer uses the same processes as a thinking person in the same task environment. The empirical answer is 'sometimes yes, sometimes no'. For example, there now exist some chess-playing computers that perform at a formidable level, so that they can be defeated by only a few hundred (at most) of the strongest human players. These programs demonstrably use processes that differ in important ways from those used by human players. While, like human players, they draw upon a considerable body of chess knowledge, they also conduct an enormous search through the tree of possible moves and counter-moves (typically a search through several million branches at each move). Human players, including masters and grand masters, seldom examine as many as one hundred branches in the game tree before making a move (de Groot 1978).

On the other hand, several chess programs have been constructed that behave in a far more humanoid manner. A program built by Newell, Shaw and Simon (1958) selected its moves by forming and pursuing goals, with a very small amount of search. It was a weak, but credible, chess player. A mating combinations program by Baylor and Simon (1966) was very powerful in searching for winning moves in sharp tactical situations, usually examining far fewer than one hundred branches and finding many of the celebrated grand master combinations that are reproduced in histories of chess. These programs can be shown to exhibit many of the phenomena of human chess thinking – tactical thinking more successfully than strategic thinking.

These investigations of chess playing can be matched by simulations of human expertise in many other task domains: solving puzzles, solving mathematics and physics problems, making medical diagnoses, detecting patterns in letter and number sequences, learning languages, understanding problem instructions, and others.

Principles of Human Problem Solving

Let me comment now on the content of the theory of problem solving that has emerged from this research. I will focus on four main principles, omitting many details.

First, most problem solving involves selective search through large spaces of possibilities. The selectivity, based on rules of thumb or *heuristics*, allows such searches frequently to reach success in a reasonable length of time, where an undirected, trial-and-error search would require an enormous time, and often could not be completed in a human lifetime. In cases of well practised skills, there may be almost no search at all, the heuristics being sufficiently powerful to select the correct path to the goal at once. The more difficult the problem and the less efficient the heuristics, the more search will be involved. (We will expect tasks demanding creativity to require a good deal of search, for by definition, the heuristics available will be weak.)

Second, some of the heuristics that guide search in problem solving are specific to the task domain, but others are quite general, applying to a wide range of domains. Because of their generality, these latter methods cannot make use of information that is specific to a given domain; hence they are generally called 'weak methods'. When stronger, domain-specific heuristics are not available to a problem solver, we would expect him or her to fall back on weak methods. Therefore, we would expect weak methods to play an important role in explorations of new territory – hence in scientific discovery.

Third, among the most important and widely used problem solving heuristics is means–ends analysis. The problem solver compares the present situation with the goal situation and notices a difference between them. Recognition of the difference cues in memory information about the operators that might be applied to remove it, bringing the situation closer to the goal. Once a new situation is attained, the same procedure is applied again, until the goal is reached. The effectiveness of means–ends analysis depends on the problem solver's ability to notice differences and to retrieve from memory relevant operators for reducing or removing these differences. Hence, in the presence of considerable domain-specific knowledge of this kind, means–ends analysis is a strong method; if there is little such knowledge, it serves as a weak method.

Fourth, the domain-specific knowledge that largely distinguishes expert from novice behaviour is stored in memory in the form of *productions*, that is to say, of actions (A9 paired to conditions (C), C → A). When the conditions are satisfied in a problem situation (e.g. when the problem solver notices the presence of certain cues), memory is accessed for actions that are associated with these conditions. (E.g in the case of means–ends analysis, the conditions are what we called differences, and the actions are operators for removing these differences.) Each execution of a production is an act of recognition. Thus, the physician, recognizing a patient's symptoms, is reminded of one or more diseases that present these symptoms and of the nature of these diseases, tests that will discriminate among them, prognosis and treatment, and so on.

The expert's skill, then, derives from a large base of productions (50 000 is a plausible number for human professional-level skills) that allow recognition of relevant cues in problem situations, combined with an ability to analyse and reason about information using means–ends analysis and similar heuristics. In this picture of expertise, there is no sharp boundary between 'insight' or 'intuition' and analysis. Insight and intuition are simply acts of recognition based on the stored knowledge of the domain, and they interact with analysis to solve problems. For many simple, everyday problems, recognition alone may be enough, and little analysis may be necessary. In more complex situations, recognition of salient cues allows analysis to take larger and more appropriate steps than if the heuristic search has to depend on real methods alone.

The claim, then, that the processes of scientific discovery are normal problem-solving processes is a claim that scientific discovery follows the four principles just enunciated. First, its basic method is selective (heuristic) search. Second it uses both general and domain-specific heuristics. Third, means–ends analysis, a heuristic of broad applicability, plays an important role in analysis and reasoning. Fourth, effectiveness in discovery depends heavily on processes of recognition, making use of tens of thousands of productions that index memory with familiar and recognizable cues characterizing common problem situations.

THE PROCESSES OF SCIENTIFIC DISCOVERY

Scientists, in their work, do a great many different things. In most sciences, there is a greater or lesser degree of specialization between theorists and experimentalists, but the specialization, formal and informal, goes much farther than this. Scientists discover and define problems, they find appropriate representations for problems, they design experimental procedures and strategies and plan and execute experiments, they obtain data by observation, they formulate laws and theories to account for data, using mathematical and other forms of reasoning, they deduce consequences from their theories, they invent instruments for making observations, and they devise explanatory theories to give deeper accounts of descriptive laws.

This may not be an exhaustive list of scientists' activities, but it will serve to illustrate the wide variety of activities that make up the scientific enterprise. My claim is that all of these are problem-solving activities that make use of the basic processes described in the previous section. Since we now have direct empirical evidence to support this claim for several, if not all, of these activities, I would like to provide some examples that will illustrate the nature of the evidence.

Deriving Laws from Data

The activity that has been studied perhaps most intensively is the process of deriving laws from data. A series of computer programs, collectively named Bacon, has successfully simulated the process whereby a substantial number of important laws of eighteenth and nineteenth century chemistry were induced from data. (For a detailed account of Bacon and related programs, see Langley et al. 1987.) In all of these cases, we know the process was an inductive one, without benefit of theory, because there did not exist, at the time of the discoveries, theories that were relevant to the derivation. For example, Bacon is able to obtain Kepler's Third Law from data on the distance and periods of revolution of the planets about the Sun. The discovery process is purely inductive, as was Kepler's, since there existed in his time no body of theory that would have led to the law – that theory had to wait for Newton, generations later. The Bacon program also obtains Joseph Black's laws of temperature equilibrium, the law of conservation of momentum, and others, and discovers atomic and molecular weights from data on chemical reactions, distinguishing between atoms and molecules along the way. It not only finds laws, but in a number of instances introduces new theoretical concepts (inertial mass, index of refraction, specific heat, atomic weight, molecular weight) to permit the laws to be stated parsimoniously. A detailed account of Bacon's successes (and limitations) can be found in Langley et al. (1987).

Other programs, also reviewed in Langley et al. (1987), derive qualitative laws from qualitative data. The Stahl program, for example, on examining information about combustion and reduction reactions, will arrive at the phlogiston theory of combustion or the oxygen theory, depending on how the reactions are described to it. (The actual history of the competition of the phlogiston and oxygen theories can be explained in these same terms.)

Our knowledge of the induction of laws from data is not limited to computer simulations of historical cases. We can also present the historical data (unidentified) to subjects in the psychological laboratory, and examine their attempts to find regularities in the data. Qin and I (unpublished) have presented 14 students with Kepler's data; four of our subjects found Kepler's Third Law in one to two hours' work. When we compare the thinking-aloud protocols of the successful and unsuccessful subjects, we find that the former, but not the latter, compared each hypothesis they formed with the actual data and then selected their next hypothesis on the basis of the specific discrepancies they found. Their heuristics in generating a sequence of hypotheses closely resembled Bacon's, as did the actual hypotheses they generated. Similar experimental data, with similar findings, have been gathered for Balmer's law, which describes the wave lengths of lines in the hydrogen spectrum, and Planck's law of black-body radiation, both foundation stones of subsequent quantum theory. Subjects were often able to find these laws in the laboratory, and the heuristics they used in the search were similar to Bacon's.

Planning Experiments

Quite different from the activity of discovering laws in data is the process of planning sequences of experiments aimed at producing data relevant to a research goal. For example, the German biologist, Hans Krebs, carried out a series of experiments over about nine months in 1931–32 that revealed the reactions that synthesize urea *in vivo*. (For details of this history, see Holmes 1980.) Of course, the experiments were not all planned in advance. On the contrary, each experiment provided information that led to the gradual (and in one case, sudden) modification of the research plan.

Krebs began with the decision to try to discover the process of urea synthesis *in vivo*, using slices of liver tissue as his experimental materials. The research problem was an important one, already well recognized in the field, that had not yielded to previously available methods of experimentation. The tissue slice method was a new one that Krebs had acquired while working as a postdoctoral student with Otto Warburg. Krebs's initial strategy was to repeat experiments that had been performed on whole organs (the method previously used) to see if he could reproduce their results. Many of these experiments involved testing the urea yield when a tissue was treated with mixtures of ammonia and an amino acid. The yields of urea were moderate until a particular amino acid, ornithine, was tested; the yield with ornithine was quite large.

Krebs now switched to a new strategy, which we might call the 'response to surprise strategy'. He first sought to determine whether other molecules similar to ornithine would produce the same high yield of urea. They did not. He then proceeded to vary the quantities of ornithine and ammonia used and to measure the changing yields, while at the same time trying to work out, using his knowledge of the chemical structures of the reacting molecules, plausible reaction paths. He discovered such a path, in which ammonia provided the nitrogen for the urea, while ornithine served as a catalyst in the cyclical reaction.

Deepak Kulkarni has constructed a computer program, Kekada, which captures many of the heuristics that guided Krebs's strategic planning. On the basis of its experience, it forms expectations about the outcomes of these experiments, and when these expectations are disappointed, it adopts a 'respond to surprise' strategy that involves delimiting the scope of the surprising phenomenon and then searching for its mechanism (Kulkarni and Simon 1988). Not too surprisingly, Kekada does a good job of simulating Krebs's urea synthesis discovery. More impressive, when provided with the appropriate initial conditions (research problem, available methods and domain knowledge), it also simulates closely Krebs's discovery of the glutamine cycle; some nineteenth century research on the synthesis of alcohols; and Faraday's research strategy after his 'surprise' in finding that changes in magnetic fields could induce electric currents.

Kekada is able to simulate these disparate phenomena because most of its experiment-planning heuristics are independent of the precise task domain to which they are applied. The heuristics for responding to surprising phenomena are critical in accounting for its success.

The historical data on the discoveries of Krebs, Faraday and others, together with the interpretation provided by Kekada, show the experimental process of very successful investigators to consist in heuristic search through a large space of possible experiments, the heuristics guiding the selection of each successive experiment. Many of the basic heuristics are, like the heuristics for exploiting surprise, quite general and independent of the specific task domain in which they are applied. Experimentation, it would appear, is a process of heuristic search resembling closely the processes that have been observed and identified in other kinds of problem solving.

Explanatory Theories

When we fit a mathematical function to data, as Bacon does, we are at best providing a parsimonious description of the data. The function, the law, does not explain why the data are as they are. Thus, Kepler described the relation between the periods of the planets' orbits and their distances from the Sun; Newton explained the relation by showing that it followed logically from the inverse square law of gravitational attraction. Balmer found a formula to describe the successive lines of the hydrogen spectrum; thirty years later, Bohr showed that Balmer's formula could be deduced from his quantum model of the hydrogen atom. Science is as interested in discovering mechanisms that explain phenomena as it is in discovering laws that describe them. What discovery processes enable explanations to be found?

Bacon, as applied to the phenomena of temperature equilibrium, throws some light on this question. Suppose we provide Bacon with some very broad theoretical concepts: that when substances are mixed together both mass and heat are conserved; and that the law describing the temperature equilibrium of such a mixture should be symmetrical in the properties of the components. Then, Black's law of temperature equilibrium can be deduced from these assumptions, in advance of any examination of data, and the data simply used to confirm the law. Without these assumptions, Bacon must induce the law from data with the help of rather arduous calculations. Thus assumptions of conservation and symmetry can be used as heuristics to reduce the search required to find laws. If the search is successful (with or without the heuristics), the heuristics then provide at least a partial explanation of why the phenomena are as they are.

Explanation often requires us to consider the phenomena of interest at a more microscopic level than the level of observation. We postulate unobservable mechanisms, to account for the observable data. The Dalton program, for example (Langley et al. 1987), assumes that chemical substances are made up of molecules, and molecules of atoms of the elements. Further, it assumes that atoms are conserved in reactions and that volumes of gases (under constant pressure) are proportional to the numbers of their molecules (Gay-Lussac's Law). Starting with these assumptions and data about the inputs and outputs of chemical reactions, it deduces the chemical formulas of the molecules involved. For example, on being told that three volumes of hydrogen and one of nitrogen produce two of ammonia, it concludes, correctly, that hydrogen and nitrogen are H_2 and N_2, respectively, and that ammonia has the formula NH_3.

These simple examples show how we can begin to understand the discovery of explanatory theories as a problem-solving process. The process starts with a representation of the phenomena (in the Dalton case, a particulate representation; in the case of Black's law, a representation in terms of conserved quantities of matter and of a substance called 'heat'). This representation imposes constraints upon the phenomena that allow the mechanisms to be inferred from the data – or even inferred deductively in some cases.

The question remains open of where representations come from. Answers to that question are just now beginning to be sought, and I will have nothing to say about them here. But you can guess what my prediction is about them: that representations are found by means of ordinary problem-solving processes.

The Invention of Instruments

I will comment on one other facet of scientific discovery that has not yet been studied in as much detail as the discovery of laws in data, the planning of sequences of experiments, or the discovery of explanatory theories: discovery that consists in the invention of new scientific instruments.

New instruments are commonly the by-products of the observation of new phenomena; and of course new phenomena are commonly the products of new instruments. How does this chicken-and-egg process proceed?

Consider the case of temperature and thermometers for measuring it. Sensations of heat and cold provide human beings with a built-in thermometer requiring no artificial instrumentation. These sensations do not provide, however, a quantitative and invariant measuring scale that could serve as foundation for the laws of heat. However, experiments of heating various kinds of materials revealed a common phenomenon: that many substances, solids and gases, expand when heated. By using standard methods for measuring volumes to determine the amount of expansion, the thermometer was created, in many forms corresponding to different substances (Langley et al. 1987, pp. 313–14). This basic idea was successively refined – for example, by using the thermometer bulb to magnify the effects – to produce instruments that we still use today.

Soon after the thermometer was invented, we find Fahrenheit and Boerhaave, followed by Joseph Black, laying down the quantitative laws of temperature equilibrium. The phenomenon of expansion on heating permitted the invention of the thermometer; the thermometer permitted observation of new phenomena of temperature equilibrium. A similar story can be told of the invention of such instruments as the ammeter and voltmeter following on the discovery of electrical currents and their magnetic effects. These instruments, in turn, permitted Ohm to find his quantitative law of the relation among current, voltage and resistance.

Heuristic search can again account for these discovery processes. One heuristic suggests looking for instruments that make use of new phenomena; another, even more obvious, heuristic suggests using instruments to find new phenomena.

INTUITION, INSIGHT AND INSPIRATION

We cannot leave the topic of scientific discovery, however, without attending directly to some of the phenomena that are most commonly introduced into evidence as a basis for claims that discovery is, so aehow, different from other kinds of problem solving. It is often argued that creative discovery depends on such processes as intuition, insight and inspiration, and anecdotal evidence is frequently brought forward to show their essentiality. Poincaré achieves an understanding of the Fuschsian functions as he steps on to the bus at Coutances, Kekulé conceives of the benzine ring as, half asleep, he watches the twisting snake of the fireplace flames grasp its tail in its mouth, and so on.

The principal phenomena that support the claims for intuition, insight and inspiration are the suddenness with which a discovery is sometimes made (often preceded by a long period of unsuccessful work followed by a longer or shorter interruption), and the fact that the discoverer often cannot explain why it occurred just then, or what path led to it. If the signatures of intuition and insight are suddenness of discovery and incomplete awareness of the discovery path, then these earmarks do not distinguish these two processes from the well known and well understood process that we call 'recognition'.

The ability to recognize particular symptoms, or stimuli, depends on their familiarity from previous experience and learning. Various models have been proposed for the recognition process – for example, the Epam model, which assumes that long-term memory is indexed by a discrimination net, which sorts the presented stimulus to find, if it is familiar, the information associated with it in memory (Feigenbaum and Simon 1984). An alternative model, the so-called Pandemonium mechanism, does a similar sorting job, but achieves it by parallel rather than serial processing.

The process of recognition has long been studied by psychologists. An act of recognition generally takes about half a second, or longer. Of great importance, while a person is consciously aware of the result of the recognition process (is aware of what or who has been recognized), he or she is not aware of the process itself or the cues that were used to discriminate the stimulus. Recognition is 'intuitive' in exactly the sense in which that word is used in the literature of discovery and creativity.

I discussed earlier the strong empirical evidence that an expert, in his or her domain of expertise, holds in memory some 50 000 different cues or symptoms that, when present in the situation, will evoke a recognition and consequent access to stored knowledge relevant to the cue. Each expert has 50 000 'friends' and extensive information about them. Compare this number with the 50 000 to 100 000 words that each of us has in the vocabulary of our native language. The evidence is compelling that the expert accomplishes most of his or her daily work by means of this capability for recognizing situations and thereby recalling the knowledge necessary for dealing with them. At all steps of problem solving, recognition is intermingled with analysis, and without it, analysis is hopelessly slow, faltering and inefficient.

The recognition mechanism can account quite adequately for Poincaré's sudden discovery as he boarded the bus. It does not, by itself, explain the possible role of interruption of incubation, but simple explanations have been provided for these also (Simon 1977, pp. 292–9). The visual aspects of Kekulé's experience (which, by the way, was first reported by him 30 years after the event) call for other mechanisms, but have nothing directly to do with the suddenness of the discovery or its subconscious origins.

Intuitions, insights and inspirations are not only sudden, but they are also frequently surprising. In our analysis of Kekada, we have seen that surprise is simply a form of recognition – recognition that one's expectations have been disappointed. To have expectations, one must have knowledge as to what to expect. As Pasteur put it, 'Accidents happen to the prepared mind.' So again, we come back to the expert's 50 000 chunks that allow a recognition that something unusual has happened.

In summary, we do not need to postulate special mechanisms to account for intuition, insight or inspiration. These phenomena will be produced by the mechanism of recognition, which we have already seen plays a key role in every form of expertise, and which is based, in turn, on the store of indexed knowledge that every expert possesses.

CONCLUSION: THE PROCESSES OF DISCOVERY

This quick and highly incomplete account of the evidence now available about discovery processes confirms both the variety and heterogeneity of the activities that make up the enterprise of science and the consistency with which these activities conform to the pattern of heuristic search – highly selective search that produces some measure of success even in large and poorly structured problem spaces. Such phenomena as intuition, insight and inspiration derive from the capacity for recognition that every expert acquires in his or her domain of expertise. No new mechanisms need be postulated to account for them.

Of course there is much room for additional study of the processes of science, and some processes, like problem representation, have hardly been touched by research to date. New research may certainly produce surprises, which will no doubt evoke the 'respond to surprise' heuristic, leading to a different picture of the process. Each person can estimate his own prior probability, based on the evidence to date, that the theory of discovery will or will not be altered in fundamental respects.

REFERENCES

Baylor, G. W. and Simon, H. A. (1966) 'A chess mating combinations program' reprinted in Simon (1979), Chapter 4.3.

De Groot, A. (1978) *Thought and Choice in Chess*. The Hague: Mouton, 2nd ed.

Ericsson, K. A. and Simon, H. A. (1984) *Protocol Analysis*. Cambridge, Mass: MIT Press.

Faraday, M. (1932–36) *Faraday's Diary*, 8 vols. London: Bell.

Feigenbaum, E. A., Buchanan, B. and Lederberg, J. (1971) 'On generality and problem solving: A case study using the Dendral program' in Meltzer, B. and Michie, D. (eds), *Machine Intelligence*, 6. New York: Elsevier.

Feigenbaum, E. A. and Simon, H. A. (1984) 'Epam-like models of recognition and learning', *Cognitive Science*, 8, pp. 305–36.

Giere, R. N. (1988) *Explaining Science*. Chicago: University of Chicago Press.

Glass, A. L., Holyoak, K. J. and Santa, J. L. (1979) *Cognition*. Reading, Mass: Addison-Wesley.

Gruber, H. E. (1974) *Darwin on Man*. New York: Dutton.

Holmes, F. L. (1980), 'Hans Krebs and the discovery of the ornithine cycle', *Federation Proceedings*, 39, pp. 216–25.

Kulkarni, D. and Simon, H. A. (1988) 'The processes of scientific discovery: the strategy of experimentation', *Cognitive Science*, 12, pp. 139–75.

Langley, P., Simon, H. A., Bradshaw, G. L. and Zytkow, J. M. (1987) *Scientific Discovery*. Cambridge, Mass: MIT Press.

Newell, A., Shaw, J. C. and Simon, H. A. (1958) 'Chess-playing programs and the problem of complexity', *IBM Journal of Research and Development*, 2: pp. 320–35.

Newell, A. and Simon, H. A. (1972) *Human Problem Solving*. Englewood Cliffs, NJ: Prentice-Hall.

Nickles, T. (1978) *Scientific Discovery*. Dordrecht: Reidel.

Popper, K. R. (1961) *The Logic of Scientific Discovery*. New York: Science Editions.

Qin, Y. L. and Simon, H. A. (1988) 'Laboratory replication of scientific discovery'. Technical Report, Department of Psychology, Carnegie-Mellon University.

Simon, H. A. (1977) *Models of Discovery*. Dordrecht: Reidel.

Simon, H. A. (1979, 1989) *Models of Thought*. New Haven: Yale University Press, vols 1 and 2.

PART THREE

New Papers

7. Subjective Rationality and the Explanation of Social Behaviour

Raymond Boudon

The title I have chosen for this chapter covers a limited objective, i.e. trying:

* to underline the importance of the notion, coined by Herbert Simon, of *subjective rationality*,
* to clarify its definition and meaning,
* to show that the intuition lying behind this notion is an implicit keypoint of classical sociological theories, and
* to suggest that this notion is crucial in the analysis of all types of social phenomena. As I must be selective, I will focus on the important case of the rational explanation of false beliefs.

WHAT SUBJECTIVE RATIONALITY MEANS

Simon (1982) has proposed several definitions of his notion of subjective rationality. One of these is the following:

> In a broad sense *rationality* denotes a style of behavior that is appropriate to the achievement of given goals, within the limits imposed by certain conditions and constraints.

And he adds:

> The conditions and constraints referred to in the general definition may be *objective characteristics* of the environment external to the choosing organism, they may be *perceived characteristics*, or they may be *characteristics of the organism itself* that it takes as fixed and not subject to its own control. The line between the first case and the other two is sometimes drawn by distinguishing *objective rationality*, on the one hand, from *subjective* or *bounded rationality*, on the other (Simon 1982, p. 8).

I am not sure this definition is entirely satisfactory. But, rather than discussing it, I will introduce the notion of *subjective rationality* by a deictic definition, i.e. by an example. I will use an example provided by Simon (1982, p. 134) himself and borrowed from Feldman's (1964) work in cognitive experimental psychology.

Subjects are asked by an experimenter to predict the outcomes of a head-and-tail game. They are informed, however, that the coin used in the game is biased and that head and tail will appear respectively with probabilities .8 and .2.

In most cases, the subjects choose a wrong solution: they generate a sequence of outcomes governed by the same probabilities as the series they are supposed to predict. In other words, they choose to predict randomly the outcome 'head' with probability .8 and the outcome 'tail' with probability .2. By doing so they predict correctly the outcomes with probability .68.[1] This is a poor result compared to the result they would get if they chose to predict head at all moves, since their probability of predicting correctly each outcome would in this case be equal to .8.

This example seems to me extremely important for several reasons.

First, it illustrates a case where the behaviour of a subject is governed by reasons which, although they are *objectively* wrong, are perceived as *good*. Very often the importance of this case is ill recognized because it runs against the current view based on an old philosophical tradition which assimilates groundedness and objective validity.

This raises of course the question as to how and with the help of which criteria these reasons, which have the curious property of being both invalid and good, can be identified. The answer to this question is not immediate, but we check readily that we recognize the existence of such *good reasons* in the linguistic expressions we use normally. Thus, we would probably explain the behaviour of the subjects in the experiment I have reported by a sentence such as 'they had *good reasons* to choose this wrong solution since . . .', rather than by a formula of the type 'they had really no reasons of choosing this wrong solution, but . . .'. In other words, we normally consider their behaviour as rational rather than irrational.

Why are the reasons of the subjects perceived as good while they are wrong? Because they tried to answer the question they were confronted with by making a *guess,* a *conjecture,* by applying a *theory* or a general *principle* valid in many cases.

Suppose for instance the experimenter asked them to predict a mathematical series governed by rules such as: y is the value of the first member of the series; add x to the nth member of the series to get the following member.

If the subjects decided to use these rules, they would guess the outcomes correctly. Or suppose they were asked to guess the outcomes of a *normal* head-and-tail game played with an *un*biased coin. In that case, the strategy which was wrong in the case of a biased coin becomes right. By tossing an unbiased coin in order to predict the outcomes obtained by the experimenter, the subject has a probability of .5 of predicting correctly the outcome.[2] This is neither better nor worse than the outcome he would obtain by predicting at each move either head or tail.

On the whole, the subjects made the conjecture that, in order to replicate a model, a good strategy is to generate the copy by applying the very rules which govern the production of the model. This conjecture is obviously valid in many circumstances. It is even valid when the model to be replicated is a mathematical series. It is even valid when the model is a head-and-tail game of the normal unbiased type. It is also obviously valid in all kinds of other circumstances. It can also be invalid, however, as here, when the head-and-tail game is biased. But, on the whole, it is much easier to create a situation where the principle in question works than those where it does not.

This explains why few people would probably accept the idea that the subjects are irrational, though their reasons were objectively ungrounded. Their reasons are perceived as *good* because they are universal in the sense that any subject in the same position, i.e. any subject who would not have been trained in probability calculus, would naturally come to the idea of using the generative rules of the model to produce the copy.

So, a first virtue of this example is to clarify the Simonian notion of subjective rationality better than the abstract definition I gave earlier. The example suggests namely that we tend normally to consider invalid reasons as good when these reasons are valid in many circumstances though not in all.

Another important point conveyed by the example is that *subjec-*

tive rationality is the product of the discordance between the complexity of the world and the cognitive capacities of the subject.

But the general conclusion to be drawn from the example is that, except in simple and marginal cases, action includes *theories, conjectures* or *principles*, in other words, that sociology as well as economics and the other social sciences should develop a more cognitively oriented theory of action.

Finally, and this will be the *Leitmotiv* of this chapter, while these conjectures, theories or principles may be true, valid or well adapted, they may also without contradiction be untrue, invalid and still grounded.

WHY THE NOTION OF SUBJECTIVE RATIONALITY IS CRUCIAL FOR THE SOCIAL SCIENCES

Why is the notion of subjective rationality crucial for the social sciences? As Max Weber (1951) and Popper (1967) among others have suggested, trying to substitute rational explanations for the irrational explanations of behaviour naturally produced by ordinary knowledge is one of the main tasks of the social sciences and even one of their main sources of legitimation.

But, as long as we do not perceive the importance of the notion of subjective rationality, and endorse a narrow definition of rationality – reasons are good when they are objectively good – we tend too easily to see behaviour as irrational. And this is true not only of ordinary social knowledge, but of scientific sociology as well.

To take a classical example: partly because he had a narrow definition of rationality (see his definition of what he calls *logical* actions), Pareto (1935) saw most social actions as irrational, as governed by feelings rather than by reasons. For the same reason many modern sociologists easily see behaviour as irrational, i.e. as inspired by causes located beyond the control of the social actor rather than by reasons.

By contrast, because he had a broad view of rationality including implicitly the notion of *subjective rationality*, Weber could defend the idea that explaining behaviour amounts in most cases to disentangling the reasons of the actors.

By combining these statements, we reach the conclusion that, *trying to substitute subjectively rational explanations of social behaviour for the current irrational explanations is a major task of the social sciences.*

In order to avoid a possible misunderstanding, it should be made clear, however, that the interest of substituting subjectively rational explanations of behaviour for irrational explanations is *cognitive* rather than *moral*. In other words, the main legitimation for trying to interpret behaviour rationally is not that this generates, say, a more optimistic picture of man. It lies rather in the fact that, when a behaviour appears to an observer as strange or unfamiliar, his first move is to interpret it in an irrational fashion, as the effect of causes rather than reasons. If he could subsume reasons under the observed behaviour, he would not perceive it as odd. This is why many important social scientific contributions take the form of substituting a subjectively rational for an irrational explanation of social behaviour.

I will take some classical examples to illustrate this point, which is particularly important since, under the influence notably of Freud, many people think on the contrary that depth and progress in the explanation of behaviour consists in discovering latent unconscious causes under patent reasons.

An Imaginary Dialogue Between Hume and Downs

My first example will introduce an imaginary discussion between David Hume and Anthony Downs.

In a fascinating text in political theory, Hume (1752) developed the assumption that political parties bring together people according to three basic mechanisms: interests, solidarity and principles.

In the first case, people are moted to affiliate to a given party because they have similar social positions and consequently common interests. To use Dahrendorf's vocabulary, political parties have in this case the function of giving a political expression to *latent groups*.

The second mechanism, that of solidarity, which Hume calls *affection*, is clear enough: people normally have a sense of belonging to social groups and wish to protect their collective identity. In this second case, political parties help maintain social groups in existence. Hume adds at this point that he has no difficulty whatsoever understanding these first two mechanisms. In other words, he would have accepted as easily the Marxian idea of class consciousness as the Durkheimian idea of collective consciousness.

But, as a good political observer, Hume remarks that parties can also be built around *ideas* or *principles*. And he adds that he has little to say on the question as to how this strange mechanism operates, but that explaining the existence of political parties grounded on principles is probably the most difficult task the behavioural sciences are confronted with: 'Parties from *principle*, especially abstract speculative principle . . . are, perhaps, the most extraordinary and unaccountable *phenomenon* that has yet appeared in human affairs' (p. 58).

At this point Hume becomes hyperbolic. He gives the reader the feeling that he has discovered in this field of political theory a fact as extraordinary as the so-called problem of induction in the field of the philosophy of knowledge.

Why does Hume find the existence of political parties grounded on principles so puzzling? Because he has in mind a narrow view of rationality. According to this narrow view there is only one way of knowing whether a political programme is good or bad and consequently whether it should be endorsed or not: determining the outcomes of this programme and checking whether they are acceptable or not, or whether a better alternative programme could be devised or not. From this point of view the parties which gather people around principles seem to walk on their heads: instead of checking whether the *consequences* of a political programme are good or not, the voters wonder whether it is grounded on the right *principles*.

In fact, Hume proposes an *irrational* explanation of this behaviour which appears so strange to him. We affiliate to ideological parties because we are pushed by obscure psychic forces to agree or disagree with other people:

> . . . such is the nature of the human mind, that it always lays hold on every mind that approaches it; and as it is wonderfully fortified by an unanimity of sentiments, so it is shocked and disturbed by any contrariety. Hence the eagerness with which most people discover in a dispute; and hence their impatience of opposition, even in the most speculative and indifferent opinions (p. 59).

But, interestingly enough, Hume is far from being satisfied by this explanation.

The paradox raised by Hume was solved by Downs (1957) when he showed that the choice between, say, two political programmes cannot be rational in the narrow sense. Anticipating with certainty what the consequences of the two programmes will actually be is very difficult. Moreover, it is difficult to know whether they will be applied in the form in which they have been presented. Finally, even if the voter knew the consequences of the programmes which are proposed to him, and even if he could be sure the programmes would be literally applied, he still can not know what is better for him. In other words, in such circumstances, evaluating the *principles* on which the two programmes are grounded is a good alternative to the impossible task of checking the *consequences* of the programmes. Exactly as for Simon's subjects, imitating the experimenter was a good alternative to the mathematical solution, which is more satisfactory but inaccessible to the subject.

Downs uses at this point the word *ideology*. The rational voter *should* be ideological: this formula summarizes the central theorem of his *Economic Theory of Democracy*, the theorem which made the book influential. It shows that what appeared to Hume as mysterious and unintelligible is in fact easy to understand.

Though he contributed to destroying the influence of the classical narrow view of rationality, Downs himself appears to be dominated by this view. This explains his unfortunate choice of the word *ideology* in the formulation of his main theorem. What Downs has taught us can be more plainly described by saying that, as Simon's subjects, the voter tries to meet the situation which faces him with the help of reasonable conjectures or theories, for instance the conjecture that a programme grounded on certain principles will probably lead to consequences congruent with these principles. Of course, this is not always true: an equality-oriented policy can bring more inequality; by aiming at a goal one can reach the opposite outcome. But the assumption of congruence is in many cases a reasonable one and, as a general guideline, better than the opposite assumption.

One could even go further: for people with an interest in politics, judging a programme on its principles can be a good conjecture. For those less interested, it can be rational to use simpler *signals*: checking whether the candidate looks sincere, for instance. In this case, the voter makes the conjecture that there is a correlation between this *signal* and the outcomes he is interested in, exactly as a businessman uses the *curriculum vitae* of a candidate to a job as a *signal* of his future unobservable achievements.

On the whole, this Hume–Downs imaginary discussion can be considered as paradigmatic for several reasons.

1. It illustrates the strength of the classical view of rationality, which even Downs does not entirely get rid of.
2. It shows that, as soon as a more liberal view of rationality is adopted, the explanation of behaviour becomes in many cases much easier: a type of behaviour which Hume considered a mystery becomes easily understandable thanks to Downs's rational theory.
3. It suggests that even though the first impression given by many behaviours can be an impression of irrationality, the actors can have *good reasons* to do what they do.
4. It shows finally that these good reasons have the status of conjectures, principles or theories which most people with the same level of information and/or interest in the question they are confronted with would endorse.

Second Example: The Explanation of Magic

A second, more paradoxical though equally classical example can be used to illustrate the crucial importance of the notion of subjective rationality for the analysis of social behaviour: the interpretation of magic. Magic is a crucial phenomenon for any discussion about rationality because believing in magic is often perceived as a canonical example of irrationality: 'how is it possible to believe in such causal relationships?'

Here, as in the previous example, however, the substitution of a subjective rational explanation for an irrational one generates a definite feeling of progress.

Magical beliefs were actually interpreted by many writers as irrational. Thus, to Lévy-Bruhl (1960), they show that so-called primitive men have a mental constitution different from ours. This would explain for instance why they interpret verbal similarities as real similarities, or verbal associations as causal relations. Lévy-Bruhl's theory of what he called the 'primitive mentality' is typically a causal irrational theory, in the sense that the behaviour under examination, i.e. belief in magic, is explained as the effect of psychic causes located beyond any control of the subject.

Many people felt uncomfortable with this type of explanation, however. For causal explanations of behaviour appear often as *ad hoc* and arbitrary, at least when the causes are not reasons. Of course, some behaviours can be explained in a genuine causal non-rational way, as when it is observed that the consumption of some chemical substance has a given effect on mood. But in this case and in similar cases, the causality can be empirically demonstrated, while in a case such as Lévy-Bruhl's it can not. Here, the cause, i.e. the so-called primitive mentality, is inferred in a circular fashion from the very effects it is supposed to explain.

Interestingly enough, those who were dissatisfied with causal explanations of magical beliefs *à la* Lévy-Bruhl tried, often, not to find a rational explanation of these beliefs, but rather to deny their very existence. This stance was taken for instance by the philosopher Wittgenstein (1975), but also by many professional anthropologists, among whom Beattie (1964) is perhaps the best known. Their common argument is that the supposed magical beliefs are actually not beliefs: they are not statements about the world, but symbolic statements about the subject's wishes. The primitive does not *really* believe that rain rituals, say, have the effect of bringing rain on his crops. Rather by these rituals he expresses his wish that rain would fall on his crop: 'die Magie aber bringt einen Wunsch zur Darstellung; sie äussert einen Wunsch', writes Wittgenstein (1975).

This type of theory is neither less nor more *ad hoc* than the previous one. As well shown by Horton (1982), it contradicts the beliefs of the 'primitives' themselves, who appear as absolutely convinced that their magical rituals are not only effective, but indispensable, even though they see clearly that these rituals are only complementary to the technical operations without which no crop would grow. But Horton has not only demonstrated that the primitive *really* believes in the effectiveness of rain rituals; he has also produced a fascinating indirect argument against it, the expressive theory of magic, when he has shown that Christianity, in spite of its success in many areas of black English-speaking Africa, has often failed to replace local beliefs because it failed in the eyes of the Africans to propose a toolbox of magical devices which seemed to them indispensable in the conduct of everyday life.

In fact, the good theory is the third one, i.e. the *rational* theory developed by several modern writers but suggested curiously enough in similar terms both by Durkheim (1979) and Weber (1922); 'curiously enough', because the two sociologists seldom agreed.

According to this theory, one should first take seriously the fact that those who believe in magic have no knowledge of a number of theories that Westerners have developed after centuries. Why would a 'primitive' African have any knowledge of the conservation of energy, or of the Fisherian designs of experiments? Moreover, everyday actions need theories, and magic is a theory which provides guidelines for the actor. According to Durkheim, magical theories would be *applied* theories derived in a more or less direct fashion from religious theories exactly as many of our technical devices are inspired by scientific theories. Of course, these guidelines are not as efficient as those of science. But showing that magic is inefficient requires the mobilization of methods of causal analysis which were developed by science.

Moreover, writes Durkheim, don't we observe that scientists often keep their faith in a theory intact even when it appears to be contradicted by facts? Anticipating very precisely ideas developed by contemporary philosophers of science, as Lakatos (1970), Kuhn (1970) or Feyerabend (1975), Durkheim (1962, p. 508–28) suggests that scientists have good reasons for doing so. They can always hope that minor changes in the theory will make it compatible with facts, or doubt whether the facts which appear to contradict are genuine facts or whether they are artefacts, etc. Moreover, a long time will often elapse before it can be ascertained which of these typical situations is created by the discovery of facts contradictory with the theory, so that it is as rational to try to save the theory as to try to replace it.

For the same reasons, magicians can keep confidence in their theories even though they do not always work. Exactly as scientists, they will without much difficulty devise auxiliary hypotheses to explain why the theory has failed.

Evans-Pritchard's (1968) work on the Azande contains many concrete examples which confirm Durkheim's theory and show that the Zande magician does not behave in a way very different from the modern scientist, as described by modern philosophy and history of science.

On the other hand, even if one can legitimately assume – again on the basis of Evans-Pritchard's work for instance – that the primitive have some intuitive knowledge of the procedures by which a causal relationship is confirmed or rejected, it must be recognized that this knowledge is often practically of no help. Even in our world where methods of causal analysis are well mastered, lots of people and among them many scientists appear to believe in all kinds of unconfirmed causal relations.

Thus many people see a causal link between all kinds of practices and state of health or length of life. The reasons for such beliefs lie simply in the fact that in such cases collinearity is often so powerful that it is practically impossible to check seriously whether or not x really has an effect on y. Thus, it has been discovered recently that the idea of stress as a main cause of stomach ulcers was for many years a magical belief. This magical belief was endorsed by many people, however, including scientists.

To this, a subtle argument explicitly developed by Durkheim (1962, p. 527) can be added. Ethnologists have observed that the rain rituals are celebrated during the rain season. Wittgenstein (1975) interpreted this fact as supporting his theory that rain rituals are perceived by the primitive as having an expressive rather than instrumental function. The alternative interpretation proposed by Durkheim is much more ingenious and interesting: the confidence of the primitive in the effectiveness of their rituals, says Durkheim, is reinforced by the fact that rain is actually more frequent in the period of the year when crops start growing, need rain and when consequently they celebrate these rituals. Durkheim's assumption is in other words that collinearity reinforces the magical causal beliefs of the primitives, i.e. that their causal assumption is confirmed by a genuinely observable correlation.

On the whole, Durkheim suggests that the magical beliefs of the primitive are not different from ours. The difference is that, because of the development of science, a number of old beliefs have become obsolete. As a consequence, when we see other people still believing in them, we have a strong feeling of irrationality. But as soon as we evoke the causal relationships in which we believe ourselves on such existential problems as health, for instance, we become conscious of the fact that magical and scientific knowledge coexist as easily in our societies as technical and magical knowledge coexist in primitive societies.

Max Weber (1922, p. 227–8) wrote that to the primitive, 'the actions of the rainmaker are exactly as magical as the actions of the firemaker'. He meant by this statement that the primitive has no reason to introduce the asymmetry between rain- and firemaking which we introduce ourselves, precisely because the process by which kinetic is transformed into thermic energy is familiar to us. Reciprocally, the primitives to whom this process is unfamiliar have no reason to see a basic difference between fire- and rainmaking.

So, Weber's as well as Durkheim's implicit diagnosis of magic is that the primitive should not be considered as less rational than ourselves. When they are confronted with existential problems they develop theories and conjectures, which they derive from the socially available body of knowledge. They are eventually led to forget them when they are proposed better theories. But as long as these theories are not available, they have good reason to believe – as scientists – even in theories which repeatedly fail. Moreover, reality can reinforce rather than contradict their beliefs, even when these beliefs are false, as Durkheim has noted in one of the most brilliant parts of his analysis of magic.

We have here an example where substituting a subjective rational theory for a set of irrational interpretations gives a strong feeling of scientific progress. By contrast with the other two types of theories, the rational theory of magic does not give this impression of being *ad hoc* and arbitrary. It rests upon a set of psychological easily acceptable statements and appearsEas congruent with available data.

Further Classical Examples

Mentioning Durkheim within the present discussion is also interesting for another reason: Durkheim is seldom seen as a writer who insists on the idea of explaining actions and beliefs rationally. But while this is true of his theoretical writings, he often offers in his empirical analyses rational – in the subjective sense – explanations of social behaviour.[3]

To take another example: when Durkheim (1962) tries to explain in his *Suicide* why economic booms appear to be associated with higher rates of suicide, he introduces an explanation of the *subjective rationality* type, not very far away from the ideal effect. Durkheim's assumption is that the anticipations and expectations of social actors are grounded on good reasons: in a stable conjuncture, they tend to start from the principle that they can expect, say, for the year to come, the same gains as the year before, while in a 'high' conjuncture, when the situation of many people appears to be improving, they will change their conjectures as to which objectives can be reached and aimed at.

Durkheim introduces implicitly at this point a brilliant hypothesis, namely that people extrapolate from the tangent to the curve at each point of time. Thus in the first part of the ascending phase, before the inflection point, their expectations tend to be under-optimistic, while in the second part, they are over-optimistic. This is at least my interpretation as to why Durkheim predicts an increase in disillusion and consequently in suicide rates in the second part of the ascending phase of the business cycle, but not in the first.

I have tried to show, with the help of a formal model (Boudon 1982), why, as hypothesized by Durkheim, but also by Tocqueville and others, a 'higher' conjuncture will in many circumstances produce less satisfaction than a stable one, because it will generate over-optimistic conjectures.

The same remarks could be made about Marx as have been made about Durkheim. In the first pages of the *German Ideology*, he develops a famous irrational theory of beliefs: people believe in all kinds of false ideas because obscure social forces bring them to see the world in a distorted fashion. But in many of his analyses, in contradiction with his general theory of beliefs, Marx produces a rational explanation. This is probably because he felt, as Durkheim, although he did not want to recognize it, that explaining behaviour or beliefs means finding the *good reasons* behind behaviour and beliefs.

Thus at one point in *Capital*, Marx (1867) wonders why workers accept exploitation so easily. A behaviour which goes against the very interests of an actor is typically explained in most cases in an irrational fashion. Against his own principles, Marx sketches in *Capital* a rational explanation, however, which I reconstruct in the following way: to know that they are exploited, the workers have to see the difference between their salary and the value of their work. But to determine the value of their work, they would have to master a complex economic theory, as well as a great deal of empirical information. As this is impossible and as they still want to know whether their salary is fair or not, they turn toward a natural substitute: comparing their salary to the salary of the individual producer. But, by so doing, they introduce a bias in their estimation, the individual producer using more time to produce, say, a pair of shoes than the worker in a shoe factory. On the whole, they will agree to leave to the capitalist the gain resulting from the division of labour. But they will do so with good reasons.

One need not of course endorse the theory of surplus value and still admire the ingenuity with which Marx explains how the social actor can with good reasons act against his own interest: even masochism can be grounded on *good reasons*.

SUBJECTIVE RATIONALITY AND THE EXPLANATION OF FALSE BELIEFS

The examples I have drawn from Weber and Durkheim as well as Marx lead to the final part of this chapter, where I shall try to underline the importance of the notion of subjective rationality in the analysis of beliefs.

Beliefs, notably false beliefs, are currently interpreted as the product of causes located beyond the control of the subject, rather than of reasons. Marx, in his theoretical writings at least, and Freud and Pareto among the classics, illustrate clearly this paradigm. In the same way, modern sociologists of knowledge mostly analyse beliefs as the product of obscure and invisible social or psychological causes. Alternatively, they content themselves with exploring the correlations between independent variables and beliefs and do so, this is at least my guess, because they endorse currently a naturalistic irrational view of men.

The notion of subjective rationality suggests, for this subject of beliefs, an alternative paradigm, which I think is potentially much more fruitful. It follows immediately from the fact that good reasons can be objectively invalid, so that the social actor can with good reasons believe in false ideas.

So, an interesting theoretical task for the sociology of knowledge would be to identify and classify a body of examples where mental procedures typical of subjective rationality produce false beliefs. While I cannot undertake this task here, I will present some examples to suggest the potential interest of such developments.

More precisely, I will consider three cases, which lead to false beliefs: respectively *sound methodological principles, sound ideas or theories* and finally *sound intellectual procedures*.

Sound Methodological Principles

We saw an example of the first case in the experiment reported by Simon which I presented earlier. The subjects started from the idea that, in order to reproduce a model, the best thing to do was to produce a copy following the rules according to which the original was built. The error comes here from a natural application of an apparently innocent principle.

Another seemingly innocent principle, a principle of vital importance which we are on many occasions entitled to follow, is this: when we have to make up our mind on an empirical question, for instance as to whether a given x is y, we normally check empirically, if we are in the position of doing so, whether or not x is actually y. If I am asked whether a given book is on a given table, the best thing to do is to look at the table and see whether the book is actually there. The application of this natural principle can lead to false views about the world, however.

To illustrate this point, I will draw an example from a polemical discussion which arose in France recently on the question as to whether the cognitive level of youngsters tends to decline or to climb as an effect of the overall increase in education. I will leave aside the trivial point that checking the cognitive level of a population is more complicated than checking whether a book is on a table or not. For, even if we assume that cognitive levels can be easily observed, strong illusions about their evolution can still appear with good reasons in many heads.

To introduce my point, I will build a highly simplified model: I will assume that there is a variable such as the capacity to learn and that in each of the successive cohorts of youngsters this capacity is distributed in the same way. I will suppose moreover that each year the number of students taking a given grade increases, and that this increase corresponds to a population located lower on the hypothetical distribution from one cohort to the next. Although this model is caricatural, it is obviously not without relation to the real world.

Suppose now a teacher is asked whether the cognitive level of the secondary school students increases or decreases. He would naturally answer this question by reference to his own experience. Now, according to the assumptions of the model his conclusion would be entirely unambiguous: he can see directly that the level of his students declines regularly from one year to the next. Moreover, he could easily check that his impression is general, since most of his colleagues would reach the same conclusions for the same reasons. On the whole, all teachers, except those who see the world through biased glasses, would consider as empirical that the cognitive level of high school students declines.

This pessimistic impression of the quasi-unanimity of our teachers is obviously not incompatible with the fact that the average cognitive level of the youngsters between, say, 15 and 20 increases regularly according to the model. For, except in the case where we would be ready to accept the very unlikely assumption that education would not only *not* increase knowledge but even destroy it, the model predicts also a general increase of the cognitive level. More concretely, the model shows that all English teachers, for example, would be convinced by their immediate experience that the level of their class in English decreases regularly over time. This opinion would be grounded on good reasons. But on the whole more people would know more English over time.

So, the false beliefs of our teachers are in no way illusions. On the contrary, they perceive the reality around them *as it is*. The false belief comes from the application of a principle which is in most cases all right, i.e. that observing whether x is y is a good way to determine whether x is y. This principle is effectively most often valid. But, as here, it can also lead with good reasons to beliefs in false statements.

Many examples in the same vein could be mentioned where subjective rationality produces false ideas or beliefs, where in other words subjects appear to endorse false ideas or beliefs with good reasons. I will add two further short examples in order to suggest that the idea is general.

According to a widely accepted point of the Keynesian theory, an increase in taxes has normally a deflationary effect, for the following reasons: it generates a decrease in the purchasing power, which in turn generates a decline in the demand for goods and services, and finally a decline in the prices of goods and services. Now, in a survey conducted by Katona (1951), a sample of businessmen was asked whether an increase in taxes has deflationary of inflationary effects. A majority of them answered that it should increase inflation. Why? Simply because they analysed the question by reference to a situation familiar to them: when taxes climb, this has the effect of increasing the costs of production the businessman has to bear. Except in the case where the demand for his products is highly elastic with respect to price, he will normally try to transfer at least a part of this increase in his costs of production to the consumer by increasing the price of his products or services. From this simple mental experiment he concludes with excellent reasons that an increase in taxation should generate inflationary effects.

Or consider another example. Many people are convinced that substituting mechanical for human work increases unemployment. Here again, this conviction can be grounded on *good reasons*. A simple mental experiment shows that, at the local level, the introduction of new machines will normally in many circumstances destroy some jobs. At the general level, however, it can have a positive net effect on employment, since the machine will have to be produced, maintained, replaced after a while by a better performing machine which will have to be devised and produced, etc. But this positive influence is visible at a general abstract level, the level at which the economist is located. At the local level where the worker is located, he will perceive on the contrary a negative effect. As in the previous examples this perception is not an *illusion*, however. What the worker sees corresponds to the reality as it is.

In other words a false belief results here, as in the other examples, from the combination of a correct non-illusory perception and of the general apparently innocent principle according to which questions of type 'does x produce y?' can be answered by checking whether empirically x produces y.

Questions of this type – 'does x produce y?', 'is y an effect of x?', 'is x a cause of y?' – are obviously questions which we ask almost as frequently as we breathe. Causal diagnoses are as vital in everyday life as they are in scientific research. Now, a principle often used to reach a causal diagnosis as to whether, say, x is cause of y, a principle generally considered as safe and valid, consists in observing whether x and y tend to appear together. If I observe a certain number of times that drinking too much wine tends to make me sleepy, I will normally conclude that wine tends to make me sleepy.

As the previous one, this apparently innocent principle can lead to false beliefs, however. This has admirably been shown by a number of experiments conducted by experimental cognitive psychologists. Here is one of them, which was conducted by Shweder (1977). A sample of nurses are presented 100 cards representing 100 supposed patients. On these cards two fictitious bits of information have been recorded: whether or not the patient shows a given hypothetical symptom; and whether or not a hypothetical disease has been diagnosed in his case. The joint distribution is the following:

		Disease		
		Present	Absent	Total
Symptom				
Present		37	33	70
Absent		17	13	30
Total		54	46	100

While the correlation is very low and goes in the 'wrong' direction, 85 per cent of the nurses thought that the symptom was an effect of the disease. Why? Because they started from the principle that a number of cases as high as 37 where the two features occurred together was sufficient to show that the disease is a cause of the symptom. After all, if 37 times I feel sleepy after drinking wine, would I not be convinced that wine makes me sleepy?

In spite of the extreme interest of his paper, I disagree with the author of the article on one crucial point. He claims that the nurses in his experiment illustrate 'magical thinking', as he writes in the title of his paper. If magical thinking is defined as it is usually, by the fact of seeing causal relationships where there are actually none, it is true that the nurses think magically. But I disagree with him when he seems to interpret the beliefs of the nurses in the irrational way in which Lévy-Bruhl interpreted the magical beliefs of his 'primitives': they see a causal relationship where there is none because they follow without knowing it the rules of a primitive logic.

In fact Shweder's interpretation was inspired in him because he perceived the answers of his nurses through the glasses of his own professional knowledge. What I mean is that, as social scientists, because we manipulate currently contingency tables with their three (once N is known) degrees of freedom, we tend to consider as normal the situations where three degrees of freedom have to be taken into account before a causal statement can be proposed. And we do not see that in many cases it is sufficient to check that y follows x frequently to reach a reliable answer to the question as to whether x is cause of y.

So, Shweder's nurses are not more irrational than Simon's subjects in the experiment I reported at the beginning of this chapter. And it is more illuminating to interpret their answer – on the *subjective rationality mode* – as dictated by the application of principles which are currently valid while in some circumstances they are not.

Finally, using sound methodological principles, such as seeing for instance whether x is y in order to know whether x is y, and seeing whether x and y appear frequently together to determine whether they are related, can and often does lead to the right ideas. But it can also lead to wrong ones. In other words sound principles can be the cause of false beliefs.

Respectable Ideas and Theories

In the same fashion genuinely respectable ideas can lead to false conclusions.

Several surveys on beliefs about supernatural phenomena show for instance a strange result. Believing in the existence of God becomes *less* frequent when the level of education is higher. But other supernatural beliefs appear as *more* frequent. Thus, believing in the existence of extraterrestrial beings or in psychic action at a distance appears as increasing with the level of education. In a survey mentioned by Renard (1988), 48 per cent of the interviewees with primary education, 62 per cent of those with secondary education and 73 per cent of those with higher education appeared to believe in extraterrestrial beings.[4]

Several interpretations can be given of these results. The first reaction of many sociologists to this type of finding is to interpret the belief as irrational: more education, less common sense. A more careful analysis shows, however, that this belief can often be interpreted as the consequence of a conjecture grounded on *good reasons*. People with a scientific education have learned that concepts, entities or mechanisms which were considered for a while as contradictory with the very notion of science have frequently been incorporated into the body of scientific knowledge later. The notion of physical action at a distance is a good example in this respect: the Cartesians developed all kinds of theories to explain by direct mechanical effects the physical phenomena which appeared as revealing the existence of forces acting at a distance, a concept which they considered as unacceptable, until Newton made the notion respectable and, by so doing, discredited the Cartesian theories.

Why could the progress of knowlege not incorporate in the same way the notion of psychic action at a distance? Why couldn't future scientific research demonstrate the existence of superterrestrial beings? As empirical sociologists have currently a naturalistic vision of the *homo sociologicus*, they seldom care about retrieving his reasons, so that I have no proof that such reasons explain the correlations I mentioned between beliefs and level of education. But it appears as plausible that the respondents with a higher education have finally good reasons to be less sceptical or critical on some subjects than those with less familiarity with the history of science. To summarize this case in an ironic fashion, I would say that the confidence in the scientific virtue of methodical doubt can occasionally lead to more credulity.

Many examples in the same vein could be mentioned. Another respectable genuinely scientific idea is the Keynesian theory according to which stimulating the demand for goods and services, for instance by distributing more purchasing power or reducing taxes, will stimulate the supply of goods and services and consequently reduce unemployment. This respectable and true idea can lead to dangerous beliefs, however, if it is forgotten that Keynes proposed it in a situation where aggregate demand was much below the potential supply. For in a situation where aggregate demand exceeds potential supply, stimulating the demand will produce inflation rather than a decrease in unemployment.

Thus false beliefs are often generated by the most respectable and sometimes by the most genuinely scientific theories. When for instance the hidden assumptions of a theory remain unperceived it can lead many people to believe with good reasons that x will produce y while it will actually produce z.

Respectable Mental Procedures

Very often, false ideas can also be generated by the confidence normally granted by the subject to the usual procedures of thought, as induction for instance. As we have known since Hume, though induction is logically ill grounded, it is vital for everyday life and currently used in science. But it can generate false beliefs as in the case of those children who were asked by Balacheff (1987) to look at two triangles similar in all respects except size, the triangle ABC being greater than A'B'C', and to answer some questions about them. When they were asked whether the side AB is greater than A'B', they answered 'yes'. 'Is BC greater than B'C'?' – answer: 'yes'. 'Is AC greater than A'C'?' – answer: 'yes'. 'Is the perimeter of ABC greater?' – answer: 'yes'. 'The surface?' – 'yes'. 'The sum of the angles of ABC?' – answer: 'yes'.

Impeccable formal deductive procedures as the syllogism, for instance, although it leads in most cases to right conclusions, will also eventually be responsible for false beliefs when they are used in an overconfident fashion. I am not thinking here of the sophistical use of correct deductive procedures which Pareto (1935) had in mind when he criticized these deductive arguments where the meaning of the same word changes from one statement to the next. Thus, he contended, the words 'nature', 'natural', etc. are used in many moral arguments to 'prove' that something is good. The arguments are often formally correct but they are sophistical because these words appear to be used with variable meanings. What I have in mind here is an entirely different case.

Take for instance the following deductive theory: on average, the social origin of an individual has an influence on his level of education, his level of education on his social status. From these statements, we conclude easily that, if the relationship between origin and status becomes weaker over time, the relation between social origin and status will also appear as progressively declining. The argument is absolutely correct. The words have the same meaning in each statement; the statements are logically connected to one another in a satisfactory fashion, so that we have all possible good reasons to accept this conclusion.

But the argument also contains, as any argument, all kinds of implicit statements. In general, these mental harmonics do not disturb the argument more than musical overtones disturb the main line of a melody. But sometimes, arguments can contain, as here, implicit statements which make the conclusion we derive from them much more fragile than we believe. Here, the argument takes for granted that each of the two relationships can change without the other changing. While this type of assumption can ordinarily be made in most cases and remains for this reason implicit, it produces here a false belief, as shown by Boudon (1974). Since the relationship between social origin and educational level cannot plausibly become smaller without the overall number of people being edu-cated increasing, the second relationship – between educational level and status – probably cannot remain constant. A false belief is generated here by the application of a generally valid procedure to a case where it is not, exactly as imitating a copy suffices in general to reproducing it with fidelity, while it can also occasionally deform it.

This example also has the interest of showing once more that, contrary to what Simon's example suggests, subjective rationality appears not only in everyday intuitive inference but also in scientific thinking. For it is clear that although scientific thinking is obviously more controlled than everyday thinking, a scientific procedure always contains, as in the previous example, invisible implicit steps beside its official controlled steps. These implicit assumptions are always present. In most cases they are both unconscious and harm-less. In other cases they lead to false beliefs.

This point is essential, since it underlines one of the basic mecha-nisms by which genuinely scientific arguments can provide the *good reasons* which inspire and consolidate false beliefs.

So, all kinds of usually valid and vital principles and mental procedures – induction, formal procedures such as the syllogism, sound principles such as the principle recommending empirical checking whether x is y in order to judge whether x is y, etc. – in other words the complex set of theories, procedures and principles which are used by *subjective rationality* are also basic mechanisms by which false ideas and beliefs can be grounded and consolidated.

Thus, the notion of subjective rationality exemplifies a paradigm within which all kinds of behaviours, including those oriented against the interests of the subject, as well as all kinds of attitudes and beliefs, including magical beliefs and beliefs in false ideas, can be more convincingly explained than with other paradigms.

More generally, the notion of subjective rationality seems to me a most important theoretical tool for all social sciences. Substituting subjective rational explanations for irrational explanations of behaviour is a sure sign of progress in the social sciences, while reciprocally irrational explanations, because they tend to be easy, *ad hoc*, circular and empty are a plague of sociology.

The fact that irrational explanations are often considered by sociologists as natural is evidenced by the fact that many studies are based on correlational analyses interpreted in a causal naturalistic fashion. Thus many sociologists will be satisfied to know that income, or class, say, has an influence on the probability of believing in God or in extraterrestrial beings, or on the probability of reaching a given educational level, and will often not even wonder whether or not reasons can explain the correlation.

The appeal of irrational explanations of behaviour to sociologists derives from several sources: the influence of the exoteric Marxian and Freudian tradition, but also the influence of the narrow definition of rationality according to which good reasons should be objectively grounded. The strength of this narrow definition is due to its deep roots in a secular philosophical tradition.

Once the importance of this concept of subjective rationality is fully recognized, the strange division of labour between economists who tend to see the *homo oeconomicus* as narrowly rational and sociologists who see often the *homo sociologicus* as basically moved by forces located beyond his control will be attenuated, this is at least my guess, and replaced by a more interesting ideal-type, I mean the ideal-type of the *motivated actor*, i.e. of an actor who in many cases has good reasons to do what he does or to think what he thinks.[5]

On the whole, the notion of subjective rationality outlines a general model which spans the various disciplines: it expresses the idea that, except in simple situations where the social actor can follow the narrow rational model, he is normally confronted with ambiguous and complex situations and masters them by using theories, principles, conjectures; in other words by being intellectually more active than both sociologists and economists recognize.

For all these reasons, the notion of subjective rationality appears to me as one of the most strategic concepts for the development of the social sciences.

NOTES

1. Since $(.8 \times .8) + (.4 \times .4) = .68$.
2. Since $(.5 \times .5) + (.5 \times .5) = .5$.
3. A point which I have tried to develop in Boudon (1981).
4. A survey conducted by Boy and Michelat (1986) leads to the same kind of observations.
5. A reaction against irrational explanations of behaviour has appeared with the so-called new economics, as presented for instance by McKenzie and Tullock (1975). This paradigm proposes to use a narrow definition and theory of rationality usual in classical economics in the analysis not only of economic behaviour but of behaviours not belonging to the traditional field of economics. Very often this

approach is presented as a reaction against the traditional sociological approach which is held as dominated by an irrational view of man. This verdict is true to some extent at least: the Weberian tradition appears as less influential in sociology than the traditions which see the social actor as irrational. But the reaction to this verdict is not the right one – it seems to me. It is true that the narrow rational model can be applied to the analysis not only of economic behaviour but to other types of behaviour as well. But this model should be held as a particular case of a more general model.

REFERENCES

Balacheff, N. (1987) 'Processus de preuve et situations de validation', *Educational Studies in Mathematics*, 18, pp. 147–76.

Beattie, J. (1964) *Other Cultures*. London: Cohen & West.

Boudon, R. (1974) *Education, Opportunity and Social Inequality*. New York: Wiley.

Boudon, R. (1981) *The Logic of Social Action*. London: Routledge; German: *Die Logik des gesellschaftlichen Handelns*. Luchterhand.

Boudon, R. (1982) 'The Logic of Relative Frustration', in *The Unintended Consequences of Social Action*. London: Macmillan; German: *Die Widersprüche sozialen Handelns*. Luchterhand.

Boy, D. and Michelat, G. (1986) 'Croyances aux parasciences: dimensions sociales et culturelles', *Revue Française de Sociologie*, XXVII, 2, pp. 175–204.

Downs, A. (1957) *An Economic Theory of Democracy*. New York: Harper.

Durkheim, E. (1962) *Suicide, a Study in Sociology*. Glencoe: The Free Press (1897).

Durkheim, E. (1979) *Les formes élémentaires de la vie religieuse*. Paris: Presses Universitaires de France (1912).

Evans-Pritchard, E. (1968) *Witchcraft, Oracles and Magic among the Azande*. Oxford: The Clarendon Press (1937).

Feldman, J. (1964) 'Simulation of Behavior in the Binary Choice Experiment', in Feigenbaum, E. A., and Feldman, J. (eds) *Computers and Thought*. New York: McGraw-Hill, pp. 329–46.

Feyerabend, P. (1975) *Against Method*. London: NLB.

Hirschman, A. (1980) 'The Changing Tolerance for Income Inequality in the Course of Economic Development', in Hirschman, A. *Essays in Trespassing*. Cambridge: Cambridge University Press, pp. 39–58.

Horton, R. (1982) 'Tradition and Modernity Revisited' in Hollins, M. and Lukes, S. *Rationality and Relativism*. Oxford: Blackwell, pp. 201–60.

Hume, D. (1752) *Political Discourses*. Edinburgh: Kincaid and Donaldson.

Katona, G. (1951) *Psychological Analysis of Economic Behavior*. New York: McGraw-Hill.

Kuhn, T. (1970) *The Structure of Scientific Revolution*. Chicago: Chicago University Press.

Lakatos, I. (1970) 'Falsification and the Methodology of Scientific Research

Programmes', in Lakatos, I. and Musgrave, A. (eds), *Criticism and the Growth of Knowledge*. London: Cambridge University Press, pp. 91–196.

Lévy-Bruhl, L. (1960) *La mentalité primitive*. Paris: Presses Universitaires de France (1922).

Marx, K. (1867) *Das Kapital*. Hamburg: O. Meissner/New York: L. W. Schmidt.

McKenzie, R. B. and Tullock, G. (1975). *The New World of Economics*. Homewood: Irwin.

Pareto, V. (1935) *The Mind and Society. A Treatise on General Sociology*. New York: Dover Publications, 2 vols.

Popper, K. (1967) 'La rationalité et le statut de principe de rationalité', in Claasen, e. M. (ed.) *Les fondements philosophiques des systèmes économiques*. Paris: Payot, pp. 142–50.

Renard, J. B. (1988) *Les extraterrestres*. Paris: Cerf.

Shweder, R. A. (1977) 'Likeness and likelihood in Everyday Thought: Magical Thinking in Judgments about Personality', *Current Anthropology*, vol. 18, no. 4, pp. 637–58.

Simon, H. (1982) *Models of Bounded Rationality*. Cambridge: MIT Press.

Weber, M. (1922) *Wirtschaft und Gesellschaft*. Tübingen: Mohr.

Weber, M. (1951) *Gesammelte Aufsätze zur Wissenschaftslehre*, 2. Auf Tübingen: Mohr.

Wittgenstein, L. (1975) 'Bemerkungen über Frazer's *The Golden Bough*', in Wiggershaus, Rolf (ed.) *Sprachanalyse und Soziologie*. Frankfurt: Suhrkamp, pp. 37–58.

8. Organizational Learning, Problem Solving and the Division of Labour

Massimo Egidi

In the course of this chapter I shall attempt to reformulate the problem of the relationship between market and hierarchies in an evolutionary context, assuming the boundaries between market and organizations as a variable and thus presuming technology and organization of a firm to be the object of decision making by managers.

The idea I shall develop is that organizations perform a more complex function than the market; i.e. they take on the function of *designing* the division of labour and the function of *coordinating* the tasks so divided, while the market limits itself to coordinating the activities of its agents within a structure of the division of labour that has already been established.

In this context I shall put forward a formal representation of the process by which new forms of the division of labour, or new *procedures*, are internally generated by organizations. On this basis I shall describe the firm as an organization which cannot be completely reduced to the market, in so far as it is able, unlike the market, to transform its own organizational forms.

To this end I shall represent the behaviour of individuals acting in organizations as 'intelligent' behaviour: decisions will be viewed as the final act of a complex process of reasoning based on inference, learning and discovery.

On the other hand, organizations will be viewed as based not only on the mutual exchange of information but mainly on a systematic generation and exchange of knowledge which gives rise to an internal creation of skills. A process of organizational learning will be assumed as the basic mechanism which generates the emergence of organizational shapes.

I shall analyse the learning process which takes place within organizations using the problem-solving approach: organizations will be described as governed by routines and procedures; and a procedure will be defined as a way of solving a problem. The organizational shape of a firm will therefore be viewed as the outcome of a learning process by which a team of agents creates procedures to the end of solving the problems faced by the firm.

Starting from recognition that a general and important way of solving problems is decomposing the original problem into subproblems, I will suggest that the form of such decomposition determines the way in which the division of labour is created inside organizations. I conclude by exploring some consequences of this approach.

PROBLEM SOLVING IN GAMES AND PUZZLES

I shall assume conditions of bounded and procedural rationality, by which I mean the attribution to the individual of the ability to summarize information, to formulate problems and solve them (or try to solve them) in an environment where information is scattered and incomplete, and where processing it is difficult because both specialized knowledge and the division of intellectual labour are required.

The notion of rationality is therefore examined from a non-traditional perspective; the central problem is no longer one of making the best choice using all relevant information, since the complex of factors governing the choice is only partially known. The problem is rather that of understanding how further information can be assimilated, how relevant information can be summarized and how the computational complexity of processing the information can be simplified.

The simplest way of portraying this capacity is by depicting individual behaviour as strategic behaviour. Since games theory provides a particularly straightforward model of strategic behaviour, it is perhaps worthwhile recalling it here.

In games theory each agent, or player, is assumed to be able to assess the different states of play that derive from applying the rules of the game itself, starting from the initial configuration. The game tree represents the whole range of alternative moves and counter-moves which the player can theoretically conceive; to any final positions of the game, i.e. to any positions that can be reached at the end of a play, corresponds a terminal node in the tree; a pay-off function evaluates every terminal node.

In analysing the game, each 'rational' player has to study in advance the full sequence of moves he will make in the course of the game. For each of his moves he has to predict all the possible responses of his opponent; he will then have to choose, for each of these responses, a counter-counter-move of his own, and so on. He thus elaborates a strategy which may therefore be a conspicuous part of the game tree.

If the number of moves made in each game is low, we know that the player is able to explore the entire game tree, and to choose – if it exists – the winning strategy. However, exploring the entire tree is not always possible in complex games (and this is the reason why people enjoy playing them!)

In an environment of some decision-making complexity, an individual is not generally able to work out all the available options exhaustively, nor is he able to choose the best one. His portrayal of the situation will usually be incomplete and local and he will attempt to examine the alternatives open to him by means of search procedures. A typical feature of these procedures is that they reduce the amount of analysis, and therefore the complexity of the calculation, by means of parameters – just as the market reduces the strategic nature of individual actions to parametric ones via prices. Chess provides a typical instance of this situation: it is a game where there exist both a winning strategy and a procedure for finding it (the von Neumann algorithm). As we know, this method requires full examination of the game tree, which has far too many states (about 10^{120}!!) for such examination to be remotely possible: this is a classical failure of method requiring unlimited computational ability.

Nonetheless the human player, using incomplete knowledge and a limited computational capacity, succeeds in winning without having found the best strategy. From this we may induce that he possesses a more powerful tool than the seemingly perfect one of Olympian rationality. This 'spontaneous method' involves a reduction of the strategic character of the game, and its partial parametrization; human players apply their analysis and strategic choices to limited 'segments' of the game tree: they explore moves and counter-moves by orientating themselves according to 'subjective' evaluators of the future state of the chess-board; that is to say, they refer to such indicators as the number of pieces in danger of being taken, the number of pieces that occupy the centre of the board, and so forth. These indicators constitute the parameters governing each player's strategic choice, move by move; they allow the players to concentrate their analysis on those situations which seem 'most promising'.[1]

Two elements should be pointed out here: the incompleteness of the analysis carried out by the players, and the subjective and imperfect character of the parameters which guide their analysis. The strategy that players develop is always incomplete because it is based upon the analysis of a limited number of moves and counter-moves. Moreover, the players do not have certain and shared criteria available with which to assess the positions they reach as the game proceeds. Their evaluations are founded on subjective criteria, are improved by experience, and in general differ from player to player.

This has a consequence of some importance. Each player radically simplifies his analysis of positions by eliminating choices which look wrong on the basis of his evaluators. And since each player evaluates the chess board according to different criteria, it frequently happens that the expectations formulated by each of them concerning his opponent's moves can fail: during the game one player may choose a move that his opponent has not predicted and this error can decide the result of the game.

In chess tournaments in any series of matches played by two grand masters of approximately the same ability, each of them loses a certain number of games. We normally consider two players to have the same ability if each of them wins approximately the same number of games as his opponent. Note that every time a player loses, he has evidently made a wrong assessment of his opponent's strategy. Consequently, if two players have the same ability, both fail in their expectations of the strategies chosen by their opponent for 50 per cent of the games in a tournament, and they are therefore unable to formulate *rational* expectations.[2] Thus the behaviour of the players is characterized by incomplete knowledge, surprise and inconsistency of expectations.

Under conditions of incomplete knowledge and inconsistency of expectations a subject will try to reformulate his knowledge by selecting new information and by revising the criteria previously used to evaluate his decisions. He will try to revise his beliefs and his knowledge base by means of *search* procedures. The most salient feature of player behaviour during the search process consists therefore in the restructuring of knowledge: this entails that players must, above all, be able to solve the problems which arise during their attempts to achieve their goals.

I will assume *problem-solving* activity to be a general frame for describing and explaining economic behaviour in conditions of uncertainty. Following Simon and Newell (1972) I shall take this activity to be a manipulation of *symbol structures*, of which a good example is provided by puzzle-solving activity.[3]

Puzzles are analogous to strategic games in the sense that both, using simple rules, generate a combinatorial explosion of different possibilities, which cannot generally be fully explored by the players. In order to find the solution of a puzzle the player has to solve the problem of how to reach a desired goal from the initial state (or configuration) by sequentially using the rules of the puzzle. If we take Rubik's Cube, for example, the aim is to achieve an 'aesthetically beautiful' configuration starting from a 'scrambled' one by means of successive state transformations.

As in strategic games, one solution to this problem is perfectly possible: exhaustively exploring all the positions until the desired one is found. But, like chess again, the extremely high number of possible permutations which have to be examined rules out this procedure.

The only difference between puzzles and strategic games is that in the former the player's strategy does not depend on decisions taken by his opponent; thus the uncertainty which derives from the inter-active character of the decision is eliminated; we may overlook this difference, however, because in the case of puzzles it is still impossible to find the winning strategy, and by consequence uncertainty arises once again from the boundedly rational capabilities of players.

Puzzles and strategic games can therefore be taken to be specific examples of the more general case of problem-solving activity; *executing* a strategy, and *seeking* a strategy (a bad, good, satisficing or winning strategy, if it exists) are the two main aspects of problem-solving activity as applied to puzzles and games.

We must attribute these abilities to players, bearing in mind that during a game, they generally need to use both, jointly or separately. There are games like the Rubik Cube, in fact, which can be successfully played by executing simple local rules, while there are other games, like chess, where this behaviour is allowed only for fragments of the game (generally its opening and closing stages) and creative behaviour is required for the rest. This is due to the fact that in some games, like chess and checkers, it is impossible to find the winning strategy or to compact it into a restricted set of rules, while in other games, like the Rubik Cube, a simple set of rules can be found by which a player can mechanically solve the problem. Once the rules for the Rubik Cube solution had been discovered, the game rapidly lost is popularity, because the search for the final configuration became a simple exercise in the speedy execution of perfectly routinized moves. Players have learnt to implement certain standard sequences mechanically and to combine them in an opportune way. They behave like machines which, having accepted the initial configuration and the desired final state of the cube as inputs, proceed to implement all steps necessary to reach the final configuration: in brief, they *execute a program*. In the opposite case of the mid-stages of chess, we can observe the creative and explorative behaviour of searching for new local strategies.

Games and puzzles are therefore a fruitful area for studying and formalizing human behaviour as characterized by two different 'extreme typologies': on the one hand the mere performance of routines; on the other, the creative and explorative behaviour of searching for new routines and for new methods to solve problems. As was shown by Cyert, Simon and Trow in a pioneering paper of 1956, this distinction is crucial for understanding of decision makers' behaviour in the real business world. As a key to understanding of decision processes they proposed the distinction between *programmed* and *non-programmed* decisions, on the basis of an empirical case study. Their analysis described the firm as an organization which works on the basis of a hierarchical structure of programs, that is to say of procedures employed to solve predetermined tasks.

A similar distinction – between *routines* and *innovative decisions* – is used by Nelson and Winter (1982) which also characterizes the firm in term of routines it has;[4] the activity of the organization's members consists of the coordinated implementation of these routines, and, most importantly, of the modification of the routines, which are adapted to the continuously changing circumstances.

SEARCH AS CONJECTURAL PROCESS OF PROBLEM SOLVING

Attributing procedural rationality to individuals is to suppose that they are able to enact *search procedures* suitable for attaining their goals; such goals will differ according to the context under discussion: a satisficing strategy in the case of strategic games, or a sequence of steps leading to the solution in the case of puzzles; two cases which are specific examples of the most general context in which these search procedures can be examined, namely that of problem solving.

In this general context a problem is represented by means of a *symbol structure*[5] in Newell and Simon's sense; and finding a solution means finding the *program* (or procedure) which leads to the desired goal.

Once more, puzzles will be used for the following discussion because they represent in a very vivid and rich way the general problem-solving context, without a loss of generality. My plan for this section is first to show that, for a given class of problems, many different solutions can be found; second to discuss their characteristics and compare their efficiency; and finally to focus on the more complex of these solutions, those based on decomposition of the original problem into a hierarchical structure of sub-problems; I will argue that this solution is a good model of how the division of knowledge comes about in the search process.

Let us turn to search processes in puzzles and strategic games. As we have seen, when the game is one of great complexity, like chess or checkers, the player 'naturally' orientates his search by using simple rules or 'heuristics': indicators that synthesize the relevant information about the 'goodness' of a given configuration of the game.[6] This suggests that a player, searching for a solution, can follow two different procedures:

1. Explore extensively the game tree according to a general search algorithm. This is a blind and uninformed procedure which requires unlimited computational capabilities of the player. Call it 'blind procedure'.
2. Selectively explore the tree, orienting the search according to *ad hoc* criteria (heuristics). This is the way many people seem to play chess and checkers. Call this the 'satisficing procedure'.

One notes with interest that for many puzzles, as for example Rubik's Cube, players follow neither of these two procedures; the blind procedure in fact is practically unrealizable for the extremely high number of moves that could be explored; the satisficing procedure does not work, because, as yet, nobody has been able to discover a good heuristic based on the characteristics of the configuration, i.e. a set of rules by which to establish which move is the 'more promising', for any given configuration.

To understand why this happens, note that a natural heuristic for puzzles is based on the idea that the closer a move brings the state of the puzzle to the goal the more it is preferable. Therefore if we are to measure the 'distance' between the state of the game and the desired goal we can use it as heuristics; the problem is that this traditional measure of 'distance' fails. It is easy to understand why the simplest indicator of 'distance', which is based upon the number of blocks already in the desired position, does not permit one to come closer to the desired configuration.

Let us assume that the final position is given by the configuration in which each side of the cube is composed of the same colour. Starting with a scrambled configuration, a player will easily succeed in arranging all the blocks of a certain colour into one identical side; but when he attempts to repeat the exercise with the second side, he realizes that he is unable to effectuate the action without muddling up the side that had already been sorted out. It will not take him long to understand, as a result, that the 'difference' between the situation in which he finds the cube and the final configuration cannot simply be evaluated by the number of sides already in order.

Spontaneously, therefore, he tries to see if he is able to move the blocks in the cube's most important points (the corners and the top blocks in every row) without altering the position of the blocks already in place or altering them just so much as to allow their replacement. This is a typical 'sub-problem', that is to say a problem which must be solved if the original task of reaching the final desired position is to be fulfilled. In the case of the cube, the problem of passing from the scrambled configuration with which one is initially confronted to the final 'desired' configuration is actually resolved by breaking the problem down into simpler, yet more general, sub-problems. Consequently we must add one more element to the list of search procedures listed above:

3. Move into the space of problems, by exploring the tree of sub-problems. The problem is posed very incompletely (a rather limited number of positions are explored) and the final result is a 'cognitive structure', i.e. a structure of interconnected sub-problems which 'explain' the original problem. Call this the 'intelligent procedure'.

Let us specify these three procedures, i.e. let us show that they can be written as three different *programs* and compared from the viewpoint of their efficiency. In order to do so, I provide an example of how they work when applied to a *Rubik Square*; this is a puzzle based on the idea of simplifying the Rubik Cube by reducing it to a square and accordingly by simplifying the transformation rules. I will briefly describe the rules, referring the reader to Dosi and Egidi (1991) for further details.

Let us reduce the three-dimensional Rubik Cube to a bi-dimensional square comprising four blocks of different colours. Each block of the square has the same colour at the front and back and can rotate along two orthogonal axes, analogously with the Rubik Cube. The problem, once again, is to reach a given configuration starting from any initial scrambled configuration.

A simple formal representation of the puzzle treats it in terms of strings of four symbols. Let A,B,C,D indicate the four differently coloured blocks of the square; any different configuration of the Rubik Square can be represented by a string composed of the four corresponding different symbols; for example the string CBAD represents a configuration where the colour C is in position 1, the colour B in position 2 and so on (under the convention that position 1 stands for the top left position, 2 for the top right, 3 for the bottom right and 4 for the bottom left).

One sees immediately that each rotation of the Rubik Square can be represented as a transformation of strings. The reader can verify that the admissible exchanges are: between symbols adjacent in the string (e.g. ABCD into DCBA) and between symbols in the left-most and right-most position (e.g. DCAB into BCAD). Thus the puzzle is represented by:

1. An initial configuration arbitrarily chosen, say BACD.
2. Some rules of transformation. We have the following rules:

ABCD---> BACD (exchanging the letters in positions 1 and 2;
call this transformation *u*)
ABCD---> ACBD (exchanging the letters in positions 2 and 3;
call this transformation *l*)
ABCD---> ABDC (exchanging the letters in positions 3 and 4;
call this transformation *d*)
ABCD---> DBCA (exchanging the left-most and the right-most
letter, i.e. the letters in positions 1 and 4; call this transformation
r)
3.   A final configuration, arbitrarily chosen.

Given an initial configuration (say BCDA) and a final one (say
ACDB) we must find the sequence of moves which transforms
BCDA into ACDB. Each of the three procedures (blind, satisficing
and intelligent) must specify a correct sequence of moves, for any
given pair of initial-final configurations. It is possible to write each
of the three procedures as a *program* which accepts as input a pair of
configurations (the initial and the final one), and generates as its
output a sequence of transformations (composed of the elementary
transformations *u*, *d*, *l*, *r*,) which produce the desired result. This
sequence therefore constitutes *a solution* to the given problem. I now
describe briefly the three procedures.

The *blind procedure* simply expands in orderly fashion all the
possible nodes, and tests, after any expansion, if the goal has been
achieved or not:[7] when a configuration which has already been
created reappears, the player does not expand further on the node,
and considers this node to be *terminal*; this configuration is considered a search failure because further expansions are useless and
the goal has not been reached. The computation proceeds until
either the desired goal has been reached (success) or all the possible
configurations have been generated without any result (failure).
Figure 8.1 shows an example of a tree created by a blind search,
starting from BCDA and searching for ABCD.

The reader can verify that the search has ended with a success;
starting from the pair (BCDA, ABCD) the blind search has produced the solution *uld*. The player has had to expand and visit
$4 + (4*4) + 4 + 2 = 26$ nodes before reaching the goal.

The satisficing procedure follows the same pattern as the blind
procedure (recursively transform the initial configuration and test

Figure 8.1   A tree created by a blind search

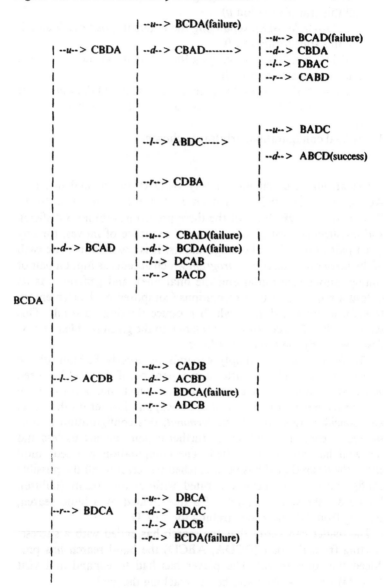

for success) but the player selects and expands only the 'more promising' nodes by means of an appropriate heuristic rule.

As usual in similar cases, let the rule be based on the 'distance' between the actual position and the desired position; decide to measure the distance by simply counting the number of letters which are in the desired position. For example, if ABCD is the goal, since ABDC has 2 letters, A and B, in the desired position, it has evaluation 2; in the same way ACDB has evaluation 1 and so on.

In Figure 8.2 for every string I have written a sequence of four binary numbers 0,1 : 1 below any letter of the string which is in the desired place; 0 otherwise. Summing the four numbers gives the 'distance' of the state from the goal. If, as happens in our example, more than one node has the same score, we simply choose the first one which has been expanded. The reader can easily verify that, as in the blind search, the player obtains the sequence *uld*, but now he has reached the goal after only 14 moves. Consider now the intelligent procedure. In order to solve the specific problem solved with the blind and the satisficing procedure, we must first find a general procedure with which to tackle the general problem of reaching any given configuration from any one initial configuration.

Clearly, if we can solve the problem of reaching the specific configuration ABCD starting from any one scrambled configuration, then we can solve any other problem.

Let the symbol # stand for 'don't care', i.e. that it does not matter which letter is placed in a given position; our problem can now be symbolized in the following form:

$$(\# \ \# \ \# \ \#)---> (ABCD)$$

This problem can be immediately divided into the following subproblems:

(P1)   Move A from the initial position in the string to position 1:
$$(\# \ \# \ \# \ \#)------> (A \# \ \# \ \#)$$

(P2)   Examine the element in position 2; if this is not B, then move B (which can only be in positions 3 or 4) to position 2 *leaving* A in the first position: $(A \# \ \# \ \# -----> (AB \# \ \#)$.

(P3)   If C and D are not in the required positions 3 and 4, exchange them:
$$(AB \# \ \#)--> (ABCD)$$

Figure 8.2   A tree created by the satisficing procedure

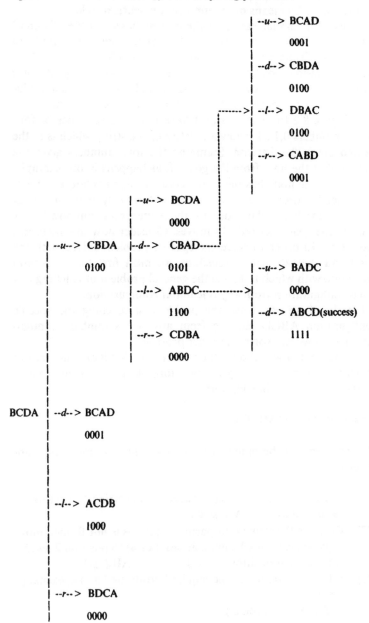

Figure 8.3   P1 decomposed into elementary problems

Can problem P1 be solved? If A is in position 2 or 4, yes, immediately, by using respectively the transformations *u* and *r*. But what happens if A is in position 3? In order to solve this problem we must be able to solve the following sub-problem:

(P11)   Move a letter from position 3 to 1: $(\#\#A\#)\text{-----}>$
        $(A\#\#\#)$

To solve the problem it is sufficient to combine two transformations: *lu* (of course, there are many other solutions; for example: *dr*). Figure 8.3 completely decomposes the problem P1 into elementary problems.

Let us turn to P2: here, either B is in position 3, and in this case the problem is solved by transformation *l*; or B is in position 4 and we must therefore use two transformations: *dl* (see Figure 8.4).

Finally, problem P3 is immediately solved by using *d*. We have now solved problem P for every initial condition by decomposing it

Figure 8.4   P2 decomposed into elementary problems

                | (A≠B≠)-----> (AB≠≠)-----> *l*
                |
(A≠≠≠)-----> (AB≠≠) |
                |
                | | (A≠≠B)-----> (A≠B≠)----> *d*
                | |
                | (A≠≠B)-----> (AB≠≠) |
                                           | (A≠B≠)-----> (AB≠≠)----> *l*

Figure 8.5   Decomposition of the original problem

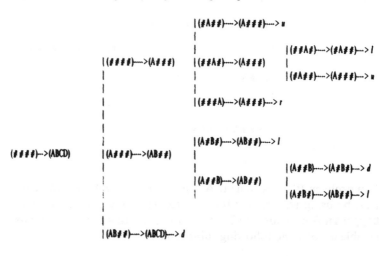

into a hierarchical structure of interconnected sub-problems. This is shown by Figure 8.5 which shows the decomposition of the original problem. The original problem has been decomposed into three sub-problems P1, P2, P3. Each of these is further decomposed until we arrive at elementary problems, i.e. problems which have been solved by means of one only elementary transformation.

Note that all sub-problems generated by a given problem are connected to each other either by an AND logical connection, or by an OR logical connection. The tree is therefore called a AND–OR tree; it represents the original problem as a 'cognitive structure', i.e. as a set of interconnected sub-problems which are either elementary ones or can be reduced to elementary ones.

We can now represent the 'intelligent' search. Assume that a player uses the procedure outlined above: he will execute the general program represented by the tree in Figure 8.5. If the problem is the same as in the blind and the satisficing procedures (transform BCDA into ABCD), then:

(P1)   The player moves A from the initial position in the string to position 1:

BCDA----> l-- > ACDB

(P2)   He examines the element in position 2; this is not B, then he moves B to position 2 *leaving* A in the first position. As B is in position 4, he uses the transformations *dr*:

$$ACDB ----- > dr-- > ABCD$$

(P3) C and D are in the required places 3 and 4, thus no further transformation is required, and the program has therefore generated three transformations with which to solve the problem:

$$BCDA ----- > ldr-- > ABCD$$

Therefore if we apply the *intelligent procedure* we reach the goal after only three steps.

Two points must be emphasized: first, many experimental observations show that real players behave *as if* they would execute the intelligent program outlined here. However, they do not *execute* the general program, applied to the specific case before them; on the contrary, as we will see later, they discover the specific solution *ldr* by creating only an incomplete, partial decomposition of the original problem. Second, it is very important to note that although the player expands respectively 20, 14 and 3 nodes, none of the three procedures can be considered 'the best', regardless of the number of times that the game is played. In fact the three procedures require a very different amount of time *to be discovered*, but how to measure the time required for the discovery of the three procedures is difficult. In order to compare the search times taken by these procedures we need a discovery program able to find them, say program D; for the discovery of each different procedure, D will use a different number of steps and will therefore provide us with a comparison between the search time of the three procedures.

The problem of the existence of procedures – like D – for creating programs is essentially the one that machine-learning theories deal with; for our purposes here suffice it to mention that there exists a wide range of such procedures, one of the most interesting being the procedure based on 'genetic algorithms' (Holland 1975, 1982). By using a simple program D, and denoting the number of steps for the discovery of the blind, the satisficing, and the intelligent procedure respectively by $N1$, $N2$, $N3$, it can be shown that $N1 < N2 < N3$. This means that – in our case – the more efficient the procedure, the more times it requires to be discovered.

Therefore in order to know which procedure is more convenient we must compare the *total* search times of the three procedures, i.e. a time computed by taking into account the number of times the procedure is used.

Let k stand for the number of times the game is played, and let respectively $n3$ and $n2$ denote the average number of steps required from the intelligent and the satisficing procedures to solve the puzzle.[8] The total number of steps required by the procedures 3 and 2 is respectively $N3 + n3\,k$ and $N2 + n2\,k$. Hence it follows that for

$$k > (N3 - N2)/(n2 - n3)$$

the intelligent procedure is more efficient than the satisficing one; this means that the intelligent procedure is preferable only if the game is repeated more than $(N3 - N2)/(n2 - n3)$ times. The same applies if we compare the blind procedure with the other two. Thus if we consider the three procedures as three different technologies for solving the same problem, the choice of the most efficient technology depends on the number, k, of times the technology is used – that is on the *dimension of the market*.

Before discussing the features of the 'intelligent' procedure in general, it is important to point out that there are many different ways by which this procedure can be used to divide a problem into sub-problems; the reader can verify that – for the Rubik Square – a way to proceed exists which gives rise to a division of problems different from the structure reported in Figure 8.5.[9]

We must now address the question in its most general sense. In the search for a program to give the solution of a problem, we can follow two different alternatives. The first is to perform a search in the *state space*, i.e. to explore (either in a blind or an oriented way) the different configurations of the given problem in order to reach the desired goal. A second approach is formally analogous with the first: move into the space of sub-problems and try to reduce the original problem to a set of solvable sub-problems. Although we are still concerned with an oriented search in a tree, the tree is no longer the game tree – the tree describing the states of the puzzle – but it is rather the *sub-problems tree*, whose nodes constitute the sub-problems which one sets oneself as the search progresses.

A notable difficulty arises here. In state space analysis there is a general procedure for identifying the best local strategy: it is sufficient to apply the rules of the game and (mechanically) generate new positions until a certain 'depth' has been reached.

An intelligent player, by contrast, cannot work in this mechanical way. His search for the solution occurs by *conjecturing* a possible sub-division of the original problem in the manner discussed above. This means that in his search the player decomposes the problem into a hierarchy of sub-problems *without knowing* whether they are solvable or not. He proceeds recursively in his division of problems until either he reaches elementary solved problems or an error forces him to revise his procedure. Indeed, errors play a fundamental role: since the error is always 'informed', the use of the information contained in the error allows the player to create new conjectures.

The example of Rubik's Cube clarifies what I have just said: the first conjecture is that he is able to sort out the cube's different sides sequentially (and independently). Were this conjecture true, the initial problem (changing the cube from its original scrambled to its final, ordered state) would be sub-dividable into sub-problems: sort out side one, side two, etc. Each of these sub-problems would be decomposable into a simpler sequence of sub-problems, and so on recursively until the player arrived at elementary problems.

However, as the search proceeds, this provisional technique will lead to failure: this is what happens when the novice player realizes that it is impossible to solve the sub-problems each independently from the other;[10] here it is precisely the error committed which shows the player that the sub-problems he identified at the start are *not independent*, and that, therefore, he must look for a new division into sub-problems which must be independent of each other. Thus the player *re-organizes* the problem.

I would like to point out that the most relevant result obtained from re-analysing the problems and decomposing them is the discovery of a new, more 'essential' representation of the same problem. Players who know that a given set of problems are solvable use them as building blocks in their further analysis and solution of problems. The problem solver most commonly operates in a situation characterized by the availability of a 'basis of knowledge', i.e. by the availability of a complex of problems which are known to be resolvable. The player is aware that some sub-problems can be solved (even if he may not know the solution) and he uses them to solve new problems. A typical example is that of proving theorems: a mathematician who wants to prove new theorems makes use of previous theorems using them as building blocks for the demonstration; he need *not* remember the proofs of the theorems every time he uses them; but treats them as 'synthetized knowledge' with a great economy of memory and thinking.

This situation shows that the conjectural division of problem solving is a process which gives rise to a division of knowledge: this division is a very efficient tool because it allows subjects to economize memory and thinking efforts, and vice versa allows a team to achieve complex goals which should be unattainable by a single individual with limited memory and rationality.

DIVISION OF LABOUR AND COORDINATION

Having previously defined the process of decision making in a more general and comprehensive way than has traditionally been the case, we need to discuss what the term 'coordinating different decisions' actually means.

A classical definition of the role of coordination has been provided by Coase:

> Outside the firm, price movements direct production, which is coordinated through a series of exchange transactions on the market. Within a firm, these market transactions are eliminated and in place of the complicated market structure with exchange transactions is substituted the entrepreneur-coordinator, who directs the production (Coase 1937).

Since a decision process essentially involves a problem-solving activity, one naturally wonders whether the coordination of different decisions will require a multi-actor problem-solving process. This multi-actor process actually exists in all institutions, but can be recognized more clearly within firms rather than outside, on markets.

Coordinating different decisions does not merely mean sending to independent individuals signals which enable them to take consistent decisions, as assumed by perfect competition analysis: we cannot trivially transfer perfect competition analysis to description of firm organization, assuming that agents are coordinated by an entrepreneur who sends consistent plans and projects, while the agents themselves are only mechanical executors.

The central reason why this model does not fit well with reality is that the activities of planning and building new projects inside the firm are *distributed* activities in an *evolving* environment: at the top of the hierarchy plans are formulated in very general terms, not in detail; at any different level of the hierarchy, the execution of plans requires the ability to interpret and adapt these general ideas or to reject them, and to solve the new problems arising from attempts to put plans into practice; a continuous process of transmission of information and knowledge among subjects is thus required and their coordination is possible only if a learning process takes place. As Chester Barnard suggested (1962), coordination involves essentially a process of organizational learning, which connects different groups cooperating to the solution of the current problems.

In order to fulfil projects and plans, the organization must therefore be able to define and re-define its internal tasks, i.e. it must define the way by which labour is internally divided. We thus come to an important point: the outcome of a problem-solving process performed by a team of individuals who want to undertake a project is the division of labour *and* the coordination among the divided parts. Coordination is the complementary part of the division of labour which follows the realization of a project; the further the division of labour proceeds, the more the different divided parts require coordination and the more information becomes dispersed.

The working hypothesis I propose is that the search in the problem space, based on the division of a given problem into sub-problems, is a model for the division of labour within the organizations. Let us emphasize that the search in the space of sub-problems is a highly uncertain and conjectural process. In fact when a problem has been decomposed into a set of sub-problems, generally not all the sub-problems will be immediately solvable and, consequently, they will in turn be decomposed into simpler ones.

The decomposition then recursively proceeds until all the 'relevant' sub-problems have been solved. The procedure 'by decomposition' is therefore a conjectural one:

- there is no set of decomposition rules which *a priori* allows agents to achieve a certain result, and
- subjects can verify the solvability of the original problem only when all the 'relevant' sub-problems have been solved.

This way of solving problems is characteristic of projecting and planning activities inside organizations: first a task is drawn up, on the presumption that it is feasible; then the main task is decomposed into different functional parts. This division proceeds recursively until every part of the project has been recognized as feasible. By consequence, the internal structure of organizations can be seen as one of the possible ways by which tasks are decomposed into sub-tasks and entrusted to functional sub-systems of the firm. The organization decentralizes tasks internally, structuring its procedures (routines) into parametrically connected sub-procedures. Note that this process of problem solving by division into independent sub-problems seems to suggest that the existence of hierarchies in organizations may be intrinsic to the method of solving problems: but it should be emphasized that there is usually more than one way of decomposing a problem, and that there are therefore an equal number of possible hierarchies; moreover, these hierarchies do not coincide with either the hierarchy of roles or of command within the organization, even though they define functional sub-systems within the system.

One point appears central: the division of problems structures tasks from 'macro' to 'micro', in the sense that whenever a certain problem is to be solved, it is represented as a combination of simpler problems, and so on recursively until a level of 'minimum detail' is reached where the problem yields an effectively executable task.

This macro–micro feature has many interesting consequences, but I shall stress here only one of them: the possibility of explaining the incompleteness of contracts. Note that when a contract is established between two agents, only very 'generic' characteristics are outlined, without entering the details; the contracts on the labour market are a striking example of this feature. In general, as Coase notes: 'The details of what the supplier is expected to do are not stated in the contract but are decided later by the purchaser' (Coase 1937).

It is easy to find actual organizations based on very different ways of defining tasks, as emerges from the difference between the Tayloristic model of organization, which defines even the most specific detail of elementary operations, and the Japanese model which allows notable elasticity for continuous definition and redefinition of sub-tasks within a general framework.

In both cases, the recursive nature of the division of problems allows for the incomplete formulation of projects and contracts presupposing, obviously, that human agents will be able to complete them, by resolving problems autonomously.

FINAL REMARKS

In the last paragraphs I have argued that the conjectural process of problem solving (the 'intelligent' procedure) can be viewed as a process of knowledge framing.

As a given problem is being solved, many different hierarchical cognitive structures of sub-problems can arise. These different hierarchies have been considered to be different structures of knowledge and it was suggested that inside organizations the division of knowledge and the division of labour proceeds in the same way. As we saw, different knowledge structures which solve the same problem cannot *generally* be compared for the purpose of establishing an order of efficiency, because the choice of the most efficient technology depends on the number of times the technology is used – that is on the *dimension of the market*.

Moreover, the division of the knowledge into independent parts allows different agents to know only a limited part of the whole problem, and therefore to develop a specific and local knowledge, as von Hayek noted (1945). It follows that the limits of memory and computation of each agent can be overcome by the organization, and complex tasks can be fulfilled. It must be remarked that plans and projects within firms are not merely executed by different subjects, but they necessarily require a multi-agent process of learning, a feature which allows us to rethink the relationship between market and hierarchies.

Within organizations, as we have seen, two complementary processes take place so that projects can be fulfilled and given tasks performed: the division of labour, and the coordination among the different divided parts. These are the two main features of the process of 'organizational learning' which any team must implement in order to perform given tasks.

The two processes are realized in very different ways by markets and by organizations. Markets mainly coordinate different activities, while organizations divide their activities into different sub-tasks and coordinate them. This difference is due to the fact that the internal organization of a firm pursues its goals in at least a partially conscious way (von Hayek 1945): to the extent that they are 'islands of conscious power' (Robertson 1930), firms are able to design the forms of cooperation which will enable them to realize their pre-established goals; that is to say, they are able to design their internal organization, and to modify this organization whenever it does not suit their purposes.

NOTES

1. See Nillson (1971, 1980) and Pearl (1984) for a deep discussion of the problem.
2. In the sense of Muth (1961).
3. It can be shown that puzzles and strategic games are special cases of a more general model of human reasoning, Post systems, which allow formalization of problem solving activity. Post invented a device – which has been proved to be equivalent to the Turing Machine – for formalizing the concept of *algorithm*. This device, now called Post canonical system, can be considered a general computational model for problem solving.

   Let $L = \{a1, a2, ... an\}$ be a finite set of symbols, called an *alphabet*. A *string* from L is any sequence $a_{i1}, a_{i2}...a_{i_m}$ of symbols from L.

   For any alphabet L we use write (as below) L^* to denote the set of all the strings from L. Denote with $S, S1, ..Sn..$ the strings from L^*.

   Post called *Production* a general rule of transformation between strings, which takes the form:

   $$g1\ S1\ g2\ S2....gm-1\ Sm\ gm \text{ ---> } h1\ Si1\ h2\ Si2\ ....Sin\ hn$$

   where:

   $g1, g2, ..gm, h1, h2, ...hn$ are given (fixed) strings; and the subscript $i1, i2, ..in$ are all from $1, 2, ...m$ and need not be distinct.

   A Post (canonical) system consists of:

   A finite alphabet L
   A finite subset of L^*, the subset A of the *axioms*
   A finite set of *Productions* of the form (1) above, whose fixed strings are in L^*.

   It can be shown that a canonical Post system is equivalent to a Turing Machine (Cutland 1980, Chapter 3; Minsky 1967).

4. Henceforth I use the word 'procedure' in a precise sense of algorithm, which (by the Church thesis) can be represented by means of a Turing Machine and mechanically executed. A computer program, or a detailed program for realizing given goals in an organization constitutes therefore 'procedures'; 'routine' is here a synonym of 'not completely specified procedure'; see also Nelson (1982), Nelson and Winter (1982), Winter (1982).
5. See Simon and Newell (1972), Chapter 1.
6. Note that there is no formal algorithm to assign these indicators, but only the experience of a large number of games; which leaves open the problem of how players can synthesize relevant information to obtain 'efficient' parameters.
7. See Nillson (1971) for further details.
8. From Figure 8.5 it is easy to see that the maximum number of steps required by the intelligent procedure is 5: the program *ludld*; $n3$ is approximately equal to 3, and $n2$ to 15.
9. See Dosi and Egidi (1991).

10. When a player has been able to arrange all the blocks of a certain colour into one identical side and attempts to repeat the exercise with the second side, he realizes that he is not able to effectuate the action without scrambling the side that has already been sorted out.

REFERENCES

Alchian, A. A. (1951) 'Uncertainty, Evolution and Economic Theory', *Journal of Political Economy*, vol. LVII, pp. 211–21.

Arrow, K. J. (1971) 'Economic Welfare and the Allocation of Resources for Invention' in Lamberton (1971).

Arrow, K. J. (1983) 'Innovation in Large and Small Firms' in Ronen (1983).

Barnard, C. (1962) *The function of the Executive*. Cambridge: Harvard University Press (1938).

Coase, R. (1937) 'The Nature of the Firm', *Economica*, 368–405.

Cutland, N. J. (1988) *Computability – An Introduction to recursive function theory*. Cambridge: Cambridge University Press.

Cyert, R. M., Simon, H. A. and Trow, D. B. (1956) 'Observation of a business decision', *Journal of Business* (29) pp. 237–48.

David, P. A. (1975) *Technical Choice, Innovation and Economic Growth*. Cambridge: Cambridge University Press.

Davies, M. (1958) *Computability and Unsolvability*. New York: McGraw-Hill.

Diamond, P. and Rothscild, M. (1978) (eds) *Uncertainty in Economics*. Orlando, Fla: Academic Press.

Dosi, G. and Egidi, M. (1991) 'Substantive and Procedural Uncertainty. An exploration of Economic Behaviours in Complex and Changing Environments', *Journal of Evolutionary Economics*, 1.

von Hayek, F. A. (1945) 'The Use of Knowledge in Society', *American Economic Review*, 35, no.4 pp. 519–30.

Hey, J. D. (1982) 'Search for Rules for Search', *Journal of Economic Behaviour and Organization*, vol. III, pp. 65–81.

Holland, J. H. (1975) *Adaptation in natural and artificial systems*. Ann Arbor: University of Michigan Press.

Holland, J. H., Holyoak, K. J., Nisbett, R. E. and Thagard, P. R. (1988) *Induction – Processes of Inference, Learning, and Discovery*. Cambridge, Mass: MIT Press.

Hopcroft, J. and Ullman, J. P. (1979) *Introduction to Automata Theory, Languages, and Computation*. Reading, Mass: Addison-Wesley.

Knight, F. H. (1957) *Risk, Uncertainty and Profit*. London: The London School of Economics and Political Science.

Lamberton, F. (ed.) (1971) *Economics of Information and Knowledge*. London: Penguin.

Lewis, A. A. (1986) *Structure and Complexity. The Use of Recursion Theory in the Foundation of Neo-classical Mathematical Economics and the Theory of Games*. Ithaca: Cornell University, Dept. of Mathematics, Mimeo.

Manna, Z. (1974) *Mathematical theory of Computation.* New York: McGraw-Hill.

March, J. G. (1988) *Decisions and Organizations.* Oxford: Blackwell.

McGuire, C. B. and Radner, R. (1972), *Decision and Organization.* Amsterdam: North-Holland.

McLelland, J. L. and Rumelhart, D. E. (1988) *Parallel Distributed Processing – Explorations in the microstructure of Cognition.* Cambridge, Mass: MIT Press.

Muth, J. F. (1961) 'Rational Expectations and the Theory of Price Movements', *Econometrica*, vol. XXIX, no. 3, pp. 315–35.

Nelson, R. R. (1982), 'The Role of Knowledge in R&D Efficiency', *Quarterly Journal of Economics.*

Nelson, R. R. and Winter, S. (1982) *An Evolutionary Theory of Economic Change.* Cambridge, Mass: The Belknap Press of Harvard University Press.

Nillson, N. J. (1971) *Problem Solving Methods in Artificial Intelligence.* New York, McGraw-Hill.

Nillson, N. J. (1980) *Principles of Artificial Intelligence.* Palo Alto: Tioga Publishing Company.

Pearl, J. (1984) *Heuristics.* Reading, Mass: Addison-Wesley.

Post, E. (1943) 'Formal reduction of the general combinatorial decision problem', *American Journal of Math.*, 65, pp. 197–215.

Robertson, D. H. (1930) *Control of Industry.* London: Nisbet.

Ronen, J. (1983) (ed.) *Entrepreneurship.* Lexington, Mass: D. C. Heath.

Shackle, G. L. (1969) *Decision, Order and Time in Human Affairs.* Cambridge: Cambridge University Press.

Simon, H. A. (1957) *Models of Man.* New York: Wiley.

Simon, H. A. (1963) 'Problem solving machines', *International Science and Technology*, 3(36), pp. 48–62.

Simon, H.A. (1969) *The sciences of the Artificial* (Carl Taylor Compton Lectures), Cambridge, Mass: MIT Press.

Simon, H. A. (1972a) 'From Substantive to Procedural Rationality' in McGuire, B. and Radner, R. (1972).

Simon, H. A. (1972b), 'Theories of Bounded Rationality' in McGuire, B. and Radner, R. (1972).

Simon, H. A. (1973) 'The Structure of Ill-Structured Problems', *Artificial Intelligence*, vol. IV.

Simon, H. A. (1979) 'Rational Decision Making in Business Organization', *American Economic Review*, vol. LXIX, pp. 493–513.

Simon, H. A. and Newell, A. (1972) *Human Problem Solving.* Englewood Cliffs, NJ: Prentice-Hall.

Stigliz, J. (1986) 'Learning to Learn', presented at the Conference on *The Economic Theory of Technology Policy.* CEPR, London, September 1986.

Trakhtenbrot, B. A. (1963) *Algorithms and Automatic Computing Machines.* Boston, Mass: D. C. Heath.

Turing, A. M. (1936) 'On Computable Numbers, with an Application to the Entscheidungsproblem', *Proceedings of the London Mathematical Society*, vol. XLIII, pp. 230–65.

Williamson, O. (1975) *Markets and Hierarchies: Analysis and Antitrust Implications.* New York: Free Press.

Williamson, O. (1985) *The Economic Institutions of Capitalism.* New York: Free Press.

Winter, S. G. (1982), 'An Essay on the Theory of Production' in Hymans, S. H. (ed.) *Economics and the World Around It*, Ann Arbor: Michigan University Press.

9. Cognitive Constraints of Economic Rationality

Riccardo Viale

Neoclassical economics is based on a theoretical hypothesis of the rational actor with the two following characteristics:

1. He knows all physically or even logically possible options, and all physically and logically possible states of the world which could be relevant to his decision.
2. As Bayes's agent, he has a coherent preference structure. Therefore, he is able to estimate his expected utility for each option and then choose the option with the highest expected utility.

In neoclassical economics, the rational agent is a maximizer.

In science there are two basic ways to control a theoretical hypothesis: (a) indirectly, by upholding the general propositions to which the hypothesis is deductively connected; (b) directly, through the control of factual, singular propositions that can be derived from the hypothesis, in the form of *explanandum* or initial conditions (according to the titular-deductive framework).

In posing the problem of controlling the theoretical hypothesis of the rational maximizing actor in neoclassical economics we can refer to either way.

CONTROL OF THEORETICAL SUPPORT OF THE RATIONAL ACTOR HYPOTHESIS

To which general propositions is the economic actor hypothesis connected in neoclassical economics?

According to Simon (1987, p. 26) this model of rational actor is mainly connected to the following hypotheses:

1. His beliefs about aims and values are given and not liable to change in time and through experience.
2. His beliefs are internally coherent.
3. The agent is capable of an objective description of the world.
4. His abilities to elaborate data to define his expectations, that is, respectively, his probabilistic and deductive reasoning, are not limited.

We could express these properties otherwise by saying that, in the neoclassical economic actor, perceptive rationality – the rationality which is assumed in the representations of informational data – and decisional rationality – the rationality which is assumed in inferential activities which lead from data to decisions – are non-limited (from the point of view of some prescriptive canons) (Viale 1991b).

These propositions of deductive support for the neoclassical rationality hypothesis may be, in principle, empirically controlled. Cognitive science has been engaged in testing them for some years, through experiments and observation.

Neoclassical *perceptive rationality* presupposes an objective representation of the world, in the form of coherently organized true beliefs.

Empirical control of this hypothesis has been effected mainly through cognitive study of perception and memory mechanisms and of the codes of representation of informational data (Viale 1991a). Up to now these controls have shown that the representation of informational data is often unreliable[1] and incoherent.[2]

Perception is a central theme in cognitive research. One of the standard approaches in the psychology of perception is based on so-called pattern recognition. People recognize the presentation of an object as an example of a certain pattern. Perception output implies a classification of the stimulus. The perceived stimulus is not a mere *qualia*, but a classification of a certain section of the environment. The perceptive stimulus is developed into a perceptive belief. Both Marr (1982) and Rock (1983) highlight different stages in perception. There is, in brief, a lower stage of 'perception of forms' in which the stimulus is not recognized and is characterized as round, elongated, etc. and there are higher stages in which access to long-term memory leads to the categorical recognition of the stimulus. All stages, however, require descriptions of the stimulus.

Perception is ultimately made up of two kinds of elaboration:

bottom–up elaboration, in which information flows from small perceptive inputs to larger units made up of those inputs, and top–down elaboration, in which background beliefs influence the interpretation of the most elementary perceptive units.

In language perception empirical evidence of the importance of context in the perception of words is available. We have, for instance, the 'reintegration of phoneme' effect when, in an experiment, the missing phonemes in a word are automatically and unconsciously restored by the listener so that they conform to the context.

The influence of memory on perception, on the other hand, has been shown by a number of experiments such as those on the visual perception of fragmented and incoherent images which, after having been identified with a given object, are then easily recognized through the previously memorized pattern.

As these examples clearly show, top–down elaboration of perceptive stimuli often tends to add something which was not present in the stimulus itself: some internal constructive process mediates between the entry stimulus and the perceptive result. This can lead to an improvement or to a decline in the reliability and truth of the perception, depending on the kind of perception and on individual mnemonic patterns.

A trade-off phenomenon between rapidity and reliability of perception is moreover evident. Strong emotions such as wishes and fears, generally related to primary needs, lead to an improvement in perception rapidity to the detriment of reliability. Partial correspondence of some portion of the perceptive stimulus with a memorized pattern having a high affective value is enough to produce a strong activation of the pattern itself and thus the recognition of the perception. For example, the child with an intense wish to see his mother will recognize her face in other women's features. At a pragmatic level such a phenomenon can have a positive value but, as far as the reliability and accuracy of our perception of reality are concerned, it is clearly not always so, and it is responsible for the production of false belief. In this case too the presence of such a phenomenon will be related to the particular emotional and affective constitution of the individual.

Another fundamental component of the correctness of informational inputs of perceptive rationality is related to the mechanisms of *memory*. The fact that an individual holds a belief now doesn't imply that he will hold it in the future. This depends on mnemonic power. In the same way, if a man has a belief today, because he thinks he had it some time ago, it is not certain that his belief is the same. That will depend on the accuracy and reliability of memorization mechanisms. The corpus of beliefs, the factual foundation of rationality, depends therefore on memory. As we know, memory can be subdivided into three sections: besides the memory of sensory information which does not concern us here, there is short-term memory (STM), where a small part of rapidly disappearing information can be stored and where the operational centre of the information processing is located, and long-term memory (LTM), which is the filing cabinet of information, with virtually unlimited capacity. I do not address myself here to the question whether short-term memory exists separately from long-term memory or corresponds to states activated by it.

The first consideration one has to make concerns which data base is used in the inference. Various experiments, as well as everyday observation, clearly show that the factual data base used often corresponds only to a part of the beliefs available in long-term memory and useful for inferences. People cannot gain access to a significant part of their knowledge and consequently the resulting inferences are generally wrong. Sometimes the individual cannot connect all elements, useful for inference, existing in his memory. If inference is a causal process in which the premises must be causally operative in producing a new belief, then, at a psychological level, only activated beliefs and not residual ones will be operative.

At the root of the problem of belief activation is apparently the codification process which determines the communications through which activation is propagated in the mnemonic system. Man codifies information in a semantic structure which goes beyond individual information. This can happen both at the time when the informative input presents itself and when the information is retrieved through memory. This often leads to a diminished reliability of memory. For instance people tend to develop the recollection of an event using information subsequent to the event itself. Moreover, one is not always able to make out the original sources of information.

Associated to memory we find the irrational phenomenon of perseverance in the belief, carefully studied by Nisbett and Ross (1980). People are inclined to preserve a belief even after it has been proved false by new evidence. The reason for this perseverance can be found in the emotional refusal of new beliefs, deemed unsatisfactory, and in the search for factual validation of old beliefs through the retrieval of supporting information from memory. This phenomenon seems to be, among other things, at the root of the confirmation bias, a phenomenon studied by the cognitive psychology of science, which points in the opposite direction to Popper's falsification rule.

There is also another characteristic of memory which goes against the rational principle of revision of beliefs in the face of new informational data. According to psychologists, long-term memory is not a blackboard from which propositions can be wiped out on the basis of new evidence. On the contrary, there seems to be no real loss of informational material from memory unless as a result of physical damage. Every piece of information memorized, and every belief acquired, is stored in memory and cannot be erased even after it has been proved false. If information material cannot be erased from memory, it will contain contradictions and time structures. The wrong steps worked out while solving a problem will be memorized together with the correct ones and may be recalled when the solution of the problem is undertaken again. Residual beliefs can, like the phoenix, always revive from long-term memory through a semantic interference with other beliefs causing an incorrect and incoherent answer. It is clear that also in the case of memory the tendency to incoherence or to accuracy of beliefs will show individual degrees of variation.

At the root of the availability of information inputs are the cognitive modalities through which information is represented. They are another powerful cognitive constraint against the hypothesis of objective representation of the world in neoclassical rationality.

One first general fact emerging from cognitive research is the pervasiveness of hierarchical organization in mental representations (Goldman 1986, pp. 228–37). Hierarchically structured representations can be identified in the structure of linguistic propositions, in semantic memory, in visual representations, in time sequences as well as in other domains, such as behaviour planning and problem solving. There is, moreover, a pervasive tendency to favour certain hierarchical organizations and certain compositions of the represented phenomena: in vision, only certain parts are recognized as such, memorized and exploited to recall the whole picture (Bower and Glass 1976); a musical sequence is hierarchically memorized – according to the laws of pictorial completeness, similar to those of the *gestalt* – and is retrieved through a top–down mechanism (Deutsch and Feroe 1981); representation of movement, too, takes place according to cognitive constraints which tend to favour the interpretation of movement of solid bodies, along straight lines and towards objects which are nearer than others (Ullman 1979).

Hierarchization can often result in errors and distortions which make of mental representations an unfaithful image of reality. On the other hand, hierarchization contributes to the power and flexibility of the cognitive activity. Since it makes it possible to move from one level to another, varying the resolution level of the analysis according to the problem and the decision maker's 'interests', it allows one to highlight only details which are significant from the contextual point of view, disregarding all others. Besides, hierarchization considerably increases the power of mnemonic retrieval. When a plan of action has to be decided upon, for instance, one should be able to represent in STM the various stages of the plan and its consequences. Because of space limitations in STM this is not possible. The bottleneck can be bypassed by sub-dividing the plan into various related parts and focusing on them one at a time. This is possible because in LTM the 'plan' macro-unit is hierarchically organized in 'stage' micro-units of the plan itself.

Substantially, many authors seem to agree on the characteristics of hierarchical organization in mental representations; opinion is more divided about the forms of the representations. A common feature shared by a number of cognitive scientists is the unvarying tripartition of representations: according to Langley, Simon et al. (1987) the three possible forms are list structures, propositional representations and images; according to Johnson-Laird (1983) mental models, propositional representations and images; according to Anderson (1983) time sequences, abstract propositions and space images; etc.

The form of representation which seems to play a central role in the peculiar human way of representing informational data is the image. As explained by Kossylin (1981) the mental image is an instrument of representation much more powerful than the proposition. It allows the simultaneous and interdependent representation of information such as shape, size, orientation and position of an object. The mental image is however susceptible to various forms of interference. Since representations having higher emotional content, concreteness, simplicity and ability to evoke other images will be preferred, distorting effects on the accuracy of the representation of reality may often ensue.

Serious cognitive constraints to the 'Olympian' pretences of neoclassical rationality have also been empirically brought to attention in regard to *decisional rationality*. In elaborating the available data to define expectations about environment and agent and to select, on the basis of these expectations, the most appropriate action, people seem to deviate from the rules underlying the neoclassical rational agent.

This is evident in many studies of *probabilistic reasoning*, which have shown that man forms estimates about the likelihood of future events, assigns numbers and percentages, combines probabilities and values in a way which does not conform to the theory of probability.[3] Only a brief reference to these empirical results will be mentioned here.

The selection of information deemed relevant for decisional purposes is not carried out through an exhaustive examination at mnemonic level of all relevant information (Tversky and Kahneman 1973). Man tends to select examples of large classes rather than of small ones, even if they are just as relevant in the decisional context (heuristic of availability).

Another tendency discovered by Tversky and Kahneman is the propensity to give counter-normative judgements according to the degree to which the salient characteristics of an object or person are representative of or similar to characteristics conceived as peculiar to some category. This is known as the heuristic of representativity. Representativity is formally described by a relation between a model M and some event X associated with that model. A sample X is more or less representative of a model M.

Four kinds of cases can be identified in which the heuristic of representativity may be present:

1. M is a class and X is one value of a determined variable in that class: the average income of the teachers in a school may be thought as representative of that class.
2. M is a class and X is an example of that class: Rita Levi Montalcini may be considered as being representative of Italian scientists.

  ` 3. *M* is a class and *X* is a sub-set of *M*: Post Office workers may be considered more representative of the category of Italian civil servants than the employees of the Ministry of Culture.
  4. *M* is a causal system and *X* one possible consequence: Keynesian economic policy (*M*) can be considered a cause of Italian national debt (*X*).

In these cases *X* may cause a counter-normative judgement of the characteristics of *M* since the judgement of *M* is completely oriented (biased) by the sample *X*, and it disregards the general characteristics of *M*.

Various studies have compared probability estimates made by people with the estimates that should be derived from Bayes's theorem. Some experiments have shown that subjects underestimate the effects of new evidence and that this underestimate is reflected in their evaluation of the subsequent probability, evaluated as lower than predicted by Bayes's theorem. This behaviour has been called conservative by Edwards (1968).

On the other hand, subjects have more often been found to ignore completely, in certain situations, prior probability. Tversky and Kahneman (1985) conducted some well known experiments on this using the 'taxi-cab problem'. Prior probability seems to combine correctly with new evidence only when the former is interpreted in a causal way and when the nature of the other evidence is not more specific than the data of the prior probability.

The importance of causal patterns in everyday reasoning has been pointed out in many experiments. Several of them refer not to statistical reasoning but to the more general phenomenon of causal attribution (Nisbett and Ross 1980). Standard interpretation of this kind of experiments differentiates between causal reasoning (from cause to effect) and diagnostic reasoning (from effect to cause). People feel more at ease with causal reasoning. Even when the information content is the same in both directions, people favour the causal pattern over the diagnostic one.

Bayes's information model, on the other hand, considers only the information content and ignores the difference between causal and diagnostic reasoning. This is another instance in which the normative model obviously breaks away from the actual decisional behaviour of people.

A decision is generally elaborated by combining probabilistic and *deductive reasoning*.[4] One implicit logical form which can often be identified in the argument at the basis of inferences is the syllogism. In it premises and conclusion can have various forms, among them universal, particular, probabilistic or hypothetical propositions, so that we can speak of categorical syllogisms, statistical syllogisms and quasi-syllogisms.

Empirical results of experiments on syllogistic reasoning have shown very low levels of performance. One of the first theories on performance in syllogistic reasoning was suggested by Woodworth and Sells (1935). With their 'atmosphere effect' theory they maintained that people cannot reason logically because of the nature of the premises which creates an atmosphere leading the subject to derive certain conclusions. More specifically, they suggest that positive premises lead the subject to accept positive conclusions while negative premises lead him to negative conclusions. If one of the premises is positive and the other negative, then the subject inclines towards a negative conclusion.

They also took into consideration universal propositions (such as, 'all As are B') and particular propositions (such as 'some As are B'). According to the atmosphere effect, universal premises predispose people to accept a universal conclusion while a particular conclusion is accepted after particular premises. The subject also prefers a particular conclusion when one premise is universal and the other particular.

The atmosphere effect theory has been questioned by Johnson-Laird and Steedman (1978). According to the atmosphere effect subjects should have been equally ready to accept each of the wrong conclusions in the following syllogisms:

1. Some As are B
    Some Bs are C
    Then some As are C
2. Some Bs are A
    Some Cs are B
    Then some As are C

The subjects in the experiment were more inclined to accept the wrong conclusion in syllogism 1 than in 2. This has been explained with the presence of another particularly strong and resilient phenomenon: the 'figural effect'. People tend to accept a conclusion having

A as subject and C as conclusion if there is a chain leading from A to B in one premise and from B to C in the other.

A further difficulty in the atmosphere effect theory comes from alternative interpretations of the same experimental results. According to some, a wrong conclusion may be accepted because of a bad interpretation of the premises. According to Chapman and Chapman (1959) and their 'conversion hypothesis', subjects commonly interpret in an inverted way both universal affirmative propositions ('all As are B' is understood as 'all Bs are A'), and negative particular propositions ('some As are not B' is understood as 'some Bs are not A').

In deductive inference the scientist does not follow some law of formal logic but appears to be developing a mental model, using whatever means at his disposal, with the aim of representing significant information in an easily accessible and manageable way. In syllogistic inference, according to Johnson-Laird (1983), first a representation of the inference symbol is developed, and then a mental model of the first premise is formed. The information of the second premise is then added to the mental model of the first premise. The conclusion finally reached expresses the relation between the symbols existing in all the models of the premises. A control of the resulting model is then enacted through the search for an interpretation of the premises which is incoherent with the model. If that is not achieved then the inference is valid.

One of the most important inference rules that has been studied till now is the *modus ponens* of material implication. It rules that given the proposition 'if A then B', and given also A, then one can validly infer B.

Most people find little difficulty in accepting arguments based on the *modus ponens*, but often have problems with another inference rule known as *modus tollens*. This rule dictates that, given the proposition 'if A then B', and given also the fact that B is false, we can infer that A is false.

Both these inference rules seem quite obvious, but people find some difficulty in applying them. The difficulty arises from the inability to behave in a way which fits with the correct interpretation of the rules, and from the inclination to draw conclusions which are not justified.

1. As far as the rule of the *modus ponens* is concerned, it is not

justified to conclude that B is false on the basis of the premises 'if A then B' and 'non-A'.

2. As far as the rule of the *modus tollens* is concerned it is not justified to conclude that A is true on the basis of the premises 'if A then B' and 'B'.

In human reasoning the drawing of false conclusions based on 1 and 2 has often been observed.

Rips and Marcus have worked experimentally using hypothetical examples (1977). They submitted all possible combinations of premises and conclusions. In the case of the *modus ponens* all subjects selected the correct conclusions. With propositions of other kinds, however, a large proportion of subjects made logical errors from the point of view of the logic of material implication.

In case 1, for instance, one cannot say that B is 'never' true since that cannot be ascertained. Yet 16 per cent of the subjects gave 'never' as an answer. This particular error is called 'fallacy in the denial of the antecedent'.

Another example has to do with case 2 which, as the former, is not a valid inference. A cannot be said to be 'always' true, even if it can be true sometimes. Yet 23 per cent of answers maintained that it was 'always' true. This error is known as 'fallacy in the affirmation of the consequent'.

Many errors were found also in the application of the *modus tollens* rule. The correct conclusion in the *modus tollens* is that A is 'always' false, but only 57 per cent of the answers were of this kind. Thirty-nine per cent answered 'sometimes'.

The conclusions of these studies seem to point to two important principles (Viale 1989, p. 123):

1. Individuals do not behave in accordance with the logical principle of trying to falsify a rule, except in particular circumstances.

2. These circumstances are those in which the interpretation of the problem is achieved through its mapping out in a description of the situation existing in memory, which successfully incorporates a suitable testing procedure. Just as problem-solving procedures are determined by the initial representation of the problem itself, the same is true of this particular test of logical reasoning.

Not only does the precise form of the problem determine the

strategies used by the subject; it has also been found that, even if a correct answer has been given to a specific concrete problem, the subject rarely behaves correctly when faced with a subsequent abstract version of the problem itself. In brief, he doesn't even appear to have learned to transfer his knowledge from the concrete situation to a structurally identical abstract one.

Logical properties of conditionals are determined by the inter-related propositions and by the kind of relation they represent. Every proposition generally defines its own context and in the case of the conditional this is achieved in three ways: once for the antecedent, once for the consequent and once for the relation between the two. According to the seemingly more plausible theory, the subject uses his beliefs and knowledge stemming from the interpretation of the conditional to develop a mental model of a scenario in which the antecedent will come true. At this point the consequent is interpreted in the light of that model and scenario (Johnson-Laird 1983, pp. 54–62).

CONCLUSION

To conclude, empirical control of the propositions at the basis of the model of rational actors in neoclassical economics appears to falsify them.

Common man's inferential and decisional performances diverge from the prescriptions of the hypotheses underlying maximizing rationality. This reason alone would be enough to reject the hypothesis itself.

Advocates of the neoclassical model could object that these conclusions apply only to the common man, while economic theory is interested in an economic actor capable of surviving in the market by learning. This, however, is merely a peripheral objection, since the results of cognitive research have established systematic limitations to the expression of maximizing rationality which are built into the psycho-physiological structure of the decision maker. These constraints are therefore present and active in various contextual and learning situations, among which are market situations (which have been the object, among other things, of experimental research in cognitive science).

For the sake of methodological completeness one could also

control the factual predictions inferred from the model of neoclassical rationality. If the predictions too were falsified by empirical data of an economic kind, one would have another strong argument against preserving the hypothesis of maximizing rationality.

CONTROL OF THE FACTUAL CONSEQUENCES OF THE RATIONAL ACTOR HYPOTHESIS

There are two main ways of controlling the factual consequences of an economic theory: through observation in artificial experiments; or through historical recording in the so-called natural experiments.

From a methodological point of view economists are rather doubtful about whether *artificial experiments* can be considered as a reliable testing ground for the rational actor theory. There are three specific constraints for an experiment to be acceptable by economists (Hogarth and Reder 1986, pp. 11–13):

1. Subjects in the experiment must have experience as maximizing actors in the specific market sector.
2. Subjects must be appropriately motivated so that rewards are a progressive function of the correctness of their answers.
3. Experimental settings must correspond with a context in which competition market forces are active.

These constraints stem from one of the fundamental conditions of the rational actor theory: only through competition do individual actions become liable to that learning feedback which forces them either to become competitive, hence maximizing, or retire.

Kahneman and Tversky (1987, pp. 90–91) have questioned the actual possibility of learning of this kind in actual market conditions: feedback is often inadequate because there is no clear connection with the results; variability of environment diminishes feedback reliability; there is often no clear information on the consequences of alternative decisions; many decisions do not occur a second time and therefore are not useful for learning purposes.

This strict methodological requirement does not therefore seem to have much foundation. However, some experiments have been carried out in recent years to try to reproduce the conditions of choice outlined by economists. Results are contradictory. In some experiments which aimed at reproducing motivational patterns in relation to the correctness of answers, results have been counternormative. Recently Thaler (1987) and Kahneman and Tversky (1987) have quoted studies in which an inverse relation between incentives and rational behaviour has emerged. Other studies, conducted on experts in experimental realistic setting, have highlighted a proportion of errors analogous to the one on non-expert groups (Eddy 1982).

Kahneman and Tversky (1987) have put forward a possible interpretation of these results, assuming the importance of the framing effect in making the problem of choice plain or opaque. When in the problem context the presence of disturbing elements does not allow the creation of a well structured problem space, then the problem becomes opaque and even the expert is inclined to behave in an irrational way.

In artificial experiments the possibility of selecting and isolating the most relevant decisional variables allows, in principle, direct control of the maximizing rationality hypothesis. Verifying the rational choice hypothesis in the so-called *natural experiments* is a different matter.

Economic science has a pre-eminently deductive nature. Given the general framework of the rational choice hypothesis – in its enlarged version of constrained maximization of the utility function or in the restricted version of maximization of expected utility – economists are interested in extending the applicable domain of the hypothesis. This is achieved through various conventional strategems, but chiefly through an abundant use of suitable, and often *ad hoc*, auxiliary assumptions, which protect the rational choice hypothesis from falsifications, without increasing the empirical content of the theory.

This protection is often also achieved in a more 'metaphysical' way through the extension of the explicative domain to areas where significant empirical control data are not available.

The confirmation of deductive consequences in neoclassical economics is therefore often reached by adding auxiliary hypothesis of a factual kind, with the function of defining the situation. As Simon (1987, p. 28) maintains, without these factual assumptions on the forms of the utility function, on the way in which agents form expectations about the future or on their attention to specific environmental variables, the maximization of utility hypothesis offers no predictive or explicative value. The limited usefulness of the maximizing hypothesis is proved by the fact that, in many cases, it can be replaced by much weaker hypotheses of 'satisficing' behaviour without any loss of explicative power. Some examples given by Simon (1987, pp. 29–38) are enlightening in this respect.

One example comes from Becker's numerous efforts at extending the rational choice hypothesis to domains outside the traditional boundaries of economic science. Becker's theory (1981) on education and intergenerational mobility, or his other theory (1981) on the dynamics in the American family after World War II are an example. In the former he aims at proving that remedial educational programmes cannot reach their purpose because parents of attending children reallocate elsewhere the resources they would have invested in their children. This is based on the assumption that the parents' utility grows in positive terms with their consumption and their children's income and that the children's income is an additive function of the parents' investment and their children's fortune. The conclusion thus does not depend on the maximization hypothesis, but from the auxiliary assumption – empirically unchecked – that the interaction between fortune and income is of an additive rather than a multiplicative kind. Maximization of utility in this case is a condition neither necessary nor sufficient for the compensatory behaviour of parents.

As far as the second example is concerned, according to Becker (1981), the steadily growing proportion of married women in the workforce has been a consequence of the growth in women's wage power as the American economy has developed. This has led to an increase of the housewife's cost of choice and has raised the relative cost of children, with a subsequent reduction in their demand.

According to Simon (1987, p. 31) the whole of Becker's explanation is based on an unexplained change in the demand curve of women's labour. In this case, too, action depends not on the hypothesis of maximization of utility but on factual assumptions about change or stability of demand and offer curves.

Among the examples offered by Simon (1977, pp. 33–4) to illustrate the fundamental – rather than merely auxiliary – role played by auxiliary assumptions, one of the clearest is the explanation of the economic cycle. Both in Keynes's (1936) interpretation and in the opposite one by Lucas (1981), the economic cycle is explained not in reference to maximization hypotheses but to the 'money illusion' which workers, according to Keynes, and businessmen, for Lucas, undergo. The former cannot differentiate between changes in real and in nominal wages, while the latter cannot differentiate between general changes in prices and changes in their own industry. Both supplementary assumptions refer to processes leading agents to form certain expectations about future events. Only by studying empirically these processes would it therefore be possible to formulate an empirical theory, capable of genuinely explicating and predicting the economic cycle.

To conclude, both the control of the general propositions at the basis of the model of rational actor and the control of the factual consequences of this theory seem negative.

The successful explanation of the economic behaviour doesn't rely only on the neoclassical theory of rational actor plus the initial conditions but needs the *post hoc* addition of new assumptions. These assumptions, in many cases, have the form of empirical psychological laws about economic decision making. These laws often add empirical content to the theory; therefore their introduction may be considered not *ad hoc* and then accepted.[5] But in many cases they rob the neoclassical theory of the rational actor of its predictive primacy. The 'maximizing' theory itself becomes an auxiliary assumption that may be substituted by the 'satisficing' one without any loss of explicative power.

In other cases the *post hoc* assumption doesn't add any empirical content nor function as a semantical device to define the situation.

These are typical *ad hoc* adjustments that show the inadequacy of the theory.

NOTES

1. The reliability of a mental activity like perception or memory may be evaluated by the rate of true beliefs it is able to generate. In this case truth may be defined as some kind of correspondence between belief–real world ('realist' position) or as some kind of internal coherence between prediction and predicted fact ('instrumentalist' position). A belief is a mental state whose content may be not only a proposition but also an image or a mixture of the two, as in the mental models (Johnson-Laird 1983).

   While it is likely to find some ways to prove the correspondence or quasi morphism between a mental image and a real fact this seems much more difficult. In this case the instrumentalist position seems much more comfortable even if not without problems (Viale 1991a).
2. A logical incoherence is usually considered a flaw which must be promptly

eliminated. There are two reasons for this: because any proposition can be derived from a contradiction; and because at least one of the two propositions must be false. The rule prescribes therefore the prompt identification and elimination of the incoherence. This is not so desirable, however, from a pragmatic and epistemic point of view. First, a coherent belief system is not necessarily better than an incoherent one, from the point of view of its truth. It could be a coherent system of false beliefs. In addition, when faced with an incoherent belief system, it is sometimes better to wait for further data before proceeding to eliminate the incoherence, so as to be sure that a true belief is not being sacrificed in favour of a false one. Sometimes, therefore, pragmatic and epistemic reasons prevail over the reasons of logic.

3. There are arguments against the pretension of adopting some theory of probability as a canon for the rationality of probabilistic inferences (Cohen 1981, pp. 319–20). The concept of probability has not found a universally accepted interpretation yet. If we take as syntactic reference point Kolmogorov's (1950) axiomatization – where probability is axiomatically defined in terms of sets and theory of measure – various definitions can be considered coherent in relation to the constraints set up by axiomatization: the frequentist definition (Reichenbach 1949; von Mises 1957), according to which the probability of an event is the limit towards which the relative frequency of the event tends when the number of occurrences tends to infinity; the subjectivistic definition (Ramsey 1931; de Finetti 1931), according to which the probability of an event is the degree of confidence that an individual has, on the basis of the knowledge he possesses at a given moment, that the event will occur; Carnap's (1950) conception of probability as logical connection between propositions; Popper's (1959) and Mellor's (1971) conception of probability as causal propensity etc. All these interpretations seem to conform to the constraints of Kolmogorov's axiomatization. The choice of any one interpretation as a rational canon is not indifferent, however. First, probability is treated as a function of propositions if it is measured as a degree of subjective confidence or established as a logical relationship; as a function of sets if it refers to relative frequencies; as a function of properties if it refers to causal propensities. These different functions are not equally appropriate to the evaluation of the probability of events. Second, while different degrees of subjective probability of an event are not considered mutually incoherent, the assertion of different relative frequencies, of different logical relationships or of different causal propensities about the same event are logically incoherent.

In the face of these differences it is difficult to decide which interpretation is viable as a theory of human probabilistic inferences without relying on an empirical evaluation, based on people's intuitive judgements of appropriateness.

Furthermore, if the syntactic characterization of Komogorov is apt for the previous semantic interpretations, its appropriateness is dubious where other, non-classical interpretations are concerned.

Finally, one can apply to these axiomatizations, as in the case of the truths of logic, the consideration that their ultimate foundation can only be of an intuitive sort. It does not seem possible to do without intuition, both when evaluating which semantic interpretation is viable as a theory of human probabilistic inferences, and where the ultimate foundations of syntactic axiomatization in the theory of probability are concerned.

4. Various arguments can be opposed to the pretension of assuming classical logic as the canon of deductive rationality (Cohen 1981, pp. 318–19; Johnson-Laird 1983, pp. 26–8, pp. 34–9; Viale 1989, pp. 111–15): if classical logic were accepted as the canon of deductive inferential rationality one would reach the absurdity of having to accept the countless conclusions, trivial but correct, which are implied

by a set of valid premises. This would have fatal consequences for man's ability to adapt to his environment. Other inferential rules are therefore needed to select and skim significant deductions from trivial ones. This seems to be the function of the heuristics which select relevant conclusions, according to feedback of a contextual and pragmatic kind, and are usually, but not always, able to preserve the semantic informational content of the premises. Secondly, it is not clear why one should favour classical logic over any of the several types of logic which have been developed in our century: modal types of logic, which offer the advantage of formalizing the concepts of possibility and necessity, or non-monotonic types of logic and 'fuzzy' logic, which can emulate the ambiguity, poor resolution and contradictoriness of human reasoning. Third, justifying the validity of a logical theory is one thing; ascertaining the possibility of its application to cognitive reality is a different matter. In the case of propositional calculus, for example, its application has to do with the meaning assigned to the logical particles 'if', 'and', 'or', based on the intuitively perceived legitimacy of deductive relations between the propositions where these particles appear. Fourth, there is one final consideration underlying this whole line of reasoning: outside intuition, there is no logical theory through the application of which one can justify the validity of human inferences, since logic itself finds its ultimate justification is human intuition. The main strategy aimed at avoiding the recourse to intuition in founding the truth of logic is obviously ineffective: the empirical–inductive strategy sets logic as an adjunct to science and grounds logical truth on the truth of the holistic system which forms scientific knowledge. This strategy is not effective both because of the classical arguments against neopositivism and for the impossibility of establishing important methodological principles in the methodology of science, such as simplicity, coherence and generality, without resort to intuition.

5. The principle of the acceptability of a theoretical adjustment on the basis of the increase of the empirical content may be found in many authors, for example in Popper (1959) and Lakatos (1970). This normative principle has found a descriptive support from some methodological and historical studies (Donovan, Laudan and Laudan 1988).

The possibility of new theoretical adjustments through the introduction of auxiliary hypotheses is allowed when the *ceteris paribus* clause is not put in the unproblematic background knowledge. In general it is always preferably a conventional decision, among the scientists, on when to put this clause on the unproblematic background knowledge and consequently on when stopping the *post hoc* introduction of new assumptions and initial conditions that may save the theory under control. Usually this decision should be taken when, after a certain number of theoretical adjustments, the new empirical content has not found any kind of empirical confirmation.

REFERENCES

Anderson, J. (1983) *The architecture of cognition.* Cambridge, Mass: Harvard University Press.

Becker, G. S. (1981) *A treatise on the family.* Cambridge, Mass: Harvard University Press.

Bower, G. H. and Glass, A. L. (1976) 'Structural Units and the re-integrative power of picture fragments', *Journal of Experimental Psychology*, 2, pp. 456–66.

Carnap, R. (1950) *Logical foundations of probability*. Chicago: Chicago University Press.

Chapman, L. J. and Chapman, J. P. (1959) 'Atmosphere effect reexamined', *Journal of Experimental Psychology*, 58, pp. 220–6.

Cohen, J. L. (1981) 'Can human irrationality be experimentally demonstrated?' *The Behavioural and Brain Sciences*, 4, pp. 318–20.

de Finetti, B. (1931) 'Sul significato soggettivo delle probabilita', *Fundamenta Mathematica*, 17, pp. 298–329.

Deutsch, D. and Feroe, J. (1981) 'The internal representation of pitch sequences in tonal music', *Psychological Review*, 88, pp. 503–22.

Donovan, A., Laudan, L. and Laudan, R. (1988) *Scrutinizing science*. Dordrecht: Kluwer.

Eddy, D. M. (1982) 'Probabilistic reasoning in clinical medicine: problems and opportunities', in Kanheman, D., Slovic, P. and Tversky, A. (eds) *Judgement under uncertainty: heuristics and biases*. Cambridge: Cambridge University Press.

Edwards, W. (1968) 'Conservatism in human information processing', in Kleinmuntz, B. (ed.) *Formal Representation of Human Judgement*. New York: Wiley.

Goldman, A. (1986) *Epistemology and cognition*. Cambridge, Mass: Harvard University Press.

Hogarth, R. and Reder, M. (1986) 'Introduction: perspectives from economics and psychology', in Hogarth, R. and Reder, M. (eds) *Rational Choice*. Chicago: University of Chicago Press.

Johnson-Laird, P. N. (1983) *Mental models*. Cambridge: Cambridge University Press.

Johnson-Laird, P. N. and Steedman, M. (1978) 'The psychology of syllogisms', *Cognitive Psychology*, 10.

Kahneman, A., and Tversky, D. (1987) 'Rational choice and the framing of decisions', in Hogarth, R. and Reder, M. (eds) *Rational Choice*. Chicago: University of Chicago Press.

Keynes, J. M. (1936) *The general theory of employment, interest and money*. London: Macmillan.

Kolmogorov, A. N. (1950) *A foundation of probability*. New York: Chelsea.

Kossylin, S. (1981) *Image and mind*. Cambridge, Mass: Harvard University Press.

Lakatos, I. (1970) 'Falsification and the methodology of scientific research programmes', in Lakatos, I. and Musgrave, A. (eds) *Criticism and the growth of knowledge*. Cambridge: Cambridge University Press.

Langley, P., Simon, H. A., Bradshow, G. L. and Zytkow, J. M. (1987) *Scientific Discovery*. Cambridge, Mass: MIT Press.

Lucas, R. E. (1981) *Studies in business cycle theory*. Cambridge, Mass: MIT Press.

Marr, D. (1982) *Vision*. San Francisco: Freeman.

Mellor, D. H. (1971) *The matter of chance*. Cambridge: Cambridge University Press.

Nisbett, R. E. and Ross, L. (1980) *Human inference: Strategies and shortcomings of social judgement*. Englewood Cliffs, NJ: Prentice-Hall.

Popper, K. (1959) *The logic of scientific discovery*. London: Hutchinson.

Ramsey, F. P. (1931) *The foundations of mathematics*. London: Routledge.

Reichenbach, H. (1949) *The theory of probability*. Berkeley: University of California Press.

Rips, L. J. and Marcus, S. L. (1977) *Supposition and the analysis of conditional sentences*. Hillsdale, NY: Erlbaum.

Rock, I. (1983) *The logic of perception*. Cambridge, Mass: MIT Press.

Simon, H. (1987) 'Rationality in psychology and economics', in Hogarth, R. and Reder, M. (eds) *Rational Choice*. Chicago: University of Chicago Press.

Thaler, R. (1987) 'The psychology and economics', in Hogarth, R. and Reder, M. (eds) *Rational Choice*. Chicago: University of Chicago Press.

Tversky, A. and Kahneman, D. (1973) 'Availability: a heuristic for judging frequency and probability', *Cognitive Psychology*, 5, pp. 207–32.

Tversky, A. and Kahneman, D. (1980) 'Causal schemas in judgements under uncertainty', in Fishbein, M. (ed.) *Progress in social psychology*. Hillsdale, NJ: Erlbaum.

Ullman, S. (1979) *The interpretation of visual motion*. Cambridge, Mass: MIT Press.

Viale, R. (1989) *Epistemologia, cognizione e razionalità deduttiva*. Milano: Feltrinelli.

Viale, R. (1991a) *Metodo e società nella scienza*. Milano: Franco Angeli.

Viale, R. (1991b) *Cognizione e razionalità delle credenze nelle scienze sociali*. Roma: LUISS.

von Mises, R. (1957) *Probability, statistics and truth*. London: Allen & Unwin.

Woodworth, R. S. and Sells, S. B. (1935) 'An atmosphere effect in formal syllogistic reasoning', *Journal of Experimental Psychology*, 18, pp. 459–82.

10. Implications for Economics

Robin Marris

The main task of this final chapter is to discuss some implications for economics of the contributions in the rest of the book. First, however, it is desirable to summarize the present author's impression of the cognitive aspects, i.e. the dominant theme, of the totality, not only as found in the progressive unfolding of Herbert Simon's extraordinary contribution from the 1950s[1] to the present day, but also as found in the other authors' contributions. In addition (before attacking the main task) it will be necessary to indicate the present author's own view of the human animal's thinking processes: despite his deep admiration for all the ideas of Herbert Simon[2] and of the other contributors, there are some aspects of their collective viewpoint on that topic with which he does not entirely agree.

Unlike the other contributors to the book, the present author was in the position to exercise, in effect, a *droit de seigneur*, in that he had all the other contributions in front of him when writing his own. Consequently the present text is illustrated with boxes containing edited paraphrased extracts from the other texts. These are not necessarily selections that would be made by the authors themselves, and in particular they may sometimes miss the deeper points of the respective papers. Rather they are selected to illustrate the points that seem salient to the present author. The 'editing' (some might say 'doctoring') has essentially been done to increase the emphasis on these points.

'UNBOUNDED' RATIONALITY

At the risk of appearing naive,[3] we find it necessary to pose yet again the question of what is the meaning of the *un*bounded antonym. Some contributors, including Herbert Simon, tend by implication to

Box 1. '*Rationality*' as conceived by Max Weber

From *The Protestant Ethic and the Spirit of Capitalism* (1904; English 1930)

Why did not . . . economic development [in other countries] enter upon that path of **rationalization** which is peculiar to the Occident? . . . [Every answer] must . . . above all recognize the importance of the **economic factor**.

From *Economy and Society* (1922; English 1968) and (last sentence) *German Politics* (1943)

[Bureaucratic organization is] always from a technical point of view the most **rational** type. For the needs of mass administration today, it is completely indispensable. The choice is only between bureaucracy and dilettantism. . . . [Nevertheless] it is horrible to think that the world could one day be filled with nothing but these little cogs, little men clinging to little jobs and striving towards bigger ones.

---

define this as, in effect, whatever bounded rationality is not. Alternatively writers refer to 'neoclassical' rationality. Such usage is reasonable among friends, but does create a few problems, of which the following three need discussion.

One problem is that economists use the adjective 'rational' differently from other social scientists.[4] Another problem concerns the relation between the meaning of rationality in 'neo-' classical, in contrast to classical, economics. The third problem is that it is in fact difficult to imagine *any* concept of rationality that does not imply a boundary or domain.

On the first point, we know that by 'rational' general users of the word (Max Weber for example, Box 1) mean, 'based on reason'. So the question at issue is the type and scope of reasoning involved. Herbert Simon would not disagree with that. He, and all the contributors to this volume, would agree that numerous different types of reasoning processes have evolved for different types of task. What must be disputed, however, is the right of some economists to appropriate the (unqualified) word 'rational' for what is by implication only one type of process and a rather narrow type at that.

The second point is that the idea of rationality as applied to economics in general and to economic theory in particular does not begin with the neoclassical age, nor does it begin with Max Weber; but rather it begins a century earlier with Jeremy Bentham. This may seem at first a controversial statement, since although Bentham invented the philosophy of Utilitarianism, his explicitly economic writings were relatively thin. Neither he nor the subsequent classical economists (from Say and Smith to Marx and Mill) had a theory of value that would permit them to assume that utility could be operationalized in the market. To Bentham, utility was concrete – in principle measurable, in principle conservable, but as likely to be increased by legal and institutional processes (e.g. penal reform) as by market processes, in which latter, in fact, writing at the end of the eighteenth century, Bentham was not profoundly interested.[5] The proof of the 'invisible-hand surmise' indeed requires a theory of market value, but you will not of course find the required theory in Smith; you must find it in Walras and Pareto.[6]

Neoclassical economics does not, however, *define* rationality; rather it postulates a particular process, namely general equilibrium in perfect markets, for *achieving* rationality. We all agree (more precisely, most people sympathetic to the present book agree) that there are profound reasons for questioning this process – the intrinsic imperfection of markets is one, cognitive infeasibility another – but these are not, in the author's opinion, questions relating to the concept of rationality, in the sense of process based on reason, as such.

The final problem can be illustrated by imagining some kind of widget, more 'intelligent' perhaps than the organism hypothesized by Herbert Simon in Box 2, no.1 but not in truth very complex. Its essential function is to help elucidate the definition of neoclassical rationality at the level of the individual, before considering society. We thus imagine a *choice-making machine*. It has been programmed with a rather simple, e.g. lexicographic, utility function containing a relatively small number of cardinal arguments, the left-hand side of which is also a cardinal number. It is placed in a fairly simple environment implying a modest system of constraints, of such a nature that a student mathematician with one year of calculus can compute the utility-maximizing solution quickly and easily. The

Box 2.   *Essences de Simon I‡*

---

(1)   *Page 41 (Chapter 3)*
Consider an organism that has a single need – food – and is capable of three kinds of activity: resting, exploration and food getting. The organism's environment is a surface over which it can locomote. At isolated widely scattered points there are little heaps of food each adequate for a meal. At any moment the organism can see only a limited circular area about the point at which it is standing. It is able to move at a fixed rate, metabolizes at a fixed rate and is able to store a certain amount of food. The problem is to choose its path in such a way that it will not starve. Now I submit that a **rational** way for the organism to behave is to explore the surface at random; when it sees a food heap, proceed to it and eat it; if and when it experiences an energy surplus, remain still. **There is nothing particularly remarkable about this behaviour except that it differs markedly from the models of human rationality proposed by economists.**

(2)   *Pages 76–7 (Chapter 5)*
In programming a computer it is substantially irrelevant what physical processes or devices are to be used ... Consequently, since the thinking human being is also an information processor, it seems that **human thinking should be explainable in information-processing terms without waiting for a theory of the underlying biological mechanisms, and that theories of human thinking may be formulated in computer programming languages, to be tested by simulating predicted behaviour with computers.**

‡These quotations are edited quotations or paraphrases of extracts from papers reproduced in the present book, heavily revised by the present author for the purpose of compression. For original texts, see pages indicated. Original author's italics, present author's bold type.

---

problem space is smooth and convex. In short, we have set up a situation which is inherently non-Simonian.

The widget, however, has been programmed not with the mathematical solution but with an iteration routine that can be seen on inspection to be sure to optimize within a reasonable computing time, say, a few seconds. In short, as compared to Herbert Simon's widget, this one is the antithesis; it is the paradigm neoclassical widget.

As far as the present author is concerned, this concept, or some analogous artifact, is both sufficient and necessary to define neoclassical rationality. If, after the few seconds, the iteration converges to the optimal solution, the widget has behaved rationally. If it does not, it has not. But how could it not? Is there a fault in the hardware, a bug in the software, or has someone inputted a different utility function from the one we thought was there – in other words has the widget changed its mind? Stripped to this level of discussion, the neoclassical concept of rationality begins to seem trivial, and is certainly gravely lacking in operationality. In any event, it is obviously severely bounded. It is bounded by the domain of its utility function and the specification of its environment. For example, it does consider God.

By contrast, as soon as we look more carefully at the problem facing Herbert Simon's widget – the problem whose characterization set up, in 1956, virtually all that was to follow – we see that the ideas that are being demonstrated are altogether deeper and subtler than the foregoing. But in the present author's view it was a strategic error to later defer to orthodoxy by renaming the topic as 'bounded' rationality, thus implying the existence of an ideal, unbounded, form. This is an example of what I have elsewhere (Marris 1990) called 'paradigmatic crucifixion', i.e. adopting part of the opponent's terminology for the purpose of communication, but, in so doing, by implication accepting part of his nonsense.

'Satisficing' was a good word, albeit troublesome to proofreaders. 'Bounded rationality', by contrast, in implying the possible existence of some form of 'unbounded' rationality, construes a contradiction in terms.

Supporters of the 'bounded' terminology may well of course argue that one begins with a domain (e.g. an economic system) over which, for some normative reason (e.g. the promotion of economic welfare) one would like to define a problem. Then one finds that owing to cognitive limitations such as discussed in this book, this or that type of social mechanism will inevitably fail to find the optimum solution of that problem. But surely this situation should properly be described as 'failed', rather than 'bounded' rationality.

In fact, as we shall further imply below, the terminology of the 'boundary' is not only inconvenient; it can also be positively dangerous. Suppose one happens to argue that a certain dysfunctional economic phenomenon is caused by a certain form of limited perception in a certain class of economic agents (see e.g. Box 4, no. 7 or Box 7, no. 2.). First there is the disturbing policy implication that all the government needs to do to cure the macroeconomic disease in question is to enlighten these agents by appropriate education. Second, and worse, there is absolute disaster if, in the event, it is shown that the phenomenon in question can be explained by another, powerful, theory, not dependent on bounded rationality. In such event, pop goes the revolution.

'INTELLIGENT' RATIONALITY

The present author therefore does not like the 'bounded' terminology. Instead he would prefer to describe the type of mental process characterized by the writing of Simon and other contributors to this book as 'intelligent' rationality. By rationality we mean a mental process based on reason. By an 'intelligent' reasoning process we mean one that is feasible and effective given the nature and circumstances of the type of reasoner who is to be supposed to do it. It follows that 'unintelligent' rationality means a reasoning process that is unfeasible and therefore, by definition, ineffective. To the present author, and to the contributors to this book, neoclassical rationality is an example!

We now set out what we have seen as the salient features of intelligent rationality as hypothesized for the human animal in his role as 'economic man'. These points are more or less directly taken from the boxes.

The starting point is the Simon widget, as described, and already mentioned in Box 2, no. 1. This paradigm example seems quite simple, yet says so much. By imposing basically three conditions on the neoclassical widget, it transforms the whole nature of the problem. Once these conditions are present, the satisficing behaviour inevitably represents the intelligent rationality. In contrast, maximizing becomes meaningless.

The conditions in question are the first two 'Simon points' in the list below. We then add other salient Simon points taken from his other papers in this book and from his exquisitely rich responses to the Discussion (Chapter 2). Then follow points from the other contributors.

Features of Intelligent (= 'Bounded') Rationality

Simon

1. The environment is complex; only a part of the information to be taken from it that is relevant to a given decision problem can be accessed at a given time; therefore relevant information must be obtained by sequential search and its processing is therefore path-dependent.
2. The computing capacity of the human brain is time-limited.[7]
3. 1 and 2 make *satisficing* behaviour (see Box 3, no. 4) inevitable.
4. 3 implies that in order to model economic behaviour we must model human thinking processes.
5. Human thinking processes are essentially researchable (Box 5).
6. But we do not need to wait until we understand the actual biological mechanism of the brain.
7. The fact that important subconscious processes are not directly observable is not an insuperable obstacle to research.
8. Intelligent (i.e. 'bounded') rationality leads to an understanding of the central role of *organizations* in economic life (Box 4, no. 8);[8]

Egidi

1. Market systems fail to resolve the problem of computing complexity for economic coordination because they do not have the incentive to produce the necessary public data base.
2. 1 is the reason for the existence of business organizations structured as administrative hierarchies.
3. Intelligent rationality uses heuristics which break down problems into parts; the division of labour in an administrative organization is an analogous process; thus organizations can be seen as collective artifacts for solving economic problems outside the market.

Box 3.   Essences de Simon II[t]

(3)   *Page 55 (Chapter 4)*
We can point to a person in a certain state and say, 'thinking is a set of processes like those now taking place in the central nervous system of that person'. Alternatively we can point to a **problem** and say, 'Thinking is a set of processes like those which enabled a person to solve this problem.'

(4)   *Page 69 (Chapter 4)*
In very well structured problem domains, formal procedures (algorithms) are available for finding the solution that is optimal by some criterion. . . . For most problems of everyday life no general algorithm has been discovered. Instead, a modest number of possible solutions can be considered: human problem solvers or computer simulation programs do not search for the 'best' solution but for a solution that is 'good enough' by some criterion. Heuristics that proceed on this basis are sometimes called **'satisficing'** heuristics.

(5)   *Page 105 (Chapter 6)*
We have every reason to believe that while some thought processes are conscious. . . . other essential processes are subconscious and not open to direct observation or even self-observation. Since the unobservable processes will be as essential to the theory as the observable ones, we are faced with the necessity of inferring their presence by indirect means. This difficulty is no different from those faced continually in all the sciences.

[t]Note as for Box 2.

Boudon
The same conditions which give rise to the idea of bounded or intelligent rationality can also give rise to *'subjective' rationality*, as displayed in phenomena such as persistence of discredited beliefs,

Box 4. Essences de Simon III[1]

(6) *Page 3 (Chapter 1)*
The term **bounded rationality** was introduced about thirty years ago to focus attention upon the discrepancy between the perfect human rationality that is assumed in classical and neoclassical economic theory and the reality of human behaviour as it is observed in economic life. The point was not that people are consciously and deliberately *irrational*, although they sometimes are, but that neither their knowledge nor their powers of calculation allow them to achieve the high level of optimal adaptation of means to ends that is posited in economics.

(7) *Pages 3–4 (Chapter 1)*
It has been shown on many occasions that for economics to deal with dynamic phenomena in general, and with the business cycle in particular, it must introduce limits upon the rational calculation of the economic actors. ... In Keynes, labour and in Lucas businessmen, suffer from a money illusion. In the former, labour confuses changes in nominal wages with changes in real wages; in the latter, businessmen confuse changes in prices in the whole economy with change in prices in their own industry.

(8) *Pages 5–6 (Chapter 1)*
The concept of bounded rationality also leads us to an understanding of the central role of organizations in economic life. ... If we look at the actual world around us, we don't find that organizations are simply small lumps in a fabric of markets and contracts. On the contrary, we see that most of all the people engaged in productive work carry out their work within organizations.

[1]Note as for Box 2.

Box 5. Simon, Galeotti and Hayek[1]

Elisabetta Galeotti
I am struck by the fact that Hayek's notion of imperfect knowledge and human limitation bear some resemblance to your concept of bounded rationality. Yet, from similar premises, very different conclusions seem to follow: in Hayek, imperfect information and limited rationality bring the rejection of planning and the defence of spontaneity. In Simon, on the contrary, the concept of bounded rationality is the basis for a theory of organization.

Herbert Simon
From one point of view, as you correctly observed, one could think of the Austrian viewpoint, particularly von Hayek's version of it, as a form of bounded rationality. Among other things, the Austrians put a tremendous emphasis on tacit and personal knowledge, and hence, have been very antagonistic to the development of quantitative and abstract formal economics. But this very same emphasis ultimately divided them from the notion of bounded rationality. In particular, it led von Mises to an extreme a prioristic position in which someone – perhaps the good Lord – told him what the Truth was, and the Truth was neoclassical theory done non-quantitatively. That led him back to utility maximization. ... So starting, as you shrewdly observed, with what looks like a very similar viewpoint, we rapidly diverge when it comes to attitudes about empiricism. I think that not only are human methods of thought and methods of learning, including tacit knowing, researchable and describable. This possibility is denied by the Austrians. And that leads us in quite different directions, for we find, when we do the empirical research, that human beings think in very different ways from those implied by neoclassical theory.

[1]Notes as for Box 2.

belief in magic and so on (Box 7).

Viale

1. The data base for rational behaviour is *memory*, which is biologically divided into short-term and long-term (see Box 8).
2. Long-term memory:
   (i) changes with time,
   (ii) can be only partially accessed at a given time (the problem of the subconscious),
   (iii) the output from long-term memory to short-term, stimulated by a given topic, will not always be the same; hence, even in the absence of new external inputs, a person's beliefs on a topic today may differ from yesterday's.
3. From 1 and 2 it follows that only active beliefs are operational in the process of inference.

To sum up, from Simon and the other contributors to this volume we learn that the profession of intelligent rationality requires us to employ explicit models of the working of the human mind, *but these can be independent of knowledge of the actual biological 'hardware'*.

The crucial constraints are *limited information* and *limited computing speed* and the crucial methodology is the use of *heuristics*, namely breaking down a total problem into sub-problems, as is done by, e.g. players of chess. One consequence is that the 'game' of economic life is *playable*, but it must be recognized that results will inevitably be of a *satisficing* (solution = good enough) rather than an optimizing (solution = maximum theoretically possible) character. Another consequence, or set of consequences, relates to organizations. On the one hand intelligent rationality explains (see Simon, Box 4, no. 8 and Egidi, Box 6, no. 1) the pervasive role of organizations in economic life; on the other, the division of labour within organizations is itself a type of heuristic. (To the present author this latter proposition of Massimo Egidi's appears to be a deeply original contribution.) It follows that organizations are themselves inevitably satisficers rather than maximizers.

THE BRAIN

The present author basically agrees with the philosophy expressed in the preceding paragraph with, however, some qualifications. These

Box 6.   Essences d'Egidi[1]

(1)   *Pages 8–10 (Chapter 2)*
Traditionally the market is viewed as an institution that coordinates individual actions. But if organizations are also ways by which individuals coordinate their decisions and organize themselves, what differentiates the role of the two forms of human organization? In the neoclassical view the role of the market is that of synthesizing the relevant information and fully reducing the computing complexity that individuals need to make rational decisions. . . . The problem is that this reduction is deeply imperfect. . . . Not all the information needed is provided by the market. . . . Therefore it is necessary to assume that the needed information is produced and exchanged. But [because information can be only imperfectly appropriated], this does not, in reality, occur. . . . There is thus a *systematic* failure of markets which is ameliorated by the functioning of **administrative hierarchies**.

(2)   *Pages 10–11 (Chapter 2)*
In chess, there is a theoretically computable winning strategy which is not practically feasible: this is a typical failure of the classical approach based on the assumption of unlimited computational capacity. Curiously, human players are able to play chess and sometimes win in spite of the fact that they have not found the best strategy. Instead . . . they detect a winning strategy by first dividing the game into sub-trees, analysing only local strategies in a bounded segment of the game; then they parametrize the strategy choice by means of appropriate evaluators . . . . Thus the reduction in complexity is achieved by dividing the tasks, **just like the division of labour in an administrative organization**.

[1]Notes as for Box 2.

Box 7. Extraits de Boudon[1]

(1) *Pages 125–6 (Chapter 7)*
Subjective rationality is the product of the discordance between the complexity of the world and the cognitive capacities of the subject.

(2) *Pages 138–9 (Chapter 7)*
According to a widely accepted point of the Keynesian theory, an increase in taxes has normally a deflationary effect, for the following reasons: it generates a decrease in the purchasing power, which in turn generates a decline in the demand for goods and services, and finally a decline in the prices of goods and services. Now, in a survey conducted by Katona (1951), a sample of businessmen were asked whether an increase in taxes has deflationary or inflationary effects. A majority of them answered that it should increase inflation. Why? Simply because they analysed the question by reference to a situation familiar to them: when taxes climb, this has the effect of increasing the costs of production the businessman has to bear. Except in the case where the demand for his products is highly elastic with respect to price, he will normally try to transfer at least a part of this increase in his costs of production to the consumer by increasing the price of his products or services. From this simple mental experiment he concludes with excellent reasons that an increase in taxation should generate inflationary effects.

[1]Note as for Box 2.

resolve around the question of the significance of the biological hardware. The currently developing biological information implies that, considered as an information processor, the brain is a processor of a very different type from the serial computer which has until recently been typical. The brain is almost certainly a parallel processor in which memory or 'data' takes (see below) a *distributed* format. This hypothesis explains many things about mental perfor-

Box 8. Viale and the significance of biological memory[1]

(Pages 176–7 (Chapter 9)

Another fundamental component of the correctness of informational inputs of perceptive rationality is related to the mechanisms of **memory**. The fact that an individual holds a belief now doesn't imply that he will hold it in the future. In the same way, if one has a belief today, because he thinks he had it some time ago, it is not certain that his belief is the same. That will depend on the accuracy and reliability of memorization mechanisms. As we know, memory can be sub-divided into **short-term memory**, where a small part of rapidly disappearing information can be stored and where the operational centre of the information processing is located, and **long-term memory**, which is the **filing cabinet of information**, with virtually unlimited capacity. I do not address myself here to the question whether short-term memory exists separately from long-term memory or corresponds to states activated by it. The first consideration one has to make concerns **which data base is used in the process of inference**. Various experiments, as well as everyday observation, clearly show that often the factual data base used corresponds only to a part of the beliefs available in long-term memory and useful for inferences. People can't gain access to a significant part of their knowledge and consequently the resulting inferences are generally wrong. Sometimes the individual can't connect all elements, useful for inference, existing in his memory. **If inference is a causal process in which the premises must be causally operative in producing a new belief, then, at a psychological level, only activated beliefs and not residual ones will be operative.**

[1]Note as for Box 2.

---

mance that had previously continued to seem mysterious and has, in the present author's opinion, important implications for cognitive science in general and for economics in particular.

The hypothesis is especially important in relation to the phenomenon of learning, of 'intuition' and of the brain's ability to make

decisions in response to unique events. It has led to a major new
industry in the construction of parallel hardware. It has also produced a literature in which the mind of a parallel, distributed, widget
is simulated in software written for serial computers.[9] But, in the
author's opinion, the fact that such simulation may be quite realistic
does not nullify the significance of the fact that it was a process of
thinking about the hardware that led to new ideas about the software. For these reasons we feel justified in discussing the whole
question of the nature of the human brain at further length.

We must all agree that if the brain is an information processor
(computer) it is a remarkable one. It can organize conferences. It can
do higher mathematics. It can compose music. It can ride bicycles
and sail boats. Clearly the brain works without a programme, or
alternatively is, especially at the highest levels, self-programming
(e.g. makes mental models; teaches itself to sail). It can use data that
are inaccurate or incomplete. It can make spontaneous generalizations. It can make inductions. It can find information without knowing precisely what it is looking for – 'content-addressing' the
memory. It records its own activities and records the recording of
them. It spontaneously creates internal mental models and at will
stores, accesses and develops these. It can transfer mental models
from one domain to another, and is thus, unlike the great majority
of 'artificially intelligent' machines, at least until recently, able to
make decisions in unfamiliar situations.

In addition to this 'fuzzy' logic, we also know that the brain is not
a bad performer in unfuzzy logic and that also, in the past half
century, it has achieved the feat of creating an artifact, the
computer, to powerfully enhance its own logical capacities, more
precisely, an artificial aid to offset its patent weakness in respect of
calculating speed and short-term storage capacity.

Up to that point, the brain had developed largely by biological
evolution, implying that its intelligence architecture was substantially completed maybe a quarter of a million years ago. At some
point there biologically evolved in man the capacity for rich language, which the highest apes, it now seems, physically do not
possess. By contrast the relatively recent developments of writing,
printing and computing are the result not of biological but of cul-
tural evolution; they are passed on not by DNA but by their own
communicating powers, from one generation to the next.

Nevertheless, the fact that the brain originally evolved by a Darwinian process is extremely relevant to everything we think and say about it. Evolution is a powerful, but untidy, form of search. Consequently it is absolutely certain that the architecture of the brain is not something that would result from comprehensive design. For example some geneticists believe that the brain evolved to meet the challenge of sight and movement. Organisms that could do complex movements and eventually could 'see' had superior fitness for survival. This could suggest that the capacity to learn complex procedures, such as skiing (not the procedure itself, of course) is a form of inherited ROM.

It is the general practice of people working in the field of artificial intelligence that they take for granted the scarcity of direct observation on the actual brain. Instead (*pace* Herbert Simon, Box 2, no. 2) we try to imitate nature, without necessarily following her. To some extent, given the experimental situation, this is inevitable. Either we do it that way or we seek other employment. But it is the strongly held opinion of the present author that we should always face up to the question, 'Is the model I am contemplating a *plausible analogy* to the way the corresponding function might be conducted by the biological brain?'

It could be that the 'intelligent' function or activity we have modelled is not, in fact, a function of the brain, but rather is something different (surely this is the case with classic expert systems?). Of course, it may well be that despite the negative conclusion, my model is nevertheless going to do something that is in some other way useful to the human race or to its organizations. Such a development has occurred recently in the case of *Parallel Distributed Processing* (PDP) where the concept, while advancing, but by no means revolutionizing, our understanding of the biological brain, has found immediate spectacularly successful applications in other fields of search-oriented computing.

PDP is a procedure for computer simulation of a *neural net*. The most general definition of a neural net is to say that it consists of a set of entities, for the sake of argument called 'neurons', that have the property that in response to inputs they produce outputs that are some non-linear function of the inputs; the plurals indicate the possibility of multiple inputs and outputs; the neuron may range in complexity from the simplest of logic gates to what amount to (in the case of actual human brain cells) an electro-chemical mini-computer.

A net consists of a layered set of neurons where every neuron in one layer is connected to every member of the next layer: the one-layer net is a limiting case. The *strength* of connections however, varies on the different pathways. The input received by one neuron in consequence of the output from another depends on both the original strength of the output and the connection strength of the pathway from the one neuron to the other. Thus inputs, outputs and connection strengths may be seen as numbers and the effective input from neuron A to neuron B is the product of the output of A (which is the same in all directions, like a lighthouse signal) multiplied by the connection strength or weight of A on B. The connection strengths are not inherently constant but rather may change through real time, i.e. may be *learned*.

Layerings may be partly circular, i.e. in a three-layer system, all neurons in the first layer are potentially connected with all in the second, and all in the second with all in the third, but the third layer, perhaps, may be connected to the first. In addition there may be exogenous inputs to individual neurons, and it may be possible to read the outputs.

With given weights, if input stimulus is applied, activity will spread through the system, and may eventually stabilize, permanently or transiently, and the resulting set of steady-state 'firings' (meaning that the pattern of firings is repeating rather than developing), as represented in the states of the neurons that have been designated output neurons, can be described as the 'output' (vector) from the original input (vector). Evidently the relationship between output and input will be essentially determined, in a complex way, by the connection strengths. It follows that the latter can be adjusted, or 'taught' (the professional term is 'trained'), to produce specific output in response to specific input. Thus nets can be trained to associate outputs with inputs. They can in fact be taught numerous pairs of associations. Thus a *single set of numbers*, namely the connection strengths, can represent numerous associations.

Because the diverse associations that have been trained into a neural net may be overlapping, the net has two crucial brain-like properties: when given a correct input it may produce the wrong output; and when given an incorrect or incomplete input it will give an output which may be the correct output and is more likely to be

Box 9. *Francis Crick*

Francis Crick, Nobel Laureate, FRS, OM, following his historic contributions to molecular biology and genetics, which began with the discovery of the helical structure of DNA in the 1950s, has for the past decade and a half devoted himself to the study of the brain, and has published a number of papers in the field and was a member of the working group which led to the publication of Rumelhart et al. (1988). In 1989 he wrote a lucid article about neural nets in *Nature*, which contains a rather choice passage, aimed primarily at psychologists, but which also aptly applies, with little modification, to organization theorists, and to other cognitive and social scientists.

It comes as a surprise to neuroscientists to discover that many psychologists, linguists in particular, have very little or no interest in the actual brain, or at least what goes on inside it. The brain, they feel, is far too complicated to understand. Far better to produce simple models which do the job in an intelligible manner. That such models have little resemblance to the way the brain actually behaves is not seen as a serious criticism. If it describes, in a succinct way, some of the psychological data, what can be wrong with that? Notice, however, that by using such arguments, one could easily make a good case for alchemy or for the existence of phlogiston. (Crick 1989)

And more recently, in what may prove to be a path-breaking paper on the nature of consciousness, Crick and his partner wrote,

The most effective way to approach the problem of consciousness would be to use the descriptions of psychologists and cognitive scientists and attempt to map different aspects of their models onto what is known about the neuroanatomy and neurophysiology of the brain. Naturally we have attempted to do this, but we have not found it as useful as one might hope though such models do point to the importance of attention and short term memory and suggest that consciousness should have easy access to the higher, planning levels of the system. *A major handicap is the pernicious influence of the paradigm of the . . . serial computer . . .* This is mainly because present-day computers make use of precisely-detailed pulse-coded messages. There is no convincing evidence that the brain uses such a system and much to suggest that it does not. (Crick and Koch 1990, italics added.)

so the less the inaccuracy or incompleteness of the input. In short, the system is capable of guessing. As in the case of humans, sometimes its guesses are right, sometimes they are wrong.

The connections strengths, *not* the neurons, are the 'memory' or 'data base' of the system. That is how it is content-addressable. If a connection strength is conceived as a piece of information, then every piece relates to every data item; it is the collectivity that makes the information. This is the 'distributed' system.

As many but not all readers will know, in the past half-decade there has been excited speculation that this is the *kind* of way a brain might work. The mass of 'white matter', i.e. connections, in a real-life brain is certainly much heavier than that of 'grey matter', i.e. the neurons. In reality, major qualifications are already apparent, of which three are especially relevant. The first is that the relevant part of the brain, i.e. that which stores long-term memory, the neocortex, could not be one vast net; it would be far too big and therefore far too slow; consequently, if the brain is neural-net-like, it must be a net of nets. The second is that the methods of 'training' adopted in the simulation models are most unlikely to be used by the actual brain. The third is that neural nets will not do logic, nor probably take decisions; there must be some other form of memory and processing for this. We may distinguish hypothetically between such a short-term or 'active' memory and a long-term or 'passive memory' (the latter being just connection strengths, the former involving the actual firing of neurons) but current knowledge about the relation between the two is limited. We do know however that there is a definite biological reason for major limitations on active processing capacity (see Crick and Koch 1990). This of course (see Simon Box 3, no. 5 and Viale, Box 8) is already recognized as a crucial factor in the situation.

In consequence, the nature of the phenomenon we call *consciousness* is fundamental to social science. It is deeply relevant to the concept of rationality. If we imagine that the experiences and associations stored in the long-term distributed memory are what, after formation into categories, informs our preferences, some difficult questions jump out.

Can we expect the resulting serially-taken decisions to be consistent? Most brain scientists will answer with a resounding negative. Given the vast capacity of the deep memory, why should not the processing capacity also be regarded as unlimited? If the limitation is in the active processing capacity, are we really saying that the decisions of humans and organizations can be informed by no more than the amount of information that can be held in the short-term stack?

In his recent paper, Francis Crick (Crick and Koch 1990) emphasizes the close connection between understanding the nature of consciousness and identifying different types of animal and human memory. In his view, consciousness, or 'awareness' involves attention, and short-term memory. The other forms of memory are not essentially involved with consciousness. Evidently, when conscious, we take information out of long-term memory and do logical operations on it. Evidently, the way data are kept in long-term memory is something much more complex and sophisticated than the way described in an elementary account, such as above, of a neural net. There must be hierarchies of categorizations, generalizations, abstractions, mental models and so forth.

How, in the condition we may timidly called consciousness, does the short-term process interact with the distributed long-term memory? Crick and his partner suggest that the answer may be 'binding', that is some way of putting in a special cross-net linkage between the involved neurons. But in the nature of things it seems unlikely that this could be effectively done with white-matter links, especially as great speed is required. The writers' dramatic suggestion is that it may be done by *synchronized firing patterns*, and, indeed, it does seem that correlated firing, creating a wave-form, around 30–50 Hz, has been observed in lightly anaesthetized monkeys, in neurons which can be proved to be associated with specific external stimuli. Thus it is suggested that consciousness is an *operating mode* of the brain that has, or will be found to have, a specific electro-chemical description. If this model is gradually validated, it will undoubtedly have a major effect of our whole way of thinking about how we think. That is to say, if we wish to postulate that thinking can be described by a certain type of cognitive model we shall need to test the idea against an increasingly definite physical model of what the brain, when conscious, actually does. Furthermore, we shall increasingly be forced to face up to the question of whether this or that type of operation which we are proposing to model is supposed to occur in this or that type of memory.

A WORKING SCENARIO

No one is required to agree with the foregoing assertions. No one can therefore be expected to accept conclusions from them. The present author, as indicated, is rather convinced. Rightly or wrongly he will therefore base his discussion on the implications of the cognitive revolution for economics on the following 'speculative facts'.

1. The brain is a neural supernet
2. 'Long term' memory
     (i) distributed in a net of nets
     (ii) total capacity extremely large
     (iii) access
          (a) content-addressable
          (b) can respond to inaccurate instructions
          (c) may give inaccurate response to accurate instructions
3. 'Short term' memory
     (i) (?)serial-like
     (ii) used for logical operations
     (iii) severely time-and-capacity limited
     (iv) comparatively accurate
4. Input–output system (IOS)
     (i) eyes, ears, etc.
     (ii) can employ language
     (iii) processing capacity much smaller than internal capacity
5. Learning
     (i) modifies long-term memory
     (ii) (?)processed via short-term memory
6. Economic preferences
     (i) only partly inherited, mostly *learned*
     (ii) reside in long-term memory
     (iii) are *activated* by consciousness

To sum up, we hypothesize that the human brain is a 'thing' that is the result of biological evolution which is born in the individual with a certain amount of inherited programming and a huge capacity for learning and future self-programming. It can do the things it evolved to do with great effectiveness but by no means necessarily in the most obvious or efficient ways. It can also learn to do new things, including things it was not biologically evolved to do (e.g. mathematics).

It appears to be some kind of gigantic parallel distributed processor, a net of neural nets, which may be tied together by some kind of synchronous process associated with the phenomenon of consciousness. It has also a short-term memory which appears to have serial and logical characteristics, but the relation between the two functions is especially unclear. Apart from learning (meaning the continuous development of new associations in the distributed memory) one of the brain's most remarkable capacities (seen from the viewpoint of the von Neumann computer) is that of seemingly being able to exploit, albeit fuzzily, albeit 'unconsciously', all the information in its (distributed) memory for the purpose of individual decisions, especially those taken in unique and unprecedented circumstances.

IMPLICATIONS FOR ECONOMICS

The foregoing will now be the 'working hypothesis' on the basis of which I propose to discuss implications of a specific subject in economics. In the early years, there was a flurry of activity in the field of the theory of the firm (e.g. Simon 1962; Cyert 1963, 1969; and Baumol 1971). Today we concentrate on a topical field which happens to be the present author's current interest, namely the *micro foundations of macroeconomics*.

From their nature, the 'macro' equations of macroeconomics are not susceptible to the behaviourist critique. They describe, or purport to describe, the behaviour, not of humans, but systems. It is increasingly accepted, however, that the causal validity of any macro model depends on the validity of the underlying explicit or implicit behavioural micro assumptions. Consequently, the two examples of the possible role of intelligent rationality in explaining such weighty phenomena as business cycles and inflation suggested by contributors to this volume (Simon, Box 4, no. 7 and Boudon, Box 7, no. 2) are potentially dramatic. It happens that, for reasons to be explained, the present author is convinced that both are quite wrong(!) but he believes that from the resulting dialectic some useful conclusions will emerge.

We therefore need to set the stage with our view of the working of a modern capitalist macroeconomy, more precisely its short-run cyclical behaviour. This is in fact a synopsis of a case set out in Marris 1991.

Goods are produced by often diversified and often large organizations, and sold by them in price-setting markets which are pervasively imperfect.[10] Although the most realistic model for the goods market as a whole is that of a chain of oligopolies, for compression of argument we here treat the whole goods market as a single industry with imperfect monopoly. Under constant macro conditions and with prices of all other products constant, each seller faces a well defined demand curve which we assume to be iso-elastic (more precisely we make no qualitative assumption concerning the cyclical behaviour of the elasticity). With given nominal wages, short-run cost curves are flat up to the point of full-capacity utilization, whereupon they become vertical: implicitly, output per worker hour (opph) is therefore constant (exogenous) at all within-capacity output levels. In the short run the number of sellers is fixed.

For the sake of argument assume that under given macro conditions the sellers engage in *maximizing* behaviour in the sense of a form of competition leading to a Nash-strategic equilibrium in prices – a *conjectural equilibrium* (see Hahn 1987) where every seller believes (correctly) that given the prices set by all other sellers, his price and resulting price profit margin maximizes total gross profits. In the equilibrium, every margin is a profit-maximizing margin. Evidently this result implies that each seller has a clear and correct perception of his demand curve, i.e. has precisely the kind of data which the behavioural critique denies. Note, however, that the seller is required to know only three numbers: the current actual price, the current actual quantity demanded and the elasticity. (Of course, in reality the assumption of iso-elasticity is likely to be untrue, but it can be shown that our conclusions will stand up provided only that the deviations are unbiased. It is the working assumption of both model builder and player.)

The profit-maximizing margin (share of profit in price) is of course the reciprocal of the elasticity. Consequently profit-maximizing price will not change unless either nominal wages change or demand elasticity changes. When the profit-maximizing margin is reached, the *real wage* is endogenous; it is equal to the exogenous opph, reduced by the amount of the margin.

Of course, the microeconomic conjectural equilibrium will not be macroeconomically stable unless the associated flow of nominal income and expenditure is just sufficient to buy the current quantities of goods supplied at their current conjectural-equilibrium prices. According to the Keynesian theory, this is not inevitable. But suppose Keynesian stability does happen to hold at an aggregate output such that producers are operating just below capacity. The level of employment is the level required to produce this output. The unemployment rate, natural or unnatural according to semantic taste, is the unemployment rate socially and institutionally associated with this level of employment and the endogenous real wage.

Suppose that some macro fiscal or monetary shock of a generally Keynesian character now disturbs the macro equilibrium downwards. Nominal aggregate demand declines and every seller experiences a leftward shift of his demand curve. But unless and until nominal wages change, given the assumption of iso-elasticity, profit-maximizing price will not change. The initial profit-maximizing response for each firm, leading to a new conjectural equilibrium, reduces *physical* outputs in direct proportion to *nominal* demand.

Subject to a small difficulty in that Keynes himself did not understand it,[11] this simple powerful maximizing model is quite sufficient to make the Keynesian cycle work. Many other behaviours, including satisficing, may be relevant, but none is actually needed.[12]

In the labour market workers will be laid off. This may possibly cause a decline in the level or rate of increase of nominal wages. Since the price level has not changed, workers will correctly perceive such change as a corresponding change in the real wage. The latter change may, or may not, produce a change in the supply of labour. But the decline in nominal wages means a decline in costs. Since the equilibrium profit margin has not changed, prices must adjust, and any real-wage effect be reversed. Unless either opph changes or demand elasticity changes, the restoration of (conjectural) equilibrium at the micro level must imply restoration of the real wage. Thus the Keynesian slump becomes dug-in. It can only be rescued if (a) *nominal* wages and prices do decline and (b) there is a sufficient part of the stock of money in the system which is not offset by short-term debt, that the Pigou Effect actually operates. In the modern economy, this is structurally and institutionally unlikely.[13]

So, in sharp contrast to Simon's suggestion in Box 4, no. 7, we have a powerful maximizing model which completely 'explains' the business cycle without any myopia or money illusion in either goods market or labour market. Where it is vulnerable to the behavioural critique is elsewhere, i.e. in the assumption that sellers can quantify the elasticity. Of course they cannot. They set a margin which is 'good enough' in the sense that, in association with the resulting demand, it yields total profit sufficient for the firm to survive, prosper and grow. We are led immediately to the empirical mark-up pricing model on which all large econometric macro models are sensibly based. The elasticity of demand for narrowly defined product brands is even less observable and quantifiable to the econometrician than to the businessman (or even to the businessman's econometrician, although we know that large corporations with research departments do make these estimates).

So we have a theory based on maximizing assumptions whose econometric implementation will necessarily require satisficing assumptions. What then is the role of the theory? The answer is that the theory is essential to meet the very serious criticism that without it the level of the mark-up lacks economic explanation. If mark-ups are purely the result of heuristics, how do we know that tomorrow they may not suddenly change?[14] There is evidence that mark-ups are higher for products where elasticity is lower; it would be a poor day for economics if that were not so. If we assume that firms do have, possibly partly unconscious, processes which keep the heuristic mark-up from deviating in the long run very far from the optimizing mark-up, we have a very strong, very realistic, yet simple theory – micro-to-macro, satisficing-maximizing – for the cyclical behaviour of the modern market economy.

The significance of mark-up pricing in relation to price/output phenomena in cyclical macroeconomics was first spotted, 25 years ago, by Richard Cyert:

> How can a firm recognise a shift in its demand curve, never having known where it was in the first place? Obviously it must look at orders, inventory and plant utilization. One response [to a change in the balance unfilled orders to inventory] of course, is to [change plant utilization]. (Cyert 1969)

Since the firm was presumed to be possessed of an, albeit invisible, demand curve, Cyert was implicitly assuming imperfect competition. But had he also implicitly assumed iso-elasticity, the 'behavioural' response he describes – namely varying output in response to the shift in quantity demanded – turns out, on our argument above, to be also the profit-maximizing response!

In effect, one can tell two stories, one of which is the 'imp-comp' maximizing story above. The other, more realistic, supposes that while firms are not quite so lost as implied in the Cyert quotation, they know only one point on their demand curve, namely the rate of flow of orders after things have settled down at current asking price. Around this point they do not even know the elasticity, but let us assume that they behave as if they thought that whatever the elasticity was, it was constant. They also believe that their current margin is satisfactory. By implication we now have a fixed relation between the satisficing margin and the maximizing margin. This means that the behaviour of holding the margin constant, while varying capacity utilization in proportion to the implicit shift in the demand curve, guarantees that the new situation will not only also be satisfactory, but will bear the same relation to maximization as in the old situation. It is therefore a 'strong' behaviour.

So we have two alternative models, one maximizing, one satisficing. They do not predict the same income distribution (profit margin) and, as far as the present author can see, it is impossible to make general statements concerning the direction of deviation in this respect. But in one crucial aspect, the predictions of the two models are identical, namely as regards cyclical macroeconomics: each can give a powerful foundation to the Keynesian multiplier. Indeed, except via secondary distributional effects (whose direction would in any case be unclear), they would both make the same *quantitative* predictions, in a Keynesian macro model, concerning the levels of output, employment and unemployment. And this is as true in realistic dynamic applications as in comparative statics.[15]

I suggest that we thus have precisely the kind of healthy relationship between maximizing and satisficing theory the economics profession needs.

We conclude by using the same model (i.e. the imp-comp Keynesian model described above) to analyse the paradox raised by Boudon in Box 7, no. 2. In this journey back to the future we must accept the business-person's answers, but we are surely permitted to adopt our own, rather than Professor Boudon's, version of Keynes. Why? Because Professor Boudon was hypothesizing the macro theory as the objective reality, to be compared with the subjective beliefs of the respondents. The objective reality, of course, is my version of

Keynes! The model I have described implies that if the government increases income tax without an increase in government expenditure there will be a fall in output and employment, possibly with no change in prices. Alternatively, the fall in the demand for labour may have some kind of decelerating effect on nominal wages which will be, the theory predicts, proportionately mirrored in effects on prices. Alternatively, if the tax increase falls mainly on indirect taxes, profit maximizing and/or satisficing prices are raised, a result which may well, through indexing, lead to a corresponding increase in nominal wages. If the government wants to keep its expenditure constant in real terms, it will have to increase nominal expenditure, so, despite the increased tax revenue, there may be no net fiscal injection or absorption of spending power. If the government allows real expenditure to decline, there will be some absorption effect and consequent negative effect on macro demand. This may lead to a fall in the demand for labour and some dampening of the nominal wage inflation process. The prediction is therefore complex but in general suggests stagflation.

So the correct answer to the question 'what will be the effect of an increase in taxation?', is 'what form will the tax increase take?'. Then, if the elucidation is, 'mostly direct', the correct response is 'recession'. Otherwise the correct response is 'stagflation'. We do not have evidence that with full elucidation the business-persons would have continued to give wrong answers. The experiment reported by Boudon took place nearly half a century ago. If respondents had been Business majors at the University of Maryland a quarter of a century later, and in consequence had been required to get Intermediate Economics possibly taught by the present author, they would *surely* have given correct answers! This remark is not totally ironic. The point at issue is that the economic question posed in the original experiment is inherently complex. The average business-person may not experience a sharp indirect tax increase falling on his own industry more than once in a lifetime. Therefore the question cannot easily be answered from experience. In consequence it must be answered from relevant education, or failing that, from received beliefs. So that although one can agree with Professor Boudon that cognitive dissonance may often be the cause of 'irrational' or 'subjectively rational' beliefs (Box 7, no. 1), they may also be the result of rectifiable ignorance. Unfortunately, at the present time, the econ-

omics profession is not helpful to the reduction of ignorance, being
itself so prone to hidden ideological bias.

NOTES

1. Apart from the papers in the present volume, there is all the more familiar work
    stemming from the 1950s, of which *Models of Man* (1957) and 'Decision Taking
    in Economics' (1959) are landmark examples.
2. The present author claims to be one of the earliest economists, and certainly the
    earliest UK-resident economist, to see its significance. In 1960/61, armed with
    the first draft of Marris (1964) he paid an academic visit to the US. Encouraged
    by his hosts to sample a new sociological experience he attended the annual
    meeting of the Southern Economic Association and there heard a business
    school professor, almost white with outrage, denounce the economics profession
    for inventing a horrible new word, namely 'satisficing'! Assuming that there
    must be something interesting about an idea that stimulated such emotion, the
    author read into the subject, was duly fascinated, and included a critique in the
    final version of his draft. On later visits he made pilgrimage to the Smoky City
    and was pleased to receive Herbert Simon's friendship. In 1970, when planning
    Marris and Wood (1971) he had intended to stage a debate on behavioural
    economics by inviting papers from Richard Cyert on the one side and William
    Baumol on the other; but Richard Cyert sadly dropped out and there appeared
    only Baumol and Stewart (1971). In the middle 1970s, having now migrated to
    the University of Maryland, he had the task of explaining to a colleague in that
    distinguished economics department the answer to the question 'who is this man
    who has today received a Nobel Prize in Economics but is not a member of the
    AEA?' (It was not easy to refrain from the reply that the questioner could not be
    a very conscientious reader of the AER.) Finally, after returning to the UK, he
    had the experience, in the mid-1980s, of hearing from his young colleagues
    about a 'new idea', called 'satisficing', the implications of which would take
    some time to absorb. The purpose of these anecdotes is to illustrate the point
    that while the cognitive revolution has had a major impact on the high thinkers
    in our discipline, its impact on the common soldiers is yet small.
3. Careful study of Hogarth and Reder (1986) has not deterred the author from
    taking this risk.
4. Compare e.g. Muth (1961) or the various contributions in Hogarth and Reder
    (eds) *Rational Choice* (1986) with the quotations from Max Weber in Box 1 or
    the approach found in the present contributions of Raymond Boudon and
    Riccardo Viale. Max Weber was a professor of Political Economy, but today, if
    he applied for work at the University of Chicago, they would of course reject
    him at the Economics Department and send him over to Sociology.
5. This statement is somewhat oversimplified. The general view of Bentham scho-
    lars appears to be that he discovered marginal utility but did not reach the point
    of relating the latter to market price. He certainly discovered the diminishing
    marginal utility of money. See Bentham (1802) and Sen and Williams (1982).
6. Walras (1874) and Pareto (1897, 1905). In (1897) Pareto devoted a paragraph to
    distinguishing 'utility' from 'ophelimity', the latter being the concept we now
    call by the name of the former. In the two books taken together he offers fewer
    than a hundred thin words on his case for denying the conservability of utility
    (ophelimity).
7. One must be reminded that the Simon widget was conceived in the computing

hardware environment of the mid-1950s, before the advent of the transistor. In Chapter 2, p. 15, Herbert Simon seems to imply that subsequent developments have not significantly changed the situation: 'Even if we had a good model of the future, if our brains wouldn't allow us to run the model as fast as time runs, we would still be uncertain about the future. (The complexity of the models used in meteorology today are limited in precisely this way – the power of the supercomputers available to run them.)'

It has to be asked whether the effectiveness of weather forecasting is actually constrained by the complexity of the modelling, or by something else. Today, with the benefit of hindsight many would say that the correct answer is 'chaos'. It is a vital question for our profession today whether macroeconomic systems are (as believed by the current Editor in Chief of the London *Times* newspaper) genuinely chaotic.

8. Younger readers may be reminded of Herbert Simon's pioneering and influential contributions to the applied economics of organization theory by reference to Simon (1957) where he invented the mathematics of the administrative hierarchy, and to Simon and Bonini (1958) which made an elegant contribution to the theory of Gibratesque processes. For more on this last topic the reader is modestly also referred to Marris (1979).
9. See for example the fascinating desk-top software found on the disk at the back of Vol. 3 of Rumelhart et al. (1988).
10. This rules out what Simon (Box 8) calls the 'Lucasian' cycle which appears to be explicitly based on price-taking and hence, in the opinion of the present author, of course, unavailable for explanations of the real world.
11. See Marris (1991), Chap. 4.
12. The past decade has seen the flowering of a small literature on imperfectly competitive micro foundations of macroeconomics. See Blanchard and Kiyotaki (1987), Hart (1982), Kiyotaki (1985), Mankiw (1988), Ng (1980, 1986), Startz (1989), Solow (1986). These are reviewed in Marris (1991) in Chap. 5. For the reasons there discussed these authors' contributions do not appear to the present author to contain an example of a simple iso-elastic imperfectly competitive properly Keynesian model such as described here.
13. For further argument, see Marris (1991), Chap. 2.
14. This echoes the aborted debate between Baumol and Cyert, as already mentioned in note 2 above, one side of which (the Baumol side) is found in Baumol (1971).
15. See the dynamic simulation model in Marris (1991), Chaps 1, 6 and 7.

REFERENCES

Baumol, W. and Stewart, M. (1971) 'On the Behavioural Theory of the Firm' in Marris, R. and Wood, A. (eds) *The Corporate Economy*. Harvard University Press.

Bentham, J. (1802) *Traités de Legislation Civile et Pénale*. Paris: E. Dumont.

Blanchard, O. and Kiyotaki, N. (1987) 'Monopolistic Competition and Aggregate Demand', *American Economic Review*.

Crick, F. (1989) 'The Recent Excitement about Neural Nets', *Nature*, 12 January.

Crick, F. and Koch, C. (1990) 'Towards a Neurobiological Theory of Consciousness', *Seminars in the Neurosciences*.

Cyert, R. (1969) 'Uncertainty, Behavioural Rules and the Firm', *Economic Journal*.

Cyert, R. and March, J. (1963) *A Behavioural Theory of the Firm*. Englewood Cliffs, NJ: Prentice-Hall.

Hahn, F. (1978) 'On non-Walrasian equilibria', *Review of Economic Studies*.

Hahn, F. (1987) 'Conjectural Equilibrium', in Eatwell *et al.*, *The New Palgrave Dictionary of Economics*. London: Macmillan.

Hart, O. (1982) 'A Model of Imperfect Competition with Keynesian Features', *Quarterly Journal of Economics*.

Hogarth, M. and Reder, M. (eds) (1968) *Rational Choice*. Chicago: Chicago University Press.

Keynes, J. M. (1921) *A Treatise on Probability*. London: Macmillan.

Keynes, J. M. (1930) *A Treatise on Money*. London: Macmillan.

Keynes, J. M. (1936) *The General Theory of Employment, Interest and Money*. London: Macmillan.

Kiyotaki, N. (1985) 'Macroeconomics of Imperfect Competition', Doctoral Dissertation, Harvard University.

Mankiw, N. G. (1988) 'Imperfect Competition and the Keynesian Cross', *Economics Letters*. Amsterdam: North-Holland.

Marris, R. (1964) *The Economic Theory of Managerial Capitalism*. London: Macmillan.

Marris, R. (1979) *The Theory and Future of the Corporate Economy and Society*. Amsterdam: North-Holland.

Marris, R. (1990) 'Imperfect Competition and the Debate on Keynesian Economics', *Rivista di Politica Economica*, Rome.

Marris, R. (1991) *Reconstructing Keynesian Economics with Imperfect Competition – a desk-top simulation*. Aldershot, England: Edward Elgar.

Marris, R. and Wood, A. (eds) (1970) *The Corporate Economy*. Harvard University Press.

Mayer, J. (ed.) *Max Weber and German Politics*. London: Faber.

Muth, J. F. (1961) 'Rational Expectations and the Theory of Price Movements', *Econometrica*, vol. XXIX, no. 3, pp. 315–35.

Ng, Y.-K. (1980) 'Macroeconomics with non-Perfect Competition', *Economic Journal*.

Ng, Y.-K. (1986) *Mesoeconomics*. Brighton, England: Wheatsheaf.

Pareto, V. (1897) *Cours d'Economie Politique*. Lausanne, Switzerland: Bibliothèque Universitaire.

Pareto, V. (1905) *Manuale d'Economia Politica*. French 1927; English 1971. London: Macmillan.

Rumelhart, D. and McClelland, J. et al. (1988) *Explorations in Parallel Distributed Processing*, 3 vols. Cambridge, Mass: MIT Press.

Sen, A. and Williams, B. (1982) *Utilitarianism and Beyond*. Cambridge: Cambridge University Press.

Simon, H. (1957) *Models of Man*. New York.

Simon, H. (1957) 'The Compensation of Executives', *Sociometry*.

Simon, H. A. (1958) 'The Size Distribution of Business Firms', *American Economic Review*.

Simon, H. A. (1959) 'Decision Making in Economics', *American Economic Review*.

Simon, H. A. (1962) 'New Developments in the Theory of the Firm', *American Economic Review*.

Simon, H. A. (1982) *Models of Bounded Rationality*. Cambridge, Mass: MIT Press.

Simon, H. A. and Newell, A. (1972) *Human Problem-Solving*. Englewood Cliffs, NJ: Prentice-Hall.

Solow, R. (1986) 'Monopolistic Competition and the Multiplier' in Heller, W. (ed.) *Essays in Honor of Kenneth J. Arrow*, vol 2. Cambridge: Cambridge University Press.

Startz, R. (1989) 'Monopolistic Competition as a Foundation for Keynesian Macroeconomic Models', *Quarterly Journal of Economics*.

Walras, L. (1874) *Elements d'Economie Politique Pure*. Lausanne, Switzerland: L. Corbaz.

Weber, M. (1904) *The Protestant Ethic and the Spirit of Capitalism*, trans. Parsons, T. 1930. London: Allen & Unwin.

Weber, M. (1922) *Economy and Society*, trans. Roth, G. and Wittich, G. 1968. England: Bedminster Press.

Name Index

Subject Index

Printed and bound by CPI Group (UK) Ltd, Croydon, CR0 4YY

16/04/2025

14658432-0001